PRENTICE-HALL

Foundations of World Regional Geography Series

PHILLIP BACON and LORRIN KENNAMER, *Editors*

GEOGRAPHY OF ANGLO-AMERICA, *Loyal Durand, Jr.*

GEOGRAPHY OF NORTH AFRICA AND SOUTHWEST ASIA,
Paul W. English

GEOGRAPHY OF THE U.S.S.R., *W.A. Douglas Jackson*

GEOGRAPHY OF EUROPE, *Vincent H. Malmström*

AUSTRALIA'S CORNER OF THE WORLD, *Tom L. McKnight*

SOUTHEAST ASIA, *Joseph E. Spencer*

AFRICA, *Donald Vermeer*

GEOGRAPHY OF LATIN AMERICA, *Kempton E. Webb*

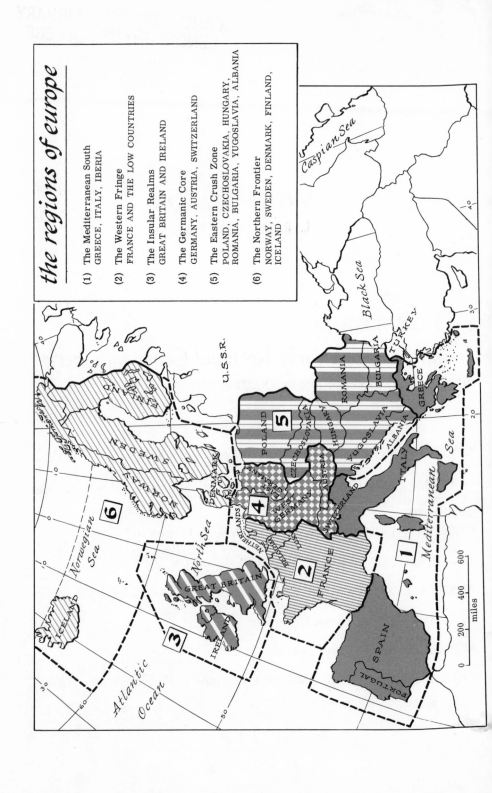

the regions of europe

(1) The Mediterranean South
    GREECE, ITALY, IBERIA

(2) The Western Fringe
    FRANCE AND THE LOW COUNTRIES

(3) The Insular Realms
    GREAT BRITAIN AND IRELAND

(4) The Germanic Core
    GERMANY, AUSTRIA, SWITZERLAND

(5) The Eastern Crush Zone
    POLAND, CZECHOSLOVAKIA, HUNGARY,
    ROMANIA, BULGARIA, YUGOSLAVIA, ALBANIA

(6) The Northern Frontier
    NORWAY, SWEDEN, DENMARK, FINLAND,
    ICELAND

Geography
of
Europe

A REGIONAL ANALYSIS

VINCENT H. MALMSTRÖM

Professor of Geography
Middlebury College

PRENTICE-HALL, INC., Englewood Cliffs, N.J.

*to the memory of a brave and beautiful
peasant girl, whose fireside reminiscenses
awakened my first love for Europe*

*born Solf, Finland, 12/11/1867
died Iron Mountain, Michigan, 8/11/1955*

PRENTICE-HALL INTERNATIONAL, INC., *London*
PRENTICE-HALL OF AUSTRALIA, PTY., LTD., *Sydney*
PRENTICE-HALL OF CANADA, LTD., *Toronto*
PRENTICE-HALL OF INDIA PRIVATE, LTD., *New Delhi*
PRENTICE-HALL OF JAPAN, INC., *Tokyo*

Contents

Maps

Foreword

As a center for cultural dispersal, Europe has touched the life of virtually everyone on earth. Through the centuries, European political ideals, scientific discoveries, and religious beliefs have had untold influence on human life. Yet it is not Europe itself, as a viable concept, that has dominated the lives of those who inhabit this region. The highest loyalty of the European has been to the state, not to Europe. As a reflection of this tradition, *Georgraphy of Europe: A Regional Analysis* seeks out those themes of homogeneity that give unity to Europe's major divisions—physical, biotic, and most important of all, cultural. Europe, as a concept, demands attention, but it is the subdivisions that are given special emphasis.

The author has selected six major regions, each defined by a distinct theme, to organize this useful contribution to Europe's regional literature. But he wisely considers the individual country as a second level of regionalization. Further, within individual countries, both natural and cultural regions are recognized.

In characterizing place, the author has dipped into history, politics, and literature to capture its personality. Yet, in this region, so frequently shattered by conflict and where the state still dominates, the new spirit of Europe shines through. The distinguished French economist and architect of the European Economic Community, Jean Monnet, put it well in reminding us that "We are used to thinking that major changes in the traditional relations between countries only take place violently, through conquest or revolution. We are so accustomed to this that we find it hard to appreciate those that are taking place peacefully in Europe even though they have begun to affect the world."

It could scarcely be more appropriate that Vincent H. Malmström was enticed to prepare this book. His credentials for doing so are impeccable. With a Ph.D. (1954) from the University of Michigan and long tenure as Professor of Geography at Middlebury College, he clearly possesses the academic qualifications needed to establish for himself a firm place in the world of scholarship. In addition, his many papers, monographs, and books, most centering on Europe, have secured for him his service stripes in the geographic fraternity. Happily, too, especially for his readers, the lively style which has always characterized his writing, is especially evident in this work. His contribution to the Prentice-Hall World Regional Geography Series, then, brings to focus Malmström's years of study, residence, travel, and research in a particularly informative, well-structured, and readable book.

PHILLIP BACON
University of Washington, Seattle

LORRIN KENNAMER
The University of Texas, Austin

CHAPTER 1 *europe:*
an introduction

Europe is a collection of irregular peninsulas and islands lying in the northwestern quadrant of the vast land mass known as the "World Island." Its northern, western, and southern extremities are defined by the shores of the Arctic and Atlantic oceans and the Mediterranean Sea. Only in the east are its boundaries indistinct, for although Europe was traditionally thought of as extending to the Urals, the Caspian, and the Caucasus, these "landmarks" are hardly realistic limits in either a physical or a cultural sense. In this volume, therefore, we have chosen to define Europe as that area lying west of the Soviet Union and Turkey. In so doing, we recognize the former country as a major world region in its own right, whereas we assign the latter to Southwest Asia, the Middle East, or "the Dry World," as it is variously known—a region with which Turkey's physical and cultural ties are strongest. (See Figure 1.)

From even this brief exercise in "boundary drawing," the reader may become aware of one of the geographer's primary concerns, namely the recognition and demarcation of *regions*. By definition, regions are "places of more or less definite extent or character." Discerning and describing the *personality* of a place—what it is like—is only the geographer's necessary first step to understanding why a region is as it is, and why it is important or unimportant. Thus, the critical second step in any meaningful regional study is an analysis of the significance of place.

Among the host of variables that contribute to the personality of any given place, the geographer recognizes two main categories: physical or natural attributes, and cultural or human attributes. Similarly, in evaluating the significance of any given place, the geographer is wont to think in terms of three anthropocentric measures: how the place is important to man *economically*, *socially*, and *politically*. To be sure, these are the

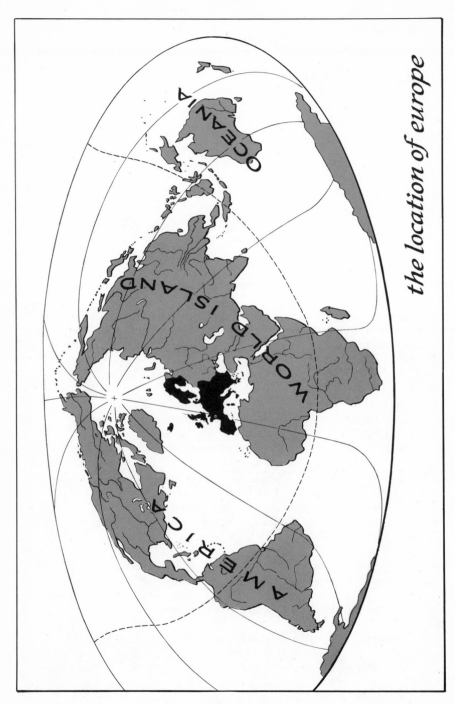

Figure 1

most dynamic aspects of geography, for while the personality of places can and does change—sometimes with surprising rapidity—the significance of places changes constantly, if for no other reason than that man's advancing technology causes him to reassess continually the earth from which he derives his sustenance.

Fundamental to both the personality and significance of a place is its *location*. Location refers not just to where a place is in terms of latitude and longitude, but to where it is relative to other places, what contacts it has with them, what impulses move between them, and how they interact. This aspect of location we shall term *orientation*, and the "impulses" that move between places, whether they be physical phenomena, people, or ideas, we shall term *innovations*. In this triad of terms —location, orientation, and innovation—we have the basic keys to understanding the personality and significance of Europe (or any region for that matter), both as it has developed in the past and as it exists today.

Sun, Sea, and Solid Rock: The Physical Setting

Take Europe's location relative to the sun, for instance. This is one of the most fundamental relationships of any region, for it is incoming solar radiation that makes life itself possible. This relationship we can state in terms of latitude, for the most intense radiation, as we know, is concentrated in the low latitudes around the Equator, and the least intense in the polar regions. Indeed, it has been calculated that up to 37° north and south of the Equator the earth's atmosphere receives more heat than it loses into space, thus building up a surplus of warmth. From 37° poleward, however, the earth is constantly losing more heat to outer space than it receives, and were it not for the atmospheric exchange of warmth between the lower and higher latitudes, it would be questionable whether life as we know it could exist in these areas farther removed from the direct rays of the sun.

Were we now to examine Europe's latitude on a map or globe, we would find that its southernmost outlier is the Greek island of Crete in the Mediterranean (latitude 35° north), while its northernmost extremity is the North Cape of Norway (latitude 71° north) on the shores of the Arctic Ocean. This represents a north-south extent comparable to the distance from Memphis, Tennessee or Albuquerque, New Mexico to Point Barrow, Alaska. Therefore, Europe occupies a position in the Old World roughly comparable to that of Alaska, Canada, and the northern two-thirds of the United States in the New World. Thus, we find that the southernmost capital in Europe, Athens, is on the same parallel as Washington, D. C.; that Rome, Italy is as far north as Providence, Rhode Island; that Paris, France is 150 miles closer to the North Pole than its daughter colony, Quebec, Canada; and that the Scandinavian capitals of Oslo, Stockholm, and Helsinki lie approximately on a line with the southern tip of Greenland.

But what does such a northerly location really imply? Not, certainly, that Europe has a climate similar to that of Canada, for it doesn't. However, one aspect of Europe's relationship to the sun is directly comparable to that of Canada, namely the length of its days and nights. Looking back at our map or globe, we will notice that the northern reaches of Europe extend beyond the Arctic Circle. Thus, in midsummer, all of Scandinavia and much of the British Isles have long hours of twilight, and in the northern areas of Norway, Sweden, and Finland the sun doesn't set at all. In fact, at the North Cape the sun circles the heavens for seventy-eight days before finally dipping below the horizon. Of course, at midwinter the opposite conditions prevail, and then the gloom of night pervades these regions as continuously as the exuberance of sunlight which it has displaced. Thus, the extremes of light and darkness are as great over northern Europe as they are in sub-Arctic Canada, even if the extremes in temperature are not.

That the climate of Europe should be so mild, despite the region's remoteness from the sun, is due to the location of Europe relative to the sea. Over the Atlantic Ocean, two semipermanent cells of atmospheric pressure are situated. One of these is the Azores High, from which warm, dry, descending air spills outward in a clockwise spiral. The other is the Icelandic Low, in which warm, moist Atlantic air masses constantly collide in a counterclockwise spiral with the colder, somewhat less moist air masses of the Arctic basin. Two more dissimilar regions of the sea you could hardly imagine. The former is calm, placid, and sunny. The latter is nearly always churning in turmoil, especially during the winter when the contrasts between the colliding air masses are even greater than in summer.

It is Europe's location relative to the Azores High that explains the prevailing wind pattern over the region. For most of the subcontinent, the predominant airflow at all seasons is from the southwest. But, because of the seasonal displacement of the Azores High, the northern and southern extremities of Europe experience certain modifications of this general pattern. In winter, for example, the southward displacement of the High brings westerly winds in over the Mediterranean region; in summer, with the northerly displacement of the High, winds are largely parallel to the coast at this latitude or away from it. The net result is that southern Europe receives almost all of its total annual receipt of moisture during the winter, whereas its summers get progressively hotter and drier the farther eastward one goes from the open Atlantic. In the northern reaches of Europe, the seasonal shift of the Azores High is reflected in more frequent intrusions of Arctic air during the winter and a generally higher frequency of storms. In summer, if the atmosphere is behaving normally, not only will there be fewer storms, but most of those that do occur will drift well past the region into the Arctic Ocean.

Thus, because Europe is dominated by maritime air masses at all seasons, it experiences a climate that is markedly milder than its latitude would otherwise suggest. In addition, because this air moves from west to east, the more exposed westerly parts of Europe are more temperate than the more continental and interior eastern regions. (The constant southwesterly airflow is also responsible for pushing the warm waters of the North Atlantic Drift all along the coast and far into the Arctic basin, so that sea ice is unknown in most of Europe. Ships can round the North Cape of Norway throughout the year, whereas Point Barrow, Alaska is accessible by water only during the summer.) Indeed, by checking some climatic graphs of Europe, you will discover that, particularly in the winter, the west-east temperature contrasts are much greater than the north-south differences. Therefore, it should not be surprising that the average January temperature in Bucharest, Romania is the same as that in Oslo, Norway. It is usually somewhat more surprising to learn that winters are no colder at the North Cape of Norway than they are in Chicago—and, aside from the darkness, probably no more unpleasant!

Summers are another matter, for then location relative to the sun reasserts itself. Even though the sun is above the horizon for many hours each day in the north of Europe, the low angle at which its light is received results in temperatures over much of Scandinavia that are largely comparable to those in northern New England or the upper Great Lakes states. On the other hand, in Mediterranean Europe, summer temperature averages rise into the middle to upper seventies and low eighties. Nevertheless, sustained heat waves like those that annually bake the more continental portions (i.e., the interior) of mid-America are of such infrequent occurrence in Europe as to warrant front page newspaper coverage when they do take place.

However, temperature is only half the climate story, if that. Moisture is another important aspect of climate. We have already noted the sharp seasonal contrast in precipitation in the Mediterranean region, with virtually the entire year's supply falling during the winter months. This we attributed largely to shifts in airflow—onshore in winter, paralleling the coast or offshore in summer. Over the rest of Europe, where winds are onshore all year long, there is no such thing as a dry season. (This does not, of course, mean that "drought" cannot occur, but an extremely dry year such as 1959 is a very uncommon happening.) Some months, to be sure, are drier than others, with annual precipitation regime usually reflecting a place's location.

Thus, over the western, more maritime portions of Europe, the contrast in land and water temperatures is greatest in the autumn and early winter, because the land cools more rapidly than the adjacent ocean as the sun retreats southward. Air moving inland from the yet-warm sea condenses its moisture as it reaches the colder land surface—usually as a slow drizzle—so that the months with the heaviest rain in much of western Europe are September and October. By the same token, the temperature contrasts between land and water are least in spring and early summer. Thus, some of the most delightfully dry and sunny weather in maritime Europe is experienced in late April, May, and early June.

On the other hand, the more continental interior portions of Europe, because they are farther removed from the moderating influences of the ocean, become much warmer during the summer than the air masses drifting in over them. They therefore tend to warm the air above them, making it unstable and triggering off convectional thunder showers. As a result, these parts of Europe receive their maximum precipitation during the late summer, usually in the form of shorter, more violent downpours than maritime Europe receives. It should also be noted, however, that because these regions have temperatures that drop below freezing in winter, such moisture as falls at that season will most likely occur as snow. Snow is only rarely seen on low ground in maritime Europe.

The lack of a dry season over most of Europe does not mean that the moisture it receives is excessive. An annual average of twenty to thirty inches is typical of much of lowland Europe—an amount corresponding to that received in such states as Minnesota and Iowa. Yet, as soon as some topographic barrier is interposed in the prevailing westerly airflow, the total rises rapidly. Hilly areas intercept over 40 inches of moisture a year, and mountains like the Alps and Pyrenees and those in Scotland and Norway catch well over 100 inches of annual precipitation. Indeed, the moisture-bearing winds have to rise so abruptly over the mountains of western Norway that more than 200 inches of precipitation fall there each year, nourishing the largest glaciers on the mainland of Europe. Yet, in sheltered valleys hardly thirty miles to the east, it is so dry that local farmers must irrigate their crops!

On the basis of such temperature and precipitation patterns, geographers have subdivided Europe into several distinct climatic regions. One such classification, recently devised by the author, defines the climates of Europe in terms of their *effective* warmth and moisture. Figure 2 shows that five distinct zones of effective warmth can be identified within the subcontinent. These are the Subtropical Zone (B), where typical crops are olives, citrus, tobacco, and cotton; the Warm-Temperate Zone (C), the northern margin of which essentially outlines the northern limits of maize and grape cultivation; the Cool Temperate Zone, (D) the poleward boundary of which marks the transition from mixed forest into the solid stands of spruce and pine that characterize the boreal forest, or taigá; the Subarctic Zone (E), the northern edge of which coincides with the treeline; and the Polar Zone (F), where deficiency in warmth permits only the growth of grasses and shrubs typifying the tundra. From Figure 2 it is readily apparent that the two principal climatic controls are latitude and altitude, a fact further substantiated by the distribution of effective moisture as depicted in Figure 3. The latter illustrates that there is a superabundance of precipitation in the upland areas of the British Isles, western Norway, and in the Alps, Carpathians, and western Yugoslavia, whereas moisture is adequate for tree growth in upland regions as far south as northwestern Spain, central Italy, and southern Greece. On the other hand, there is generally a deficiency of moisture in the lower lying regions of southern and southeastern Europe, especially in the "rain shadows" of the areas discussed above. In these regions the characteristic vegetation is scrub forest, or maquis, in the Mediterranean basin and grass in the basins of the lower

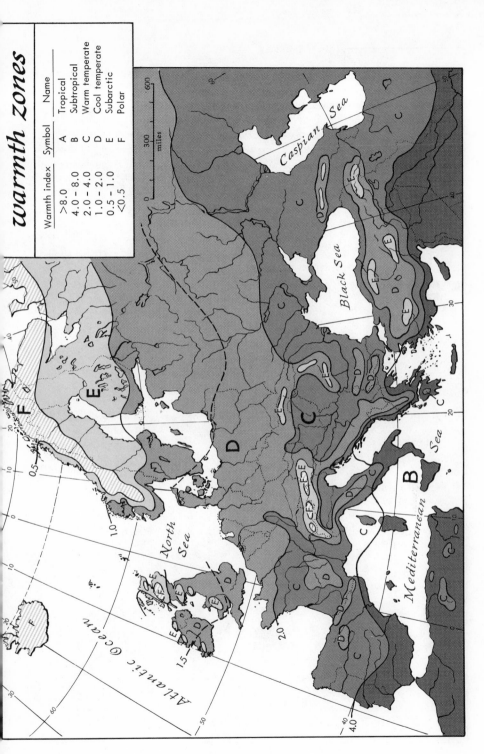

Figure 2

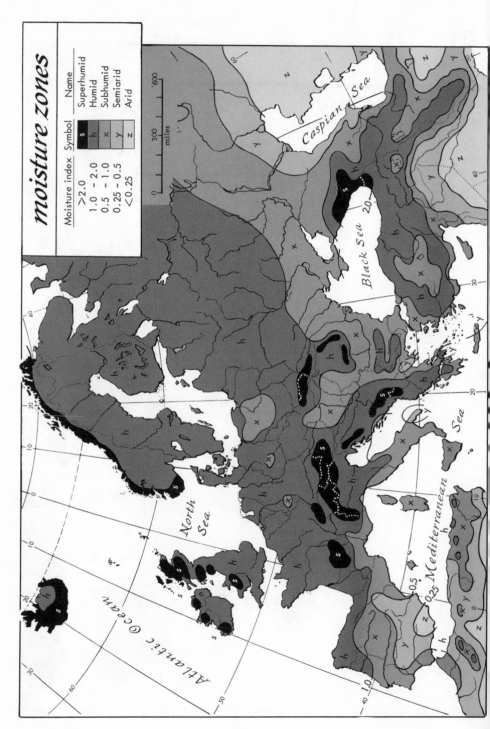

Figure 3

Danube valley. Figure 3 also reveals several small "dry pockets" in the forest regions of central Europe, particularly in low-lying areas of Poland and Germany.

The alert reader has no doubt detected that although we began by discussing climate, we seem to have ended up talking about vegetation. Indeed, because the natural vegetation of an area is one of the best single indicators of its climate, most of the critical boundaries of this climatic classification were drawn with this fact in mind. However, the seasonal distribution of moisture markedly influences its effectiveness, for as we have already noted, the subhumid (x) areas of southern Europe (which have winter rains) are clothed by an evergreen scrub forest, whereas similar regions in the lower Danube valley (with summer rains) support only a grass cover. In the semiarid areas of southern Europe (y), especially in Spain but also in sheltered pockets of eastern Italy and Greece, a short-grass, or steppe, vegetation is likewise dominant. On the other hand, in southeastern Spain—the part of Europe with the lowest total effective precipitation—a true desert condition prevails. Where effective warmth is the crucial factor, as at higher elevations and higher latitudes, the broadleaf deciduous forest gradually gives way to the conifers, which are themselves replaced by the grasses, heather, and low, flowering plants common to the alpine meadows and the tundra. Indeed, it is interesting that the words "alp" and "tundra" (from Finnish *tunturi*), despite their altered shades of meaning today, both derive from the same phenomenon—mountains that extend above the treeline.

If we were to follow our "chain reaction" from location to climate to vegetation one step farther, we would find that the broad zonal patterns of soil constitute a further link. For example, in the Mediterranean region, high temperatures combined with winter rains result in the rapid chemical breakdown and leaching away of most soluble minerals in the soil. Since the scrubby thorn forest native to the area adds little in the way of organic matter, or humus, most Mediterranean soils take their color from the insoluble minerals that remain, namely iron and aluminum. As a result, they are usually red or yellow—the color of bricks—and they take the name *laterite* from the Latin word for brick (*latus*). Not only are laterites inherently infertile soils to begin with, but, being exposed as they are to winter rains on almost vegetation-less slopes, they have been subject to frightful erosion through the ages. Actually, the most fertile soils within the Mediterranean basin are those derived from such parent material as alluvium, volcanic deposits, and some lime-rich limestones. This accounts for the fact that some of the region's heaviest concentrations of farmland and of population are along river valleys and on the flanks of the volcanoes in southern Italy.

The cooler, damper climates prevailing over the rest of Europe produce what soil scientists term *podsols*. Though chemical decomposition proceeds more slowly in these regions, the soils tend to be heavily leached of soluble minerals. Where the leaf mold of the broadleaf deciduous forests has been incorporated into the soil as humus, we find the so-called grey-brown podsols—the brown color coming from the organic matter. However, where the native vegetation is coniferous forest, there is no such addition of humus, and as a consequence, the soils have the ashy-grey color of a true podsol. As a further consequence, they are even less fertile than the grey-brown soils.

To be sure, there are local exceptions within these zonal soil groups as well. The richer alluvium of the river valleys has always attracted the farmer, as have those areas whose soils are derived from lime-rich limestones—the so-called *rendzinas*. With proper drainage, some of the bog and half-bog soils of the damper regions of maritime Europe have been turned to productive use, and another concentration of farming activity has been in the rich loess (wind-blown) soils of central Europe.

By far the richest soils in Europe are found in the subhumid regions of the southeast, where the famous chernozems, or blackearths, have developed beneath the grasslands of the lower Danube valley. Here a deficiency of moisture has resulted in the concentration of soluble minerals at some depth, while the heavy sod formed by the native grass cover provides an abundance of organic matter. With the exception of the chernozem and the few local exceptions noted elsewhere, we must conclude that the soils of Europe are not among the most *fertile* in the world. However, the reasons why they are among the most *productive* soils in the world remain to be clarified when we examine individual countries.

So far, an intimate relationship between climate, vegetation, and soil has been demonstrated. Indeed, the cause-and-effect linkages between these aspects of the atmosphere and the biosphere might well lead us to term them the "locative" factors of the physical setting, for they all trace their origins to their location. Unfortunately, we can demonstrate no such interrelationships amongst the various aspects of the lithosphere, for like gold in the old adage, such things as bedrock, landforms, and other minerals are "where you find them." For want of a better term, we might therefore call these the "non-locative" aspects of the physical setting.

Perhaps before we go too far in discounting any kind of "system" in the location of the major topographic features of Europe, we can indulge ourselves in drawing some very broad generalizations. For example, the oldest rock in Europe, the core around which the subcontinent seems to have taken shape, is to be found in the so-called Fenno-Scandian Shield. As its name suggests, the Fenno-Scandian Shield underlies Finland and much of the Scandinavian Peninsula, and it has been around so long that it has the unimpressive profile of a Viking's shield lying on the ground. Erosion has taken such a toll of its once-proud mountains that all we find today are the planed-off stumps of ranges that rivaled the Himalayas in their day—the Gotides in western Sweden, the Svecofennides in central Sweden and southern Finland, and the Karelides along the present Soviet-Finnish frontier. Composed chiefly of granites and other crystalline rocks, the ancient Shield has largely been stripped of any more recent sedimentary rocks it may have borne. As a result, it is fairly rich in primary metallic minerals such as iron and copper, but it is totally devoid of fossil fuels such as coal, oil, and natural gas. Its soils, too, apart from those developed on scattered remnants of Cambro-Silurian limestones and shales, are among the coarsest and most infertile in Europe.

On the western edges of the Shield a great structural trough, or geosyncline, early became the recipient of thousands of feet of sediments which, when compacted by the throes of the earth's crust as it shrank, were buckled into mountains that rimmed the North Atlantic basin from Ireland through Britain, Norway, and Svalbard to Greenland. The trend-lines of these so-called Caledonian Mountains are still to be seen in these regions today, and one of the sharpest lines of cleavage is the fault valley that breaks diagonally across Scotland from southwest to northeast, separating the Northwest Highlands from the Grampian Mountains. Elsewhere along the southern and southeastern edges of the Shield, such deposition as took place was largely in the form of a veneer over the submerged roots of the Shield itself.

However, if one goes far enough west or south from the stable old Shield, one finds himself in the youngest, most turbulent parts of Europe, geologically speaking. Here, in relatively recent geologic times, a series of dramatic events have added some of the most spectacular lineaments to Europe's physiognomy. Chief among these was the Alpine Orogeny, which threw up a bulwark of mountains along the entire length of the Mediterranean basin and on into the Middle East and central Asia, where it culminates in the Himalayas. So, far from having a "soft underbelly" as Churchill once described it, southern Europe has the highest, most rugged mountains in all the subcontinent, including the Sierra Nevada, the Pyrenees, the Alps, the Apennines, the Carpathians, the Transylvanian and Dinaric Alps, the Balkan ranges, the Rhodope, and the Pindus. Some of these—notably the Alps—show signs of having been compressed from the south, as if the land mass of Africa had pushed northward against the old Fenno-Scandian block. In any event, the Mediterranean basin remains an area of active crustal deformation today, as witnessed by its frequent earthquakes and occasional volcanic eruptions. Not only has this deformation culminated in the loftiest and most jagged mountains in present-day Europe (Mont Blanc, 15,600 feet), but its "shock waves" were transmitted into the older geologic formations to the north. Here the earth's crust was cracked and buckled too, but in lesser degree because it was farther from the source of the disturbance. (Location, orientation, and innovation play their roles even here.) Thus, encircling the alpine ranges of southern Europe we find a broad, discontinuous band of shattered landscapes that we can best call the Central Mountains and Plateaus region—the Massif Central of France, the Vosges and the Ardennes, the Jura and the Black Forest, the varied ranges of central Germany and the border ranges of Bohemia. Also included are the uplifted plateaus of Spain, southern Germany, and Czechoslovakia, as well as the downfaulted valley of the Rhine (the Rhine graben) and the local volcanic outbreaks in the Auvergne of France and the Vogelsberg of Germany.

A further step to the west and north, we find that the effects of the Alpine Orogeny have diminished to mere ripples. Here the sedimentary rocks were gently warped into domes and basins, of which the London and Paris basins are perhaps the best known examples. However, most of the surface was left undisturbed enough that it retained the character of flat-lying plains. Thus, we can speak of a fourth major landform region of Europe—the Central Lowland (or perhaps we should call it the Northern Plain). At any rate, it extends in an unbroken arc from the base of the Pyrenees in southwestern France through the basins of Aquitaine and Paris, the lowlands of eastern England, the Low Countries, northern Germany, Denmark and southernmost Sweden, into Poland where it broadens into the vast expanses of the plains of Russia. This vast arc of lowland is not only laced by large navigable rivers but also underlain in several places by deposits of high-grade coal and occasional pockets of natural gas and oil. Significantly, the coal measures are most accessible on the upturned edges of the plain, where it abuts against the ancient highlands of Britain and against the younger uplands of central Europe.

About the same time that the Alpine Orogeny was convulsing much of the mainland of Europe, a convulsion of proportionate magnitude was gripping the North Atlantic. There, great fissures opened in the floor of the ocean and layer after layer of basalt poured out to form a gigantic island which geologists have named Greater Iceland. At its maximum extent it stretched from northern Ireland through western Scotland, the Faeroes, and Iceland into central Greenland, and as far north as Jan Mayen. So much molten rock was erupted (some 15,000 feet in thickness) that a large portion of the earth's crust faltered and collapsed, forming the abyss now known as the Norwegian Sea. At the same time, the old Shield area was uplifted along the downfaulted edge of the sea, giving the Scandinavian Peninsula its present asymmetrical profile—a steep western declivity and a long, gradual slope toward the east. Subsequent displacements of the earth's crust reduced the core of this island to more nearly the present proportions of Iceland, in the center of which active volcanism has continued ever since. Indeed, Iceland has the distinction of being the only part of the mid-Atlantic ridge that rises above water, and hence the only place that the slow, inexorable drifting apart of the blocks of the earth's crust can be studied at first hand.

Hardly had the Alps and Iceland appeared or the ancient Shield been uplifted when a marked change in the climate began to manifest itself. In all of these upland regions so much snow began to accumulate in winter that it did not melt during the summer. Gradually great ice sheets took form and started grinding their way down-slope, both through the alpine valleys of central Europe and across the Shield of northern Europe. During the Pleistocene period, such glaciers engulfed much of Europe on at least four different occasions, with the maximum advance taking place the second time. Then ice from north central Scandinavia pushed as far south as the Thames and Rhine rivers and ground to a halt against the uplands of central Germany and southern Poland.

Drastic as the effects of the recurrent advance and retreat of the ice sheets were on the climate, vegetation, and animal life of Europe, perhaps the most permanent traces of the Ice Age are to be found in the landforms and soils. Over the mountains of Scandinavia the ice was so thick as to have blanketed virtually everything, subduing the landscape into polished, streamlined forms that contrast sharply with the jagged, nonglaciated peaks of such mountains as the Alps. Over the Shield most of the original soil cover was stripped away, and where the glacier halted (the last time in Denmark, northern Germany, and Poland) it dumped great ridges of unsorted sand, gravel, boulders, and clay. The melt-water streams from the wasting ice built up extensive outwash plains in front of these; yet further removed from the ice margin the wind deposited the fine dust (loess) it winnowed from the vegetationless areas at the base of the glacier.

Thus, especially across Northern Europe, one finds rapid changes in the nature and composition of the soil—moraine, outwash, and loess all deposited in more or less concentric arcs from the ice-scoured core of the Shield. Though the Shield itself was gouged into lakes and swamps and veneered with moraine by the glacier, it did benefit in some degree from the after-effects of glaciation. The crushing weight of the ice had so depressed the surface of the Shield that after the glacier melted, the rising sea levels invaded its periphery, laying down a thick layer of heavy marine clay. As the Shield itself rebounded, its clay covered fringes emerged as extensive coastal plains, becoming in the process the most conducive areas for later settlement and agricultural use. Indeed, the boundary between the moraine and the clay—the so-called "highest marine limit"—is one of the most important natural boundaries to be found anywhere in northern Europe today.

The Afro-Asian Prelude: Prehistoric Impulses

So far, we have examined Europe solely in terms of its physical setting, almost as though man didn't enter into the equation at all. Of course, man did not come upon the European scene until rather late in his history after many long and important chapters in the human drama had already unfolded in Africa and in Asia. Lying as it does in what was one of the more uncongenial corners of the World Island for primitive humankind, Europe was decidely peripheral to the arena where man's first faltering steps were taken.

Because of its location, Europe was most accessible to early man and his innovations from the south and east. As a result, four distinct avenues of approach came into use, three by land and one by water (Figure 4). Probably the most important entryway into the subcontinent was that leading over the land bridges of Asia Minor and the Balkan Peninsula, linking southwest Asia with central Europe by way of the Danube valley. Of scarcely less importance, however, has been the broad avenue of grassland that sweeps around the Black Sea and opens on the one hand

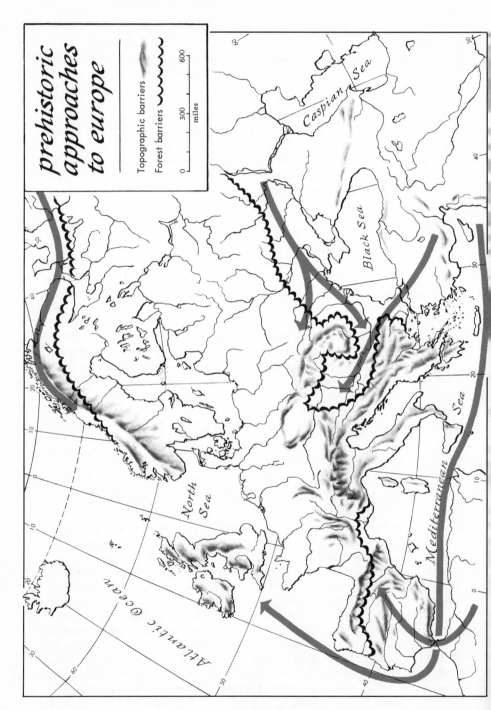

Figure 4

into the North European plain and on the other, into the Danubian corridor. Somewhat more offside was Europe's third land approach, namely that skirting the western end of the Mediterranean Sea across the Iberian Peninsula. Finally, the Mediterranean itself afforded a much-used water route to the western outposts of Europe, whence early seafarers turned northward along the Atlantic shores, penetrating on occasion as far as the North and Baltic seas.

Along all of these arteries, it should be remembered, the earliest impulses of men and ideas moved primarily *from* Asia and Africa *to* Europe, that is, east to west and south to north. (A fifth, but much less used, approach to Europe was along the tundra fringes of the Arctic Ocean. The earliest settlers in what today is Scandinavia appear to have been a circumpolar people who moved into this ice-free region during the waning stages of the last glaciation.)

Although Europe represented a relatively remote and inhospitable corner of the Pleistocene world, it was probably here that Homo sapiens finally emerged. Certainly, Cro-Magnon men who moved into Europe across the Iberian land bridge following the third advance of the glaciers were in every respect the physical equals of modern men and equipped with full-sized brains. Nevertheless, there is good evidence that Cro-Magnon man adopted many skills and customs from Neanderthal man, who likewise pushed into Europe late in the Third Interglacial Period from the southeast. However, when the glacier began grinding southward once again, Cro-Magnon man beat a hasty retreat for the warmer climes of southern France, Spain, and North Africa, leaving Neanderthal man to "over-winter" the Fourth Ice Age by himself. For a time this sturdy creature seems to have held his own, but then suddenly—during a relatively warm spell about 80,000 years ago—Neanderthal man disappeared. What caused his abrupt demise, no one has yet discovered.

The long-headed Cro-Magnon hunters who moved into Europe as the glacier melted back a fourth time remained the dominant, perhaps the sole, inhabitants of the subcontinent until about 8000 B.C. By that time the climate had grown so warm that marked changes in the patterns of vegetation and animal life were manifesting themselves. In the moist regions of maritime Europe the forest was becoming so dense and impenetrable that the larger game species on which the hunters had come to depend for their sustenance were becoming extinct. In these regions, therefore, man was increasingly obliged to seek his livelihood along the seacoast and in the tidal marshes by fishing and fowling. The advances in technology that resulted from this shift in orientation ushered in a new cultural level, the so-called Mesolithic Period, or Middle Stone Age. About the same time, however, a new wave of people, apparently of shorter stature and with round heads, began moving into Europe from the central Asian region, where the growing warmth had resulted in progressive dessication. Entering Europe over land bridges from the east, they spread up the Danube valley into central Europe, where their descendent's comprise the so-called Alpine physical type. In the process they wedged themselves into the midst of the existing long-headed peoples of Europe, separating the Nordics in the north from the Mediterraneans in the south. The latter groups were already being progressively differentiated from each other by their pigmentation: light hair, eye, and skin color was coming to the fore in the relatively sunless north, in contrast to the dark hair, eye, and skin color of the sunny south.

The beginnings of the Mesolithic Period in western Europe were paralleled by the development of an even higher cultural level in southwestern Asia. There the domestication of plants and animals and the making of pottery and textiles were ushering in the Neolithic Period, or New Stone Age and were permitting man to become an active producer of food rather than merely a gatherer of the bounties of nature. This innovation did not reach even the most exposed southeasterly fringes of Europe (the island of Crete) until about 4000 B.C., and it took another two millenia for the techniques of farming and stock raising to diffuse through the Danube corridor and into the northwestern margins of Europe. During the latter part of this period another innovation, ostensibly of eastern Mediterranean origin, reached the coastlands of northwestern Europe by sea. This was the Megalithic, or "big-stone," culture, of which such remains as those as those at Carnac in Brittany and Stonehenge in southern England are outstanding examples.

Already the ripples of a new wave of cultural innovation were spreading over the southeastern regions of Europe. This was the Bronze Age, whose introduction into the subcontinent about 2000 B.C. seems to be related to the in-migration of Indo-European peoples. The latter were responsible not only for initiating the making and use of metals in Europe but also for creating the major lineaments of the subcontinent's linguistic patterns (Figure 5). Thus, Greek- and Illyrian-speaking peoples spread southward through the Balkans and Italic-speaking peoples moved into peninsular Italy, escaping in the process the thrust of other Indo-Europeans still behind them. The Celts, on the other hand, were pushed the entire length of the Danube corridor and out into the Atlantic fringes of Europe by succeeding groups of Teutonic-speaking peoples, who occupied central and northern Europe, and Slavic-speaking peoples who settled in eastern Europe. Of the previous inhabitants of Europe, the only ones who preserved their language in the face of this Indo-European deluge were the Basques, who found refuge in the western Pyrenees.

The Bronze Age had hardly reached the outlying regions of western and northern Europe when the Iron Age, which had its origins in Asia Minor, began to flourish in the Danube corridor, especially in what is present-day Austria. Dating back to about 1000 B.C., the European Iron Age essentially coincided with the emergence of a European-based center of innovation in its own right. No longer was this peninsular projection of the World Island only a passive recipient of peoples and ideas born in other places; from then on it began to make its presence felt by creating new forces of its own. This is not to say that the main themes of civilization would not continue to emanate from the south and east for some time to come, but now, to these themes, Europe would begin adding some counterpoint of its own.

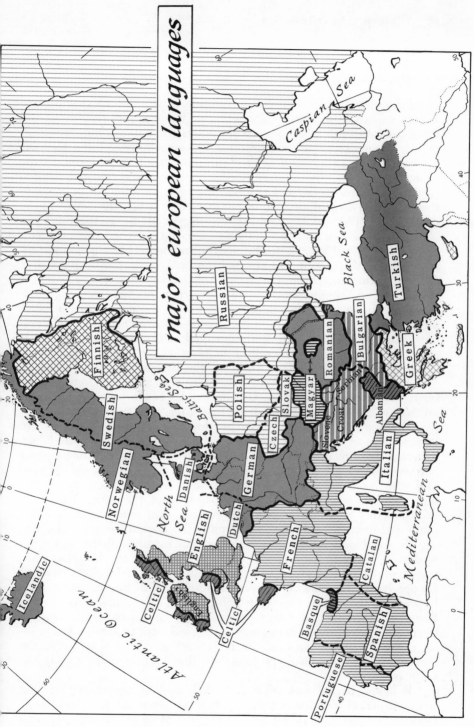

Figure 5 *After Zaborski,* Goode's Atlas, *13th ed., (Rand McNally), p. 128.*

The Emergence of Europe:
From Periphery to Center

For reasons of location and orientation, it was Greece that became
Europe's first cultural hearth, spreading its influence not only south and
eastward into the earlier centers of civilization but carrying the torch
northward into the Black Sea region and westward through the Mediterranean as well. In addition to their magnificent intellectual and artistic
achievements, the city-states of Greece gave a new *regional* dimension
to the economic, social, and political life of civilization, as opposed to
the essentially *local* dimension of civilization as it first developed in the
exotic river valleys of Mesopotamia and Egypt. Rome, as the European
successor to Greece and the "ultimate" city-state, carried this process a
giant step forward by maintaining its civilization on literally a *continental* scale. By the time it had reached the peak of its power, Rome had
pushed its frontiers to the borderlands of Scotland and to the banks of
the Rhine and Danube rivers, as well as having annexed the entire Mediterranean basin. And, though the empire itself did not endure, a religious innovation from Palestine, which Rome first sought to extirpate and
later came to embrace, ultimately emerged as the one great force that
gave continuity and permanence to the prestige and significance of what
is now known to the western world as "the Eternal City."

About the same time that Christianity was invading Rome, in the
far northeast of Europe Finno-Ugrian peoples began pushing into what
are today Estonia and Finland. In the latter area they gradually displaced toward the north a docile hunting folk, whose descendents are
known to us as the Lapps but who prefer to call themselves the *Same*.
Although this invasion in a sense completed the ethnic variegation of
northern Europe, it was merely a prologue to the great torrents of peoples who began to spill across eastern and central Europe during the
fifth century. Sweeping in from the Asian steppes, the savage Huns sent
the Germanic tribes of the North European plain scurrying toward the
south and west, overrunning and toppling the Roman Empire and infus-
ing Teuton blood into the veins of peoples ranging all the way from
western Norway to Tunisia and Sicily. By the time the *Völkerwander-
ungen*, or Great Migrations, were over, the ethnic and cultural map of
Europe had been redrawn. Even the church, one of the few institutions
to weather the storm, had been split, and a new center—"the second
Rome"—had formed at Constantinople. In the safety of its marine-
oriented location, the eastern church managed both to survive the prob-
ing thrusts of Bulgar horsemen in the seventh century and to escape the
impact of Magyar nomads pushing into the Danube valley during the
tenth century.

Religion, or the lack of it, provided most of the theme for that
troubled period of European history that we often call the Dark Ages.
Christian Europe soon found itself in the jaws of a pincers, with Moslems
beating on the gates in the south and pagan Vikings pillaging the towns

and churches of the north. Thanks to the general chaos prevailing within Europe itself, both of these peoples literally got as far as their respective vehicles would take them—the Moors as far into Iberia as they could manuever their horses (the fact that Charles Martel "defeated" them at Tours in central France is probably less responsible for turning them around than the thickening forests they encountered), the Vikings as far up the estuaries and embayments of western Europe and as far down the river systems of Russia as their sleek ships could sail. It was religion that finally pacified the north, a fact evidenced by the inclusion of the Christian cross in all the national emblems of northern Europe, and it was religion that served as a rallying cry for a renewed European thrust toward the south and east. The reconquest of Spain, a 700-year war to regain what Islam had captured in seven; the German "drive to the east"; the Swedish conquest of Finland; and, above all, the Crusades to liberate the Holy Land—all had a religious veneer, if not a religious core, for commercial, military, and political motives soon emerged as well.

The gradual revival of long-distance trade sparked the growth of such cities as Venice, Genoa, Pisa, and Florence. New centers of crafts and commerce arose in Flanders and merchants from all the corners of Europe flocked to the great annual fairs held in such strategic places as Champagne and Leipzig. In the north of Europe, a group of German port towns formed an alliance (the *Hanse*) that soon came to dominate the trade of the North and Balitic Sea regions. Yet, with all the irony of a Greek tragedy, it was also this revival of long-distance trade that virtually wiped Europe off the map. In the three years between 1347 and 1350, from one-half to two-thirds of the population of the subcontinent succumbed to the Black Death, introduced from Asia by way of the Black Sea region into the seaports of western Italy.

In its way, the Black Death probably did as much, if not more to set the stage for the ferment in Europe during the fifteenth and sixteenth centuries as did the fall of Constantinople to the Turks and the closure of the eastern trade routes. It may be said that its disastrous effects shook the established beliefs and institutions of Latin Christendom so thoroughly that in the process it helped create the intellectual atmosphere that ultimately resulted in both the Renaissance and the Reformation. In any event, from 1500 onward Europe began reorienting itself westward, looking beyond the Pillars of Hercules for a new way to the east. In the process the New World was discovered, and new political constellations came into being.

Now the most remote margins of Europe found themselves center stage, for the Atlantic had become Europe's front door instead of its back stop. Portugal, Spain, France, England, Holland, and to a lesser degree even Denmark and Sweden, began investing their energies in the acquisition of empires in America, Africa, and Asia. Western, maritime Europe became imperial Europe, snatching up colonies from which to extract wealth and to which to export the superfluous or unwanted elements of their populations (such as criminals, paupers, and religious dissenters). At last Europe had regained the momentum it had lost with the fall of Rome. No longer was religion the sole allegiance of the European, nor even the major one. Indeed, following the Reformation and the long bloody struggles it engendered, Europe's religious allegiance was split in three ways: the south retaining its ties to Roman Catholicism, the east dominated by the Greek Orthodox faith, and the northwest becoming Protestant (See Figure 6). Moreover, the city-state had been supplanted by the nation-state as the fundamental economic and political entity, and its geographic dimensions were no longer entirely regional or even continental, but in some instances were taking on global proportions. The epitome of European colonial expansion was reached by Great Britain; there is little doubt that Brittania not only "ruled the waves" from 1800 on, but also dominated much of the world's economic and political life.

The Commercial Revolution that was responsible for Britain's rise to world leadership also paved the way for the Industrial Revolution, which had its birthplace in Britain. The rising demand in the colonies for cloth, in particular, encouraged the acceleration of textile output through mechanization. Mechanization in turn encouraged the development of inanimate sources of energy, first as water power in mountain streams and later as steam power generated from coal. This development spurred the production of iron and steel from which to make the machines and the boilers, and it was not long before steam was harnessed to wheels and propellers as well, to create the first really new means of transport the world had seen since the domestication of the horse and the invention of the sail. Britain became "the workshop of the world" as country folk swarmed to the growing towns to take jobs in mines and factories. Soon other countries, especially those with the necessary coal and iron ore deposits, began emulating the British, and gradually industrialization spread eastward across Europe and westward over the Atlantic. On the European subcontinent itself, Britain's strongest competition came to the fore in Germany, a nation-state whose tardy unification had largely denied her a role in overseas empire building. The economic rivalry between Britain and Germany, these "have" and "have not" nations respectively, was largely responsible for the unleashing of the two World Wars of the twentieth century, after the second of which all of Europe was prostrate and Britain had been reduced to second-rank status. In 1945, for the first time in over 400 years, the world's power center was no longer in Europe, but had divided between two Europe's former "hinterlands," the United States and the Soviet Union.

Since World War II, Europe's major energies have been expended in reconstruction and various forms of regional integration. At the same time that the nations of Europe have been trying to work out a *modus vivendi* with the superpowers that flank them, they have also been striving to develop a "European" consciousness to supplant the ruinous nationalism that has largely been their undoing. However, in a region that was the very cradle of the nation-state, progress toward the latter goal has been slow and erratic.

Despite its grievous sufferings since the dawn of the Industrial

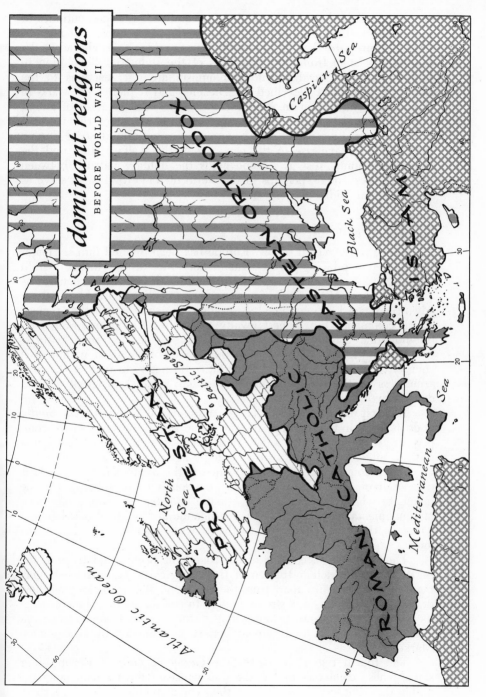

dominant religions
BEFORE WORLD WAR II

Figure 6

21

Revolution—indeed, in large part because of them—Europe continues to be a major wellspring of innovation even today. It is ironic, but not difficult to appreciate, that the two main opposing ideologies abroad in the world today stem from the early days of the Industrial Revolution in western Europe. Socialism and communism are but reactions to the unbridled capitalism described by Dickens—and deplored by Marx—in nineteenth century Britain. The abuse of labor, the creation of slums, and the despoliation of the landscape are but a few of the ills that gradually stirred a sense of social consciousness within industrial Europe and gradually gave rise to the concepts of the welfare state and the planned economy. Just as Europe holds the military balance between East and West today, perhaps in the world of tomorrow it can serve as an ideological bridge as well.

The Regions of Europe

In the pages which follow, Europe has been divided into six major regions (see map facing page 1), each defined by a distinct theme. Within each region, it seemed appropriate to consider the individual country as a second level of division, for despite Europe's remarkable postwar advances toward supranational association, the state is still the "region" which commands the highest loyalty from most Europeans. Moreover, the individual countries have been further subdivided into such "natural" or "cultural" regions as have been traditionally recognized within each country, or where such regional identities do not form part of the consciousness of the country's inhabitants, into general geographic areas defined by location.

The first major region of Europe, the so-called *Mediterranean South,* finds its unity in the fact that all four of the European states which comprise it are dominated by a dry, subtropical climatic pattern that has a critical influence on their overwhelmingly agricultural way of life.

The second region we have defined is the *western fringe,* which is composed of three major countries (overlooking Luxembourg for the moment) whose location on the Atlantic doorstep of Europe has been of fundamental importance to their economic and political development —that is, they are continental footholds with essentially maritime outlooks.

The third region consists of the islands of Britain and Ireland, *the insular realms* which by reason of their physical isolation have largely managed to live a life apart from the continent, at least as long as they, or especially Britain, was strong enough to enforce its detachment. (Today, on the other hand, Britain's long history of non-European orientation is being used as an argument against its admission to the Common Market.)

The fourth region comprises the *Germanic core* of Europe—four states whose common bond is the dominance of the German language within their borders. In addition to their common cultural heritage, these countries share a central location near the heart of the sub-continent—a location that has exposed them to precisely the kinds of involvement that the insular realms have largely succeeded in avoiding.

Similarly, the fifth region, termed the *Eastern crush-zone,* has by virtue of its position been buffeted by every people, philosophy, and political tide that has flowed between peninsular Europe and the borderlands of Asia. But unlike the "Germanic core", it has become culturally fragmented to an extreme degree. The region's unity, therefore, has been its very disunity, at least until the end of World War II when for the first time all the countries of Eastern Europe were forceably unified into an ideological buffer by and for the Soviet Union.

The sixth and final region, the *northern frontier* is composed of five countries with strong cultural and historic associations—five states unified by their location on the poleward margins of the *Oekumene, or* habitable world; five states which, despite their niggardly resource endowment, have managed to achieve the highest overall levels of living of any major region in Europe.

This, then, is the framework of the discussion to follow: a description of the personality and a measure of the significance of six regions that hopefully will enable the reader to grasp and to understand Europe as a whole.

CHAPTER **2** *the mediterranean south*

Jutting southward out of the land mass of Europe are three irregular peninsulas, the smallest and most articulated in the east, the largest and most massive in the west. Although all are bathed by the waters of the Mediterranean Sea, none is exclusively "mediterranean" in either physical setting or culture patterns. At some time in their past, each of these peninsulas has held within its territory the economic and political center of the western world, but today all of them contain states which, at best, must be reckoned as third-ranking powers.

The countries of the Mediterranean are "old" lands in relation to Europe as a whole, for they were among the earliest to be occupied by man and consequently among those that have been most altered by his hand. In all of them, the long continued growth of population has placed heavy pressure on a resource base with some rather severe limitations, both for agriculture and for industry. Indeed, apart from regional exceptions within individual countries, all the Mediterranean states are essentially under-developed industrially; as a result, they have some of the lowest per capita incomes in Europe. The region's economic backwardness and poverty is reflected in its political instability, for totalitarian regimes today hold the reins of government in three of the four states (Spain, Portugal and Greece), while in the fourth (Italy), where a recent flirtation with fascism ended in fiasco, a fragile experiment in democracy is now underway.

Owing to their latitudinal location, the peninsulas of Iberia, Italy, and Greece experience a climate characterized by mild, wet winters and hot, dry summers—but only in the lowlands. At higher elevations, as in the Meseta of central Spain, it is often bitterly cold in winter, and heavy snowfalls are frequent both in the Apennines of Italy and the Pindus of Greece. In the lowlands the summer drought restricts the vegetation to plants especially adapted to retain the water they receive in winter, with the result that there are many evergreen varieties with waxy leaves or thorns for leaves, extensive root systems, or thick bark. Among the economically important plants native to the region are the vine and the olive, and, in a fairly restricted area of southwestern Iberia, the cork oak. On the higher, cooler, and moister mountain slopes, both broadleaf deciduous and coniferous forests may be found, at least in those areas where the depredations of man and his livestock, especially the goat, have not gone too far.

The lack of rainfall during the warmest months of the year, when both plants and animals need it most, is one of the most critical factors in the Mediterranean way of life. The availability of water is all-important in determining what land shall be used and how. In rich alluvial lowlands, the presence of water from streams, wells, or springs permits intensive cultivation of citrus fruits, vegetables, maize, and rice, and along some of the damper riverine meadows there are luxuriant pastures for cattle and horses. Back from the rivers, however, on the higher and drier land, the cultivation is chiefly of grains such as wheat and barley, which are planted in the autumn, soak up moisture from the winter rains, and are ready to harvest during the dry, sunny days of early summer. Where these unirrigated over-wintering crops cannot be grown, or where the land is temporarily left fallow, we find poor pasture for the more adaptive forms of livestock such as swine, sheep, goats, and burros—all of which are more characteristic of the Mediterranean region than are the cow or horse. Finally, in areas where there is an absence of both water and relatively flat land for cultivation, the native tree and vine crops—the olive and the grape—are the dominant elements of the agricultural landscape.

Few aspects of life in Mediterranean Europe have escaped the impact of the region's distinctive climatic regime. The diet and dress of the people, their choice of building materials and architectural styles, the densities and patterns of settlement, all reflect in large measure man's adaptation to the alternating cycle of cool-season rain and warm-season drought. It can perhaps be said that in Mediterranean Europe only the dictates of religion, the requirements of defense, and the inroads of industry have influenced man's relation to the land and to his fellow man to the degree that climate has.

Greece

Greece as we see it on the map today is a relatively recent creation, dating essentially from the time of World War I. Following its glorious heyday as the zenith of Western civilization, it languished for centuries under the yoke of foreign invaders, among them Romans, Venetians, Crusaders, and Turks. Not until 1830, with the assistance of such partisans as England's Lord Byron, did Greek nationalism revive sufficiently to acquire a territorial base of its own. Indeed, it is hardly an exaggeration to state that Greek independence was largely sponsored by an imperialist maritime Britain, which saw in the articulated Greek peninsulas and islands many excellent harbors, control of which by hostile Turks or Russians it could not tolerate. (In fact, for a time Britain exacted the rights of a naval base in the Ionian Islands, which it relinquished only after it had secured control of Suez and Cyprus.) Following World War II and the dissolution of its empire, Britain no longer found it possible to secure its strategic interest in Greece, and so the United States had to assume this responsibility—or so, at least the Americans came to believe. Through the Truman Doctrine, the United States helped to put down the communist civil war in the north and later it encouraged the admission of both Greece and Turkey to membership in the North Atlantic Treaty Organization.

Outside political interest in Greece is a manifestation of the strategic geographic location the country occupies, commanding as it does the Aegean Sea and, through it, the approaches to the Black Sea. It may well be, however, that the strategic value of Greece to the West may have been seriously compromised, thanks to the establishment of Soviet naval bases in Arab countries fronting on the Mediterranean. In any case, in classical times the Greek hold on the Aegean extended even to the eastern (i.e., Anatolian) mainland, as witnessed by the ruins of such cities as Miletus, Ephesus, and Aphrodisias, to name just a few. Following World War I, however, there was a mass exchange of populations, with Greeks being expelled from Asia Minor and Turks being deported from peninsular Greece and the islands. Thus, today Turkey has sovereignty over the mainland, but all the offshore islands, with two exceptions near the entrance to the Dardanelles, are Greek. (A notable exception is Cyprus, which, as a British colony, did not undergo the exchange of populations. Today, as an independent nation, it is dangerously split by the two ethnic groups.)

THE REGIONS OF GREECE.   Greece can be divided into five main regions, three of which essentially formed the classical nucleus of the country and the other two of which were then and are now somewhat peripheral to its national life (Figure 7). The core of Greece is really the mainland area lying between the mountain bulwark of Othris and the Gulf of Corinth; this region we shall call the Center. The second component of classical Greece was the South—the irregular peninsula of Peloponnesus—while the third region consisted of the Aegean Islands, including the Cyclades, the Sporades, the Dodecanese, and Crete. More remote geographically, and hence culturally, was the North, comprising the plains of Thessaly and, more particularly, of Macedonia and Thrace. Cut off from the rest of the country by the Grammos and Pindus Mountains is the West, composed of Epirus and the Ionian Islands.

The Center.   For being the core of Greece, the central region would hardly seem to have offered a very auspicious physical setting for any human activity, for not only is it one of the driest areas in the country, but it is also largely composed of rugged and barren limestone mountains. The latter, however, are broken by a number of small plains, the

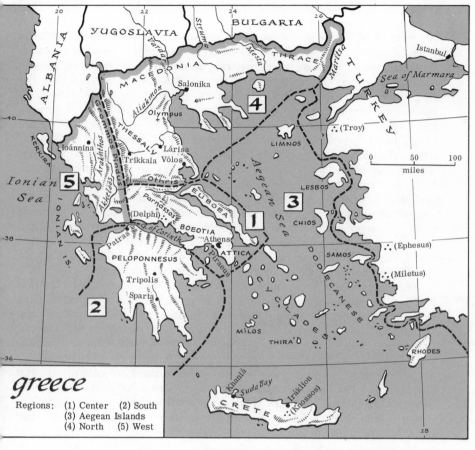

greece

Regions: (1) Center   (2) South
           (3) Aegean Islands
           (4) North   (5) West

Figure 7

most extensive of which is the interior lowland of Boeotia, the remnant of an old lake which was drained in about 1900. Of the coastal plains, the most auspicious is that of Athens (Attica), which is oriented toward the south and thus protected by mountains from the cold northeast winds of winter. Near the middle of the plain rise some irregular hills, one of which the Athenians chose as the nucleus of their city-state, the site of the Acropolis. Initially this location had defensive advantages, and sustenance for the city could be drawn from the farms of the surrounding lowland. However, as both the population and ambitions of Athens grew, it soon found the base of its power (the plains) too small, and it began looking beyond the sea for most of its necessary foodstuffs and raw materials. In the process, the port of Piraeus was spawned, and with it the lifeline of Athens, protected in its maritime reaches by a vast navy and in its final landward leg by a heavily fortified corridor. Following the eclipse of classical Greece, however, Athens virtually disappeared along with the rest of the Greek cities, and in 1830, when it was chosen as the capital of a newly independent kingdom, it was a miserable little town of scarcely 20,000 people, filled with dilapidated monuments to its illustrious past. Athens' rebirth as the administrative center of Greece came as slowly as the emergence of Greece itself, for by World War I it had grown to hardly 150,000 inhabitants. Its most explosive growth by far has taken place since World War II; modern Athens and Piraeus have coalesced into one great population node occupying the entire plain. The nearly 2,000,000 people who reside in this urban agglomeration make up almost one-fourth of the entire Greek population. Whereas Athens has essentially retained its functions as an administrative, cultural, and commercial center, Piraeus has become the country's leading port and industrial center. Fully 40 per cent of the exports of Greece move through it, as do 70 per cent of its imports and some 90 per cent of its passenger traffic. Its industries include everything from textiles and food processing to shipbuilding, chemicals, and oil refining. As the one real urban node that Greece has, this area enjoys the highest per capita income in the country, about twice the national average.

Although the silver mines at Lavrian, southeast of Athens, helped finance the Athenian navy in its days of grandeur, the chief mineral of importance in central Greece today is bauxite, which is dug from the slopes of Mount Parnassos not far from the famed oracle site of Delphi. At present, most of the raw ore is exported through the Gulf of Corinth, but Greece plans to start producing some aluminum of its own.

The South.   Within about twenty miles of the Gulf of Corinth, the mountains of the Peloponnesus rise to more than 7,700 feet. From these heights they fall off gradually toward the south in four jagged, fingerlike ridges. Between each finger of mountains lies a pocket of lowland: the plain of Argos in the northeast, the valley of the Eurotas River in the center, and the plain of Messenia in the southwest. In classical times each of these lowlands was, like the plain of Athens, the site of one or more city-states, but today none of them supports so much as a town of any consequence. On the seaward edge of each, however, a small port has come into existence—chiefly in this century, after the age-old problem of drainage, with its attendant malarial conditions and difficult maritime access, was solved. These ports act as outlets for the olives, citrus fruits, and currants that are produced in their hinterlands. However, the largest plain in the Peloponnesus is that flanking the wetter west coast, where again, disease and difficulties of access precluded settlement in earlier times. Today the city of Patras serves not only as a collecting point for the agricultural produce of this plain, but also as a terminus for ferry services to Corfu, Italy, and Yugoslavia. Its population now approaching 100,000 inhabitants, Patras is the third largest city in Greece and the successor to Corinth (from which came our word "currant") as the chief exporter of this commodity. In the mountainous interior of the Peloponnesus there is some cultivation in the basin of Tripolis (wheat, corn, and melons) but otherwise much of the land is fit only for grazing sheep. On the highest slopes, beyond the Mediterranean climatic region altogether, there are still stands of fragrant pine forests, amid which bee keeping and the making of honey is a local source of revenue. Even so, the average per capita income throughout the Peloponnesus is hardly one-fourth that of the Athens area.

The Aegean Islands. With the exception of Crete, few of the Aegean Islands were large or productive enough to support a city-state in classical times; much less can they give sustenance to a town of any size today. Apart from Milos and Thira (the latter also known as Santorini), which are volcanic and have small mineral industries based on pumice, barites, and emery, the Aegean Isles are chiefly metamorphic and largely barren. The larger islands near the Turkish coast are high enough to intercept more moisture. Consequently, they have some forest cover, but even here agriculture is primarily of the dry-land Mediterranean type with olives, grapes, and wheat. Chios is famous for its tobacco, Kálimnos for its sponge industry and Rhodes has become a fashionable resort center, especially for North Europeans.

Fifteen centuries before the birth of Christ, the island of Crete boasted the largest city in Europe: Knossos, the capital of the Minoan civilization, is estimated to have had some 80,000 inhabitants at its peak. Like all early Mediterranean cities, it was located on a hill, set back from the sea for defense against surprise attack, and from this lonely hill its ruins peer down today. None of the contemporary towns of Crete—all of them seaports founded by the Venetians in small, protected harbors along the north coast—is as large as Knossos once was, though Iraklion, just below the former Minoan capital, now has about 63,000 people. With the exception of one spring-fed valley in the south, most of Crete is fit only for the cultivation of the three dry-land Mediterranean crops, or, where the soils are too thin and stony for these, the grazing of sheep and goats. However, the island's strategic location on the outer fringe of the Aegean has made it a clear choice for a NATO military installation, and a large naval base is situated in Suda Bay, just to the east of the port of Khaniá.

The North. In the north of Greece, the plains area is considerably more extensive than elsewhere, but mountains continue to dominate the landscape. Indeed, in Thessaly block-fault mountains break the plains into two distinct basins and almost wall them off from the sea. The lower basin is centered on the town of Lárisa, a market and transport node of about 60,000 people, while the upper basin focuses on Trikkala, which is about half as large. Thessaly's chief town is the port of Volos (about 70,000 people), a center for an irrigated farming district and the outlet for the region's wheat and tobacco.

Stretching away from the northern slopes of Mount Olympus is Macedonia, an ill-defined region divided between Greece, Yugoslavia, and Bulgaria. Beyond that in turn lies Thrace, equally ill-defined and again split three ways, between Greece, Bulgaria, and Turkey. The most productive parts of Macedonia and Thrace are the broad deltaic plains formed by the Aliàkmon and Áxios (Vardar) rivers in the west and

Struma and Mesta rivers in the east. Here rich alluvial soils have been reclaimed by drainage, and a variety of crops is grown, including grains (winter wheat, corn, and rice), oil seeds (sunflower and sesame), and cotton. The chief cash crop and largest single export is tobacco, but because it does not find as much favor in world markets as the milder American varieties, its production is being gradually cut back. The intervening hill lands of Macedonia and Thrace are given over to the cultivation of fruits (plums, figs) and nuts (almonds and walnuts), as well as to grapes, mulberries, and pastoral use.

Such promise for expansion in agriculture and industry as Greece may have seems largely to lie in the North, for here the land is less crowded and inherently more productive than in other regions, and there are large rivers that can be harnessed to generate electric power. One of the beneficiaries of the region's recent growth has been the ancient port of Salonika, which now has a quarter of a million inhabitants and ranks as the country's second largest city. As the metropolis of the "New Greece" it not only boasts such industries as food processing, textiles, chemicals, and ship repair, but is also a growing transportation hub. Since the "normalization" of relations with Greece's northern neighbors, Salonika no longer finds its hinterland cut off by political boundaries, and increasingly it is coming into use as a transit port for both Yugoslavian and Bulgarian goods.

The West. The final region, the West, is the most peripheral of all, for the mountains that separate it from the rest of Greece are traversed by only three extremely poor roads, none of which is passable during the winter. The orientation of this region is westward to the sea, so Epirus and the Ionian Islands truly lie at the "back door" of Greece. Also, because of its westward exposure, this is by far the wettest region in Greece, but it is not necessarily the greenest, for the mountains are chiefly composed of porous limestones and the water is soon lost to the use of plants on the surface. The lowlands near the mouths of the Arakhthos and Akhelóös rivers were hardly more attractive than the mountains for settlement, for until they were drained, they were malarial marshes; today they support extensive corn and tobacco fields. One inland lake basin has given rise to the market town of Ioannina, but otherwise the region is sparsely populated, supporting only a sprinkling of sheep- and goatherders. The offshore Ionian Islands have far greater population densities, for there the cultivation of olives and currants is combined with small-scale fishing. Most of the settlements on the islands, the largest of which is Corfu, or Kérkira, lie on the drier, more accessible eastern side. The harbor of Corfu is still guarded by a Venetian fortress, built in the days when this island's strategic location commanded what were then the most important trade routes of the western world. Today, however, the Ionian Islands—especially those south of Corfu—are the poorest part of Greece, with per capita incomes only one-third as great as the average of the country and one-sixth of those in the Athens area.

CONCLUSION.   Poverty is perhaps the correct note on which to end when describing Greece, for its overall levels of income are today the lowest of any country in Europe. Greece has always been poor, for even the earliest city-states quickly outgrew their means of support and began spalling off colonies in all directions. Indeed, man and the land in Greece have been waging a running battle for two millenia, and almost inevitably man has lost, either by forsaking the land to become a fisherman or a sailor, or by forsaking Greece. The soils of Greece have never been able to support her people, nor does her subsoil, with its lack of fossil fuels, hold any great promise for major industrial development. On the sea, a large but rather antiquated Greek merchant fleet competes for the cargoes of world trade in the continuing effort to balance the country's meager agricultural exports against a longer list of more costly industrial imports. Even remittances from Greek laborers in northwestern Europe cannot be counted on as a steady source of income, for when business crises loom, it is the unskilled foreign worker who is let go first. Inevitably, Greece must fall back on itself, for poor though her land is, it possesses incredible beauty, a rich cultural heritage, and a proud people. Tourism is fast becoming the country's largest single industry as the people of Greece share their sunny skies, blue water, and white rocky islands with increasing numbers of foreigners each year. Both emerge the richer—the Greeks in money, the foreigner in the realization that his own hectic way of life has cost him many of the simple, heartfelt human pleasures that can only come from knowing want—and waging a ceaseless struggle to overcome it.

However, since the military coup in 1967, Greece—the hearth of Western democracy—has borne the additional and ignominious burden of dictatorship. Martial law, censorship of the press, political persecution, banishment, and torture occasioned such a reaction from the European Commission on Human Rights that the Athens regime withdrew from the Council of Europe in December, 1969, rather than be expelled. At the same time as American military aid was being poured in to bolster a staunch anticommunist ally, the economy of Greece was showing signs of faltering. A contract with Litton Industries to develop Crete and the western Peloponnesus was cancelled by the government, due to Litton's inability to attract sufficient foreign capital, and receipts from tourism have continued to drop each year. Having become pawns in the Great Power struggle for control over the eastern Mediterranean, the proud people of Greece have ironically been obliged to give up their freedom in the name of defending the "Free World."

Italy

The inspiration for the Roman god Janus may well have been taken from the Italian peninsula itself, for the latter looks both eastward to the Adriatic and Ionian seas and westward to the Tyrrhenian and Ligurian seas. In the distant past, the eastern face was decidedly the more important, for it was from this direction that the first impulses of civilization came, and they were first felt in the south, in Sicily and in the "instep" of the Italian "boot." When an indigenous civilization arose, however, it took root on the western face and in the center of the peninsula. Yet, today the real economic heart of Italy is in the north, beyond the traditional limits of the Mediterranean region altogether. Thus, despite its two-faced orientation, Italy can perhaps be thought of as consisting of three broad geographic regions—each with its own physical setting and each with its own cultural heritage—the South, the Center and the North.

THE REGIONS OF ITALY

The South. If one were to cut off the Italian boot just above the "spur" and include with it the islands of Sicily and Sardinia, one would essentially define the region we have termed the South. (See Figure 8.) Within a region so defined there are, of course, several subregions. The two islands are obvious ones, and the mainland can quite properly be divided into at least three parts: Calabria, "toe"; Puglia, the "heel"; and Campania, the "shin."

Of the larger islands in the Mediterranean, Sardinia is perhaps the least typically Mediterranean in its physical character. Much of the island is an eroded, crystalline plateau, strewn with boulders, dotted by clumps of prickly pear, and laced by dry stream beds. Its thin, stony soils yield such meager harvests of wheat that most of the land is used for pasturing sheep and goats. In the southwest is an alluvial lowland, the Campidano, where grains (corn and rice, as well as wheat), sugar beets, tobacco, and vegetables are grown. Where the Campidano opens southward into the sea, the island's chief port and town, Cagliari (pop. 205,000) has developed. The far-southwest corner of the island is mountainous again, and contains a variety of minerals including lead, zinc, iron ore, and lowgrade coal, most of which are exported to the mainland.

In contrast to sparsely populated Sardinia, with its 1,500,000 inhabitants, Sicily, with some 5,000,000 people, has long felt itself overcrowded. Before World War I it became the source of a massive out-migration. Because it is also more strategically located than Sardinia, it has been coveted by every power whose orbit embraced the central Mediterranean, from Rome and Carthage on. So troubled has been the island's history that, for their own protection, the large land-owning families bound themselves together to form the Mafia, an organization which to this day holds a "life or death" grip over most of the peasants, because of its control over the allocation of irrigation water.

Topographically, the water divide in Sicily lies almost immediately adjacent to the north coast. Because the prevailing wind direction also has a northerly component, most of the island's rainfall is in the mountainous northern third of the island, leaving the lower southern two-thirds in something of a rain shadow. This phenomenon accounts for sharp contrasts in land use and population density on the island, for only on the well-watered northern slopes is there intense cultivation of vegetables and citrus fruits. Indeed, about nine-tenths of Italy's lemon crop is concentrated here, and close to three-fourths of its oranges are likewise grown in this district. Here, too, is the island's capital, chief port and commercial center, the city of Palermo, with some 660,000 inhabitants. Over the divide to the south most of the land is in wheat, and where the hillsides are too steep or eroded for wheat, olives are grown

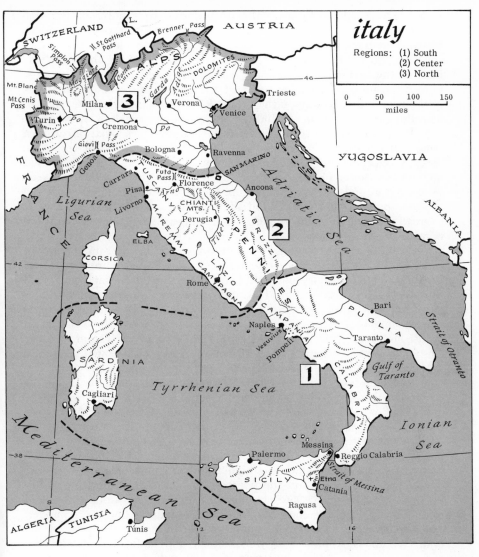

Figure 8

or sheep and donkeys are grazed. Sicily's largest plain is that of the Simeto River near Catania, but for reasons of flooding and drainage it has not been much used. However, the higher, drier hillsides are given over to typical Mediterranean tree and vine crops, including almonds and peaches. Mount Etna, to the north, has erupted on several occasions, destroying Catania in the seventeenth century and threatening it at other times. The entire island is also subject to violent, if infrequent, earthquakes, such as those in the west during the winter of 1967–68. Dramatic as such occurrences are, however, the basic problems of Sicily stem from its inbalance between man and the land. Apart from small oil and gas fields near Ragusa and Gela in the south, the island has little in the way of raw materials, power or skilled labor to encourage industrialization. The choice for most young Sicilians remains, as it has in the past, either to stay on the family farm and eke out an existence or migrate, either to one of the industrial cities of the north or overseas.

Across the narrow strait of Messina from Sicily lies Calabria, an area whose problems and prospects are little different from Sicily's. Like Sicily, Calabria is rugged and mountainous and the land is intensely used only on the wetter (in this instance, western) side, leaving the drier east in olives, figs and wheat, or as pasture for sheep. Out-migration siphoned off some population before World War I, but it only temporarily slowed a growth which in some districts has resulted in densities of over 700 persons per square mile.

Puglia is quite different. Not only does it lie in the rain shadow of Calabria, but it also consists essentially of a low-lying, porous limestone platform. Thus, it is dry not only climatically but also edaphically, and the combination has produced a largely treeless, waterless plain dominated by wheatfields, vineyards, and sheep grazing. In a narrow coastal strip around Bari there is some market gardening, while Bari itself is an industrial center with food processing and oil refining. Taranto, in the "instep" of Italy, is the site of an oil refinery and an integrated steel mill, both sponsored by the government's "Fund for the South" program. The detached limestone block of Monte Gargano, which forms the "spur" of the Italian boot, is today an important source of bauxite.

The final subregion of the Italian South is Campania, an area of fertile volcanic soils watered by the Volturno River and numerous springs coming out of the southern Apennines. Here the combination of water, level land, and good soil has resulted in very intensive market garden and citrus cultivation, while the higher and drier hillsides are, as usual, devoted to vine crops, and the poorest uplands to sheep grazing. Campania has long been the site of a dense settlement, of which the ruined city of Pompeii on the southern flanks of Vesuvius is but one reminder. Today, Campania's center of population—indeed, the metropolis of the entire South—is Naples, long the political and cultural capital of the region, it largest seaport, and now its chief industrial nucleus as well. With a population of 1,200,000, Naples serves chiefly as an import port for raw materials; its exports of agricultural products are considerably smaller in volume. Its industries include food processing, textiles, chemicals, steel, shipbuilding, and electronics.

The region we have called the South embraces about two-fifths of Italy's area and almost an equal proportion of its population, yet it earns little more than one-fifth of the country's total income. As we have seen, it is a region with many problems and, basically, little potential. A difficult physical setting has been rendered more difficult by man's destruction of the forests and by his livestock's overgrazing the hills, causing frightful erosion in many areas. The shortage of water and level land complicate farming, while the general absence of minerals and power have discouraged industry. A long history of political instability and absentee landownership and a rapidly growing population have aggravated the social problems of the region. In recognition that its geography and history have definitely left the South behind in its development, the government of Italy undertook in 1950 to correct some of the region's economic and social ills through the Fund for the South. This has sought not only to institute land reform, but also to check soil erosion, undertake reclamation schemes, build houses and highways, and, insofar, as possible, to absorb the surplus rural population into industrial employment. The South is Italy's Appalachia and the Fund for the South is an imaginative program to share with it the wealth of the more geographically favored North. Since there is no democracy in nature, only time will tell whether this plan, and others like it elsewhere, can effectively succeed in helping to create a more equitable distribution of wealth.

The Center. The Center of Italy is much more than just the peninsula's geographic midsection or a transition zone between North and South. It has long been the heart of the country politically, culturally, and economically, though in the latter regard it has been decidedly superseded by the North within the last half century. The Center is both geologically and topographically diverse, and though it is dominated by the arc of the northern and central Apennines, which in the Abruzzi district east of Rome climb to over 9500 feet elevation, the Chianti Mountains of Tuscany reach heights of almost 5700 feet between the valleys of the Arno and the Tiber (Tevere). The latter are the region's two largest rivers, and their valleys long accounted for the most extensive areas of usable lowland within the Center. In contrast, the poorly drained alluvial lowlands near their mouths—the Maremma south of the Arno and the Pontine marshes south of the Tiber—were avoided because of malaria and have been reclaimed for agricultural use only since the 1930's. (The Maremma, in particular, offers a good example of a man-made wasteland, for there is good evidence that the coastal regions of Tuscany were rather densely populated during Etruscan times, only to have their drainage impaired by the massive erosion that resulted from the deforestation of the Tuscan hills.) As a result, apart from Pisa at the mouth of the Arno, the Center was essentially a region without seaports. Even Pisa—a serious rival of both Venice and Genoa in the eleventh century—became a casualty of erosion, for it had silted so badly by the sixteenth century that the Medici built a new port, Livorno (Leghorn) to replace it upcurrent from the Arno's mouth. (As a general rule, the coastal currents in the Mediterranean run counterclockwise, meaning in the west coast region of central Italy, from south to north).

Because of its varied geology, the Center has a greater diversity of minerals than any other part of Italy. Carrara, just back of the Ligurian coast, is synonymous with fine, white marble; in the Tuscan hills a number of metals are found, including tin, copper, pyrites and mercury. The island of Elba, just offshore, has one of Italy's largest iron ore deposits.

Nonetheless, agriculture is still the mainstay of the economy: wheat is grown in the valleys of the northern Apennines and vines, olives, corn, and tobacco in the warmer southern valleys. In Umbria, where a series of old lake basins have been drained to the sea by the Tiber, elevations are too high and therefore temperatures too cool for the cultivation of olives, and here almonds become an important crop. The area's chief town, Perugia, grew up on the main Roman route to the eastern end of the Po valley. It is noted for its university and as a center of tourism, art industries, and confectionery products. Similarly, Tuscany's main town has always been Florence (Firenze), which developed on the main Roman route leading through the Futa pass to the western Po valley. A city of some 450,000 people today, Florence is best known as an art and cultural center, and as a cradle of the Renaissance. Consequently tourism provides its largest source of income as well as the principal market for its specialty crafts, such as glass, jewelry, leather, lace, metal goods, and high-quality woolens. It has not been bypassed by the modern industrial age, however, for it also produces some machine tools, scientific and electrical instruments, and chemical products.

The central Apennines culminate in Abruzzi, a region high enough to have been glaciated during the Ice Age and also to receive a heavy precipitation of both rain and snow. As a result, it serves as an important source of hydroelectric power for central Italy, as well as being a choice summer grazing area for sheep—some of which are driven all the way from Puglia—and as a popular winter ski resort for nearby Romans. Although there is some industry in its lower valleys, Abruzzi remains a poor, and by Italian standards, sparsely populated area.

Yet, by the same token, if one were to judge by the rather undistinguished appearance of the volcanic hills of Lazio (Latium), which are given over to the typical crop combination of vines, olives, and wheat, or of the generally sterile soils of Campagna, which support little more than heather and scattered clumps of pine, one would certainly wonder how the metropolis of Italy could have risen in such an unpropitious region. The answer, of course, lies in the fact that Rome, like Athens before it, very quickly outgrew its local hinterland and came to derive its sustenance first from the tributes of a far-flung empire and later from the tithes of all Latin Christendom. In the long centuries between the fall of the Roman Empire and the unification of Italy, Rome had only its religious function to sustain it; in point of size, at the middle of the last century it was exceeded not only by such cities as Naples and Milan but even by Palermo in Sicily. Like Athens, Rome received its modern impetus to growth only after it was chosen as the country's political and administrative center, and today its 2,500,000 inhabitants give it a comfortable lead over second-place Milan. Its industries are essentially limited to food processing, fashions, furniture, film making, printing, and light engineering. Because of its political function, it also became the chief railway hub of the Italian peninsula. Its many tourist attractions and its strategic location have likewise made it the leading air traffic center in Italy and an important stop on international routes between northwestern Europe, the Middle East, and Africa.

The North. There is little doubt that the modern economic heart of Italy lies in the North. Here, in a region that comprises one-fifth of the country's area, live over two-fifths of her people, who in turn earn nearly three-fifths of Italy's total income. Two subregions make up the North, the larger being the triangular wedge of the Po valley, the smaller comprising the foothills and southern flanks of the Alps. The dominant role that the Po valley plays in the agriculture of Italy can be judged from the fact that it produces one-third of the country's wine, half its wheat, three-fourths of its corn, sugar beets, and rye, and over nine-tenths of its dairy products and rice. In large measure its agricultural excellence is due to its lowland character, its rich alluvial soils, and its abundant summer moisture (for this region lies beyond the limit of summer drought and hence is not typically Mediterranean); but man, too, has done much to improve its productivity through drainage, irrigation, and fertilization. The very patterns of land tenure are different from those in the rest of Italy, for the more recently reclaimed areas are larger in size, more commercially oriented, and more dependent on seasonal paid labor than the older, family-type operations elsewhere in Italy. Within the valley there is also considerable areal specialization, with hay and dairying being concentrated in the coarser soils in the western section between Milan and Modena, while cereal cultivation dominates the finer alluvial soils in the eastern delta region. The milk of the former area is used to make the famous Gorgonzola and Parmesan cheeses, as well as butter and ice cream. In the central part of the plain, pigs are fattened on corn and skimmed milk, and many of them eventually end up in the sausages for which Bologna is famous.

Important as the Po Valley is to Italian agriculture, it is even more important to Italian industry. From modest beginnings in Roman times, manufacturing experienced its most rapid growth following the country's unification, thanks to the development of abundant hydroelectricity in the adjacent Alps and of an excellent communications network, which provided access to the raw materials of both agriculture and forestry and to a relatively prosperous regional market. Under Mussolini, Italy strove to achieve national self-sufficiency, which further spurred the industrial growth of the North. Since the war, Italian industry has concentrated on exporting to an international market in order to help solve the country's domestic problems of poverty and underemployment. This latter phase of development coincided with the discovery of a sizable deposit of natural gas near Cremona, which has materially reduced Italian imports of coal and provided cheap fuel for domestic cooking and heating, as well as for the chemical industries and the generation of electricity. Today the most important branches of industry located in the North are food processing, textiles, metallurgy, and engineering—the latter including everything from automobiles and motor scooters to farm machinery, sewing machines, typewriters and calculating machines.

The Po Valley already was the site of many towns in Etruscan and Roman times, and most of these urban centers have had their growth spurred by the coming of industry. Ravenna, for example, was imperial Rome's chief seaport and naval base on the Adriatic, but because it was located on the "wrong" side of the Po delta (i.e., downcurrent from it) it quickly silted up and now lies seven miles inland. Although it is still accessible from the sea by smaller ships using a canal, its future seems assured by the location there of Europe's largest synthetic rubber factory. Bologna, at the northern entrance to the Futa Pass, became the largest of the "gap towns" that line the northern flanks of the Apennines because it commanded the most important transmontane route, that linking Florence and Rome. A city of some 480,000 persons today, its industries include textiles and fertilizers but are chiefly related to the processing of foods: flour milling, sugar refining, and the preparation of meats, sauces, essences, and preserves.

Venice traces its origins to the fall of Rome, for its original inhabitants fled to the small islands and lagoons of the Po delta to escape the barbarians sweeping down from the north. Gradually, they turned this defensive site to commercial advantage by becoming a leading trading power in the Adriatic and eastern Mediterranean during the Middle Ages. As long as the main trade routes ran between Central Europe and the Near East, Venice was in an incomparable position to capitalize on this commerce, but once they were oriented toward the west, Venice was quickly displaced by its ancient rival, Genoa. Today it is a "museum city," incapable of growth and living largely on its glorious past, as a tourist attraction. Such modern industry as has come to the area has grown up on the mainland at Mestre, where there are shipyards, oil refineries, and chemical plants. Today the Venice-Mestre complex ranks a poor third to Genoa and Naples among the seaports of Italy.

In contrast, the port of Trieste affords a good example of the effect of political boundaries on the fortunes of a city. Originally built as the principal outlet of the Austro-Hungarian Empire in the latter half of the nineteenth century, Trieste was acquired by Italy after World War I. In the process, it lost most of the hinterland it was intended to serve. After World War II, the Yugoslav-Italian boundary was adjusted along ethnic lines, effectively reducing Trieste to the city itself. Without a region to serve, Trieste today is stagnating, for its industries, which include a shipyard, a steel mill, an oil refinery, and a paper plant, fulfill no function for Yugoslavia or Austria and are too remote to have any real importance to Italy.

In many ways, Verona is the northern counterpart of Bologna, because it commands the entrance of the Adige Valley and the Brenner Pass, the lowest crossing of the Alps leading into Central Europe. Milan's is a much more strategic location, however, for upon it converge routes from northern and western Europe by way of the St. Gotthard and Simplon passes. The construction of railway tunnels through these passes in 1882 and 1906, respectively, further strengthened the city's position and rendered it the most important international rail center in the country. Today, Milan is likewise the hub of Italy's *autostrada* system and its second busiest airport. It is the site of annual trade fairs and design shows and its stock exchange is the country's largest and most active. Milan is the home of the famed La Scala Opera as well, but the city's chief importance today is as Italy's foremost industrial center. Many of its 1,750,000 inhabitants work in factories producing everything from food products and textiles to pharmaceuticals, steel, and automobiles. The latter industry, however, is primarily associated with Turin, (pop. 1,200,000) Milan's "junior partner" to the west. Although Turin produces vermouth, leather goods, and textiles, most of its growth and present employment is associated with FIAT, Italy's industrial giant, which now ranks as the fourth largest producer of motor cars in the world (exceeded only by the American "Big Three"), and also builds locomotives, airplanes, and marine engines.

Genoa, lying physically south of the Apennines, is functionally as much a part of the North as either Milan or Turin. Indeed, were it not for their access to the port of Genoa through the Giovi Pass, it is doubtful that either Milan or Turin would exist as we know them today, because most of their coal, iron ore, and other heavy raw materials are imported through Genoa, and most of their finished manufactured goods exported through it. Backed as it is by the Apennines, the Italian Riviera on either side of Genoa is typically Mediterranean in its aspect, with olives, figs, vines, citrus fruits and flowers being grown on terraced hillsides, while the coast itself is lined by tourist resorts. Genoa's 850,000 people, however, support themselves chiefly by the industry and commerce of the rich hinterland of the Po, for the port annually handles about one-fourth of all Italian seaborn traffic. The relative prosperity of the North, especially of this industrial triangle at its western end, is reflected in per capita incomes of over $900 yearly compared to about $765 for the country as a whole and to about $275 in Calabria and the "instep" of the Italian boot in the South. In many ways, it can be said that the North resembles the countries it adjoins in western and central Europe more than it does the rest of Italy.

As we indicated earlier, the Po plain constitutes the nucleus of the North but not its entirety, for though Italy's Alpine areas are small in area and in population, they are of major importance to the economic life of the region, and therefore of the nation. Not only is about half of Italy's hydroelectric power generated in the foothills of the Alps, but this area also produces a sizable share of the country's wood and paper products. Furthermore, it is growing in importance as a tourist playground. In summer the focus is on beautiful glacial lakes like Como, Maggiore, and Garda, that grace the lower valleys, and in the winter, on the higher ski resorts, especially those set amongst the jagged Dolomites. The Alpine area also poses Italy's major minority group problems, though in the French-speaking area of Val d'Aosta, the problem has already largely been resolved by granting the region a measure of local autonomy. However, in the Alto Adige region, or South Tyrol as the Austrians know it, there was a conscious effort by Mussolini's government to submerge the

German-speaking majority through the importation of Italians to work in the large electrochemical, electrometallurgical, paper, and engineering industries built there. The result was that the German-speaking group became the minority, and, in Austrian eyes was being doomed to cultural extinction. Ironically (but for obvious economic reasons) Italy, the country that put the word "irredentism" into the vocabulary of political science, has steadfastly refused to entertain any Austrian irredentist claims for the region's return. However, in December, 1969, the two countries signed an accord agreeing to submit any further disputes to arbitration by the World Court. In addition, Italy agreed that the region should henceforth be known by its older German name and that the Italian-speaking district of Trentino be separated from it, allowing the German-speaking group to regain its majority status. Inasmuch as they were also willing to permit a wider scope in the use of the German language, the Italians have shown themselves amenable to meeting all of their neighbor's demands short of the territory's actual return to Austrian sovereignty.

Italy can be viewed as a country whose geographic center has shifted progressively northward and whose principal economic ties are with the countries of northwestern Europe, through the Common Market. It has not yet been possible for Italy to support her large and rapidly growing population through her own economy, phenomenal though its growth has been since the end of World War II. Thus, the problems of poverty and unemployment are still present, especially in the South, and large-scale emigration and the export of laborers continues to provide a safety-valve. So do the earnings of the Italian merchant fleet and the country's immense revenues from tourism, for Italy's list of imports (including petroleum, foodstuffs, and industrial raw materials) remains longer and more costly than the list of exports (automobiles, textiles, and apparel). Perhaps one of the most telling observations of contemporary Italy, encapsulating both its problems and its prospects, is that in the summer, one out of every three people one sees is a tourist, and in the winter (when most of the tourists have gone home) one out of every four people one sees is a Communist.

Iberia

Unlike the peninsulas of Greece and Italy, Iberia was never the site of an indigenous classical civilization. Owing to its location, however, it often found itself within the orbits of such centers, for both the Phoenicians and the Greeks planted colonies on its shores and both Carthage and Rome vied for its control. It was the triumph of Rome that gave the peninsula its languages and religion, its legal system, and its land ownership patterns, as well as many of its great architectural monuments. However, like the rest of the empire, Iberia was overrun by Germanic tribes during the Great Migrations, only to fall to the Moors two centuries later. Not until the year that Columbus set out on his fateful voyage was the reconquest of Spain completed by the Christians. The timing could hardly have been more propitious, for freed of a long, bitter struggle at home, Spain could devote its full energies to building an empire of its own, as the Portuguese had already begun to do. For a brief century or two, the kingdoms of Spain and Portugal ranked as world powers of great wealth, but neither of them had the resource base to secure their status and both of them soon fell back into their original roles as adjuncts to the great powers. In common with Greece and Italy, Iberia has seen industry come late and slowly; as a result, most of its people still earn their living from the land as farmers and pastoralists. By the same token, the per capita incomes in Spain and Portugal are among the lowest in Europe. Of course, these vary markedly from place to place, so it is our task now to delimit some of the major physical and cultural regions of the peninsula (Figure 9).

THE REGIONS OF IBERIA.   Again, as in Greece and Italy, it is perhaps most convenient to think in terms of general location. Thus, let us call the regions of Iberia the East, meaning essentially its Mediterranean coastlands; the South, embracing the ancient province of Andalucia; the North, comprising those areas beyond the Cantabrian Mountains that front on the Bay of Biscay and the Atlantic; the Center, synonymous with the interior plateaus, or Meseta, of Castile; and finally, the West, the country of Portugal.

The East.   Whereas the peninsula of Greece has essentially a single orientation, eastward toward the Aegean, and the Italian peninsula has two faces, the massive square block of Iberia looks out upon the world with four—north toward the Bay of Biscay, west toward the Atlantic, south toward Africa, and east toward the Mediterranean. It was the latter face that first felt the impact of the classical civilizations.

Most of the eastern face of Iberia is not really "Spanish" at all, but Catalan. The Catalan people have a distinct language, literature, and history of their own. They have always been a sea-oriented people, and for a time their political power was commensurate with their widespread commerical activities, for they held control over the Balearic Islands, Sardinia, Sicily, and the southern mainland of Italy, as well as over most of the Mediterranean coast of Spain. Catalan navigators were among the first to develop and use the famous *portolan* charts, and Barcelona was famed as a center of nautical studies and maritime law as early as the thirteenth century. When Spain turned its attention to the New World, Catalonia not only found itself oriented in the "wrong" direction, but also consciously discriminated against, for the king, a Castilian Spaniard, first granted a monopoly on colonial trade to Sevilla and later to Cádiz. Under the short-lived Spanish republic (1931–36), Catalonia was granted a large measure of autonomy, but this was quickly abrogated when Franco emerged triumphant in the Civil War. Although even most Catalonians will concede that their region could never be a viable economic entity in itself, their bitterness against the central government for its conscious repression of their "national" spirit dies hard.

Most of the Catalonian coast is paralleled by a range of low moun-

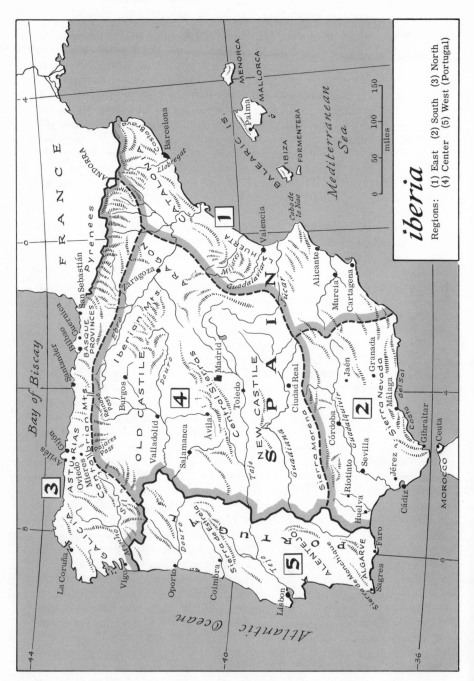

Figure 9

tains, so rivers such as the Ebro and the Llobregat, near the mouth of which Barcelona is situated, must break their way to the sea through narrow gorges. North of Barcelona, the red crystalline rocks of the coastal range form the picturesque Costa Brava, a favorite beach resort region of northwest Europeans. Such pockets of lowland as exist are largely devoted to market gardening, whereas the interior valleys tend to specialize in cereals, including wheat, corn, and rice. The latter crop is also important on the Ebro delta; in the higher and drier areas olives and vines take over.

About 2,000,000 of Catalonia's roughly 3,000,000 people live in the Llobregat lowland immediately surrounding Barcelona. Some 1,700,000 are numbered as residents of the city itself, which today ranks not only as Spain's largest seaport but also as its leading industrial center. Barcelona owes its premier industrial position to a variety of factors, including the energy and commerical-mindedness of the Catalans themselves; its seaside location, allowing it to import the necessary fuel and raw materials; and easy access to hydroelectric power both from the Pyrenees and more recently from the Ebro. From cotton and woolen textiles, which developed earliest, Barcelona has branched out into chemicals, paper, and a variety of engineering industries including railway equipment, shipbuilding, diesel engines, and automobiles. The main plant of the latter industry is a subsidiary of FIAT, deferentially known in Spain as CEAT (Compañia Española de Automóbiles de Torino).

South of Castellón the rugged coast gives way to a hundred-mile-long sweep of alluvial lowland, in large part formed, and, to this day watered, by three rivers—the Mijares, the Guadalaviar, and the Júcar. This is the famed "garden of Valencia," *La Huerta*. Here, land use patterns reflect soil, drainage, and slope conditions as dramatically as anywhere in the Mediterranean basin, for the contrasts are not only great but also abrupt. On the outermost coast the waves have thrown up a sandy beach whose low dunes are covered with pines and between which fishermen draw up their boats and tourists pitch their tents in summer. Back of the lagoon are extensive rice fields laced by a network of drainage ditches to carry off the surplus water. Farther inland, where the land is somewhat higher and the water table is lower, are the irrigated market gardens of citrus fruits, tomatoes, and onions for export, as well as of cereal, tobacco, and fodder crops for local consumption. Finally, as the land rises out of reach of the irrigation water, the vine and tree crops take over, including grapes for raisins, olives, and almonds. Beyond this, in turn, the land becomes so barren as to permit only the grazing of sheep. In the midst of La Huerta lies Spain's third largest city, Valencia, which now has more than half a million inhabitants. Its industries include food processing, textiles, leather goods, and engineering, and its chief exports are the famed Valencia eating oranges and some iron ore from the Teruel district back in the mountains.

Once the Cabo de la Nao is rounded, the landscape takes on virtually a desert character. (Indeed, Figure 3 reveals that the southeastern corner of Spain is the driest region in Europe.) Temperatures are high and the precipitation is so meager and erratic that it is risky even to grow wheat without applying water to the fields. Where water is available, however, lush oases are found in which vegetables, cane, peanuts, cotton, mulberries, citrus fruits, and even pomegranates, bananas, and dates are grown. Such oases comprise only a small fraction of the total area, however, for irrigation water is so limited that in most of the region the farmers can rely solely on tree crops (figs, almonds, and olives) and vines. This corner of Spain was first exploited by the Phoenicians for its metals, and some silver, lead, iron ore, and pyrites are still produced in the interior. Indeed, it was Phoenicia's daughter colony, Carthage, that founded the first town in the area, Cartago Nova, now Cartagena. Besides a small iron industry, Cartagena has a naval base and, thanks to its location between Middle Eastern and North African oil fields and the urban market around Madrid, it has the country's only oil refinery.

The Balearic Islands have long been culturally and commercially oriented to Barcelona, as they still are today. Tourism now dominates the local economy, but market gardening and the production of wine, cheese, and handicrafts continue to occupy the majority of the people.

The South. It was in the South of Spain that the Moors arrived first, there that they stayed the longest, and hence, there that their impact has been most enduring. Under their skilled hands, the great Guadalquivir lowland was brought to a level of prosperity through irrigation that it has never since enjoyed. Near the apex of that lowland they founded the capital of their western domains, Córdoba, which ultimately became one of the greatest cultural centers of the Islamic world. Among the many architectural masterpieces the Moors bequeathed to Spain, none is more jewellike than the Alhambra palace in Granada. In comparison, the Christians who finally expelled them were little more than ruffians, who let the great irrigation works fall into disrepair and who, in their religious fervor, destroyed many of the Moslem monuments and bastardized most of the rest. (One of the most dreadful examples is to be seen in the mosque at Córdoba.)

The Christians founded their chief city at the lowest bridging point and the head of navigation on the Guadalquivir. Sevilla became not only the country's chief colonial seaport but also, when the wealth of the Indies became apparent, the site of the Royal Treasury. Indeed, were it not for Castile's jealously retaining the center of political power up in the midst of the bleak Meseta, there can be little doubt that Sevilla, lying as it does in the heart of the country's richest agricultural lowland, might well have been fated to be the capital of Spain. However, as with so many other port cities before and since, Sevilla found that as ships grew larger, its river grew more shallow and gradually its trade was diverted to a new port (originally a Phoenician settlement) established upcurrent of the Guadalquivir's mouth at Cádiz. Only as recently as 1926 did Sevilla get a new lease on life, with the completion of a canal to the sea. Today it is a city of about 475,000 which exports some agricultural produce and minerals but capitalizes largely on its past as a center of tourism. Córdoba, less than half its size, has food processing and electrical industries. Cádiz (130,000) is a naval base and the chief export port for olive oil and sherry wines, the latter produced in the Jérez district a few miles inland to the east. While Granada (160,000) serves as a market center for the largest intermontane plain, or *vega*, at the base of the Sierra Nevada, its primary income is derived from tourists who come to see the Alhambra and the gypsies, most of whom reside in caves cut into the hillsides opposite the ancient Moorish palace. Málaga (310,000) is the commercial capital of Spain's entire southern coast, the Costa del Sol, and as such is a major tourist center in its own right. As a seaport, however, it not only carries on an active trade with Morocco but also ships early vegetables, fruit, wine, and olive oil to western Europe.

But important as these cities are, Andalucia, in common with the rest of Spain, is still predominantly rural and agricultural. From the rich alluvial soils of the Guadalquivir lowland come good yields of sugar cane, cotton, tobacco, peanuts and corn, while part of the swampy region (Las Marismas) near its mouth has been reclaimed for the cultivation of rice. Most of the oranges produced in the region are of the small, sour Sevilla variety used for making marmalade. As usual, the drier interfluves are in wheat, olives, and vines, with sheep grazing taking over on the higher mountain slopes. Near Jaén the specialized breeding of bulls is carried on to meet the demand of Spain's largest spectator sport. Because most of the land of Andalucia is owned by absentee landlords, chiefly resident in Sevilla, the bulk of the labor is provided by landless hired hands who are lucky if they find five months of work a year. With labor already in oversupply, there has been little incentive for mechanization, and as a result, poverty and underemployment are as much a part of Spain's richest agricultural area as they are of some of Italy's poorest ones.

The mountains to the south intercept enough moisture in their western portion to permit the growing of wheat, olives, and grapes, but the east is so dry that only sheep can find enough forage to pasture on. The small irrigated *vegas* and coastal *huertas* stand out, of course, as lush oases of both temperate and subtropical produce, including alfalfa, sugar cane, cotton, tobacco, and citrus.

The mineral endowment of Andalucia is chiefly concentrated in the Sierra Morena (not properly a mountain range, but rather the southern faulted edge of the central plateau), to the north of the Guadalquivir. Here, especially in the Rio Tinto district, pyrites, lead, copper, and mercury are mined. Most of the holdings are by foreign companies and most of the ores go into export, through either Sevilla or Huelva to the west.

The North. Because the North of Spain is so diametrically different from the other regions, it might be well to examine it next just to emphasize the contrasts. Within the North it is possible to recognize at least four subregions, but all of them share a mountainous terrain difficult of access; a climate that is moist the year round; a green, forested landscape; and the cultural distinction of having been little, if at all, influenced by the Moors. Indeed, it was in large part the rugged, forested mountains of the North that deterred the horse-riding Moors and permitted the Christians not only to continue their resistance as guerrillas but eventually to use this region as the springboard for launching the reconquest of the entire peninsula. This same isolation had earlier enabled the Basques to retain their ethnic identity despite the waves of Indo-European peoples that swirled around them. This isolation has since fostered the political separation that not only gave rise to the vest-pocket state of Andorra, but also to the strong regional antagonisms against the central government that continue to manifest themselves today.

The Pyrenees constitute the most rugged and least populated subregion of the North. This 250-mile bulwark of mountains is crossed or skirted by only nine roads and four railways in its entire length; of these, four roads and two railways are located near its lower, western end. Because the Cantabrian Mountains, which are almost continuous with the Pyrenees, are also lower at their eastern end, the principal approach to the Meseta of central Spain is across the upper headwaters of the Ebro River. Indeed, it is also the source of the Ebro that affords access to Reinosa Pass (2877 feet) and through it, to the port of Santander. The only other break of any importance in the Cantabrians is at Pajares Pass (4524 feet) to the west, which provides a link between the north coast province of Asturias and the central plateau. In Galicia, Spain's northwestern province, an ancient granite upland is broken by east-west faults, some of which have been inundated by the sea to form embayments known as *rias,* giving the region a profusion of excellent harbors. However, the only easy land approach to Galicia is by way of the Sil River Valley, from which roads and railways branch out to reach the main towns of the province.

Few people inhabit the Pyrenees; those that do support themselves chiefly from dairying in the moister western regions and from sheepherding in the drier eastern and colder upland areas. The greatest economic asset of the Pyrenees is its water, used both for irrigation in the tributary valleys of the Ebro and for generating electricity for the industries of Catalonia and the Basque provinces. The latter area is perhaps the most climatically favored area of Spain, in the sense that it knows no drought. Its luxuriant meadows support numerous dairy cattle, and its hillsides are largely devoted to hay, clover, potatoes, apples, and corn. To a larger degree than those of any other region of Spain, save perhaps Catalonia, the farms of the Basque provinces are oriented toward commercial production, for their meat, milk, eggs, fruits, and vegetables find ready markets in the nearby urban centers. Despite the general prosperity of their farms, however, the Basques were early noted for their whaling and fishing expeditions to places such as Svalbard and Greenland. Today manufacturing provides employment for those who forsake the family farm, for Bilbao (pop. 340,000) has built a diversified industrial structure on textiles, steel, shipbuilding, chemicals, glass, and fish processing. Its heavy industries basically stem from Bilbao's function as an iron ore export port, and the importation of British coal in return.

Today most of these heavier cargoes must be handled by Bilbao's outport of Portugalete, for its own harbor is too shallow and narrow to handle large, modern vessels. San Sebastián is another port city located in the Basque provinces, but it is not *of* the Basque provinces. It is basically an international resort town, made fashionable when the monarchs of Spain made it their "summer capital." Today it is the principal road and rail gateway to Spain from the rest of Europe.

Such autonomy as the Basque provinces had received under the Spanish Republic was revoked by Franco, so there is little love lost on the central government in this region. Moreover, the Basques recall all too vividly how Franco called in German dive bombers to obliterate their town of Guernica during the Civil War—an atrocity commemorated by Picasso in one of his paintings.

Santander, farther to the west, originally developed as a wool export port when Spain was linked to Flanders, but like Bilbao it is characterized today by heavy industries such as steel, chemicals, and zinc refining. The cities of Asturias, yet farther to the west, are likewise centers of industry, for Spain's most important coal deposits are situated at Mieres. Most of this coal is exported to other regions of Spain through the port of Gijón, which in itself has such industries as fish processing, chemicals, and glass. Halfway between the coal mines and the seacoast, at Oviedo, the province's capital, there are steel mills based on imported scrap iron and coking coal that is mixed with the local coal. However, the discovery of a large deposit of iron ore near the coast at Avilés has prompted the Spanish government to erect a larger, more modern steel mill on this seaside site, where the imported raw materials can be assembled and the finished steel exported more conomically. In Asturias, however, as in Catalonia and the Basque provinces, there is strong animosity against the central government, for it was here that Franco first achieved national notice for the ruthless way in which he put down the striking coal miners in the early 1930's—a tactic his government has repeat several times since.

There are exceptions to every rule, and Galicia breaks the pattern that most of the rest of the North seems to have set. Its rugged hillsides have a surprisingly high population density, and the region has a long history of out-migration. The laws of equal inheritance have been so scrupulously observed that most farm properties are almost minuscule, and anyone with title to as many as two or three acres is technically a large landowner. So far has this subdivision of real estate gone that one researcher claims to have found an instance in which three farmers shared the same tree! The mixed farming is of a subsistence nature, with cows used for draft animals as well as for milk and manure. Corn, oats, barley, and rye are grown as fodder for the livestock, while cabbages, potatoes and other root crops make up the primary foodstuffs for human consumption. With such a pressure of population on the land and such excellent harbors opening out onto the sea, it would seem natural that the Galicians would early turn to fishing to supplement their diet, and they did. About one-fifth of the total Spanish fish catch is landed at the ports of La Coruña and Vigo; sardines are taken in local waters and cod is caught on the Grand Banks off Newfoundland. Because Galicia has no fuels or metals, its industries are limited to food processing (chiefly fish preserves) and shipbuilding. However, the Spanish government is attempting to spur the region's industrialization through harnessing hydroelectric power and erecting large fertilizer and wood pulp plants. Finally, in one other important respect Galicia differs from the rest of the North, for its political sentiments are markedly pro-Franco. One explanation might be that he was born at the naval base town of El Ferrol—now known as El Ferrol del Caudillo (*caudillo* being the Spanish word for leader or chief, similar to the German *der führer*, as applied to Hitler).

Thus, with the exceptions noted, it is seen that the North, like Catalonia, is markedly industrialized compared to the rest of Spain—and also restive in its political sentiments. For many good reasons, the North and Catalonia feel that they are being held back by the central government and at the same time made to "carry the ball" economically for the rest of Spain. What happens in this region when the Franco era ends promises to be of interest to students of both economics and politics.

The Center.   South of the Cantabrian Mountains, stretching away in monotonous, treeless plains, is the rolling surface of the Meseta, Spain's central plateau. The Meseta is divided roughly through the middle by a series of small but rugged mountain ranges, collectively known as the Central Sierras, and it is bounded on the east by the major water divide of the peninsula, the Iberian Mountains. The northern and higher half of the Meseta is drained by the Douro River and comprises the region known as Old Castile. The southern, and generally lower, half of the Meseta essentially makes up New Castile, though this region is broken by mountains in its midsection into two separate drainage basins —that of the Tagus (Tajo) to the north and that of the Guadiana to the south. The southern edge of the Meseta, as we indicated earlier, breaks off abruptly into the plain of the Guadalquivir to form the so-called Sierra Morena.

A third subregion of central Spain may be identified in the Ebro basin, to the east of the Iberian Mountains. Although it is lower than the Meseta, it lies in the rain shadow of the Iberians and consequently has the same arid landscape as the plateau. Also, being cut off from the Mediterranean by mountains, it is something of a "frost-pocket," because cold air drains into the basin in winter and is trapped. Irrigation water in this region can therefore scarcely be used to create any exotic oases; it is used rather to insure the success of such crops as wheat and sugar beets. Zaragoza, the capital of the old kingdom of Aragon and the region's largest city, is situated at a strategic bridge-crossing in the middle of the Ebro basin. Today many of its 360,000 people work in engineering industries making machine tools, railway equipment, and motor cars.

Without doubt, the Meseta is the bleakest, least hospitable region in all Iberia. Some notion of its climate can be gained from the old Spanish proverb that speaks of Madrid as having "six months of winter and six months of hell." If the region ever supported so much as a vegetation of Mediterranean scrub trees, they have long since been replaced by steppe grasses and xerophytic shrubs. Water is in such short supply that there are few irrigated huertas to be seen, and most of the land is used for growing wheat or vines or for grazing sheep. Indeed, in some areas it is so dry that the farmer will count himself fortunate to get one wheat harvest in every three years. Toward the southwest the country-side takes on a more forested appearance because the farmers allow the cork oaks to remain in the midst of their wheatfields and pastures. On the other hand, toward the southeast, in La Mancha, the legendary home of Don Quixote, it is so arid that there are extensive areas of salt flats. In the huertas around Ciudad Real, however, there is a specialized produc-tion of saffron, a food coloring that must be extracted from the flowers before sunrise. Due to the limited production of this commodity, and the delicate handling it requires, it is small wonder that saffron retails for over $90 pound!

Understandably, few cities of any size have arisen amid surround-ings such as these. The largest in Old Castile is the provincial capital of Valladolid, with 165,000 people. It has some food processing industries and a Renault assembly plant as its principal twentieth century features. Burgos (pop. 75,000), which guards the Meseta's approaches from the northeast, has food processing, paper, and fertilizer factories and is slated for a nuclear reactor as well. Salamanca, at the opposite corner of the northern Meseta, is a university town that had more life in the Middle Ages than it does today.

It was in New Castile that the Germanic invaders of Spain, the Visigoths, founded their capital at Toledo. Situated in a gorge-like bend of the Tagus River, Toledo had a magnificent defensive site and was known in the Middle Ages for the superb quality of its steel swords. However, like Venice it had no real place to expand, and consequently it remains a "museum town," now set aside as a national monument.

In contrast, the site of Madrid is undistinguished, but its situation—its relation to its surroundings—is most strategic. Madrid is located on the plain just beneath the entrance to the Puerto de Guadarrama (5008 feet), the chief pass through the central Sierras, and as such was a com-manding position for the Christians to acquire and hold in their long southward advance against the Moors. Its centrality within Spain like-wise made it an effective control point for dominating the many diver-gent areas of the country—a position greatly reinforced by the building of the Spanish railway network.

Were it not for the fact that its political power is geographically situated in its center, Spain might well be likened to a doughnut, for the parts that otherwise matter are all on the borders. Castile is the empty heart of Spain, but by virtue of the political power vested in Madrid, it has managed to impose its language, culture, and values on most of the rest of the country. The fact that many of these values are more ap-propriate to the age of Don Quixote and Sancho Panza is only one of the irritations that peoples like the Catalans and Basques have had to learn to live with. Despite the niggardliness of its surroundings, Madrid has been elevated to Spain's largest city (pop. 2,600,000), almost, it would seem, by administrative fiat. Beyond its political-administrative and transportation functions, however, Madrid has managed to draw some industries, including the manufacture of electrical machinery and trucks, over and above the customary consumer industries one would expect in a city of this size.

The West: Portugal. The western face of Iberia, which comprises the country of Portugal, is the only one that has escaped political domination by Castile. This may be due in part to the fact that Portugal was a product of the same forces and events (the Reconquest) as Castile, but if this were the case, then Catalonia and Aragon might be expected to be sovereign states as well. A more likely explanation is to be found in its geographic location, for with its Atlantic orientation, Portugal occupies a decidely more strategic facet of the peninsula than any other coastal region. It also has a larger proportion of lowland than any other part of the peninsula, a fact that may have helped to speed the advance of the Reconquest in this region, for the last Moors were evicted from Portugal almost a century and a half before they surrendered their last mountain stronghold in southern Spain. It was at this juncture, after Portugal had won its independence and before Spain had been "liberated," that England chose to contract a treaty of "friendship and mutual defense" with the Portuguese. This treaty is the oldest international agreement still in force. Whether we can ascribe long-term geopolitical thinking to the English or not, the fact remains that it has been in British interests ever since to guarantee the sovereignty of their Iberian ally, if for no other reason than to hold the Spanish in check.

As might be expected, Portugal demonstrates the same contrast from well-watered north to arid south that Spain does—but without the intervention of the bleak, inhospitable Meseta. When the Reconquest began, the core of Portugal lay between the Minho and Douro rivers, adjacent to the Spanish province of Galicia. Not surprising, then, is the fact that the Portuguese language is closely related to that of Galicia, and that the boundary between Spain and Portugal is linguistic rather than dependent upon physical features. (Indirectly, of course, it can be argued that the Portuguese penetrated as far up the valleys as they conveniently could, and that ultimately the edge of the Meseta stopped them.)

The farms of northern Portugal are extremely small, like those in Galicia, for the population densities are high and the amount of cultivable land is limited. Those on the lower and warmer coastal plain concentrate on the subsistence production of corn, beans, and melons during the summer and use the same land to pasture cattle during the mild winters. The steeper areas are devoted to tree crops, including apples, apricots, figs, and olives. Grapes are also grown on trellises beneath the trees, but because they do not receive enough sunshine to ripen properly, they produce a sourish vintage known as "green wine." The country's best-known vintage, Port wine, comes from grapes grown on the terraced hillsides of the upper Douro Valley. After the grapes are pressed, brandy is added to arrest fermentation and then the wine is shipped down river to be stored in caves opposite the port of Oporto, whence it is finally exported. Although the higher land back from the coast once supported a forest cover, it has long since been cut over and replaced by a heath landscape, fit only for the summer pasturing of cattle and sheep. Temperatures are so cool in the interior mountain districts that rye and potatoes are among the few crops that can be grown.

The largest city of the north and the country's second city is Oporto, with about 320,000 people. Not only does it dominate the commerce and industry of the North, but, as might be surmised, it is also the "port" from which the wine and the country both take their names. However, Oporto is now so badly silted that much of its exports of wine and fish move through its outport of Matosinhos.

South of the Douro many of the coastal sand dunes have been planted with pines to hold them in place, and many of the lagoons behind them are used as salt pans. Sardine fishing is important along the coast, while the alluvial river valleys are intensively utilized for growing rice, corn, vegetables, and fodder crops. The poorer, more rugged land of the interior once had extensive forests but is now used for the cultivation of vines and rye and for the grazing of sheep. The chief town of this region is Coimbra, seat of the country's oldest and most renowned university.

South of the Serra de Estrela, a mountain range whose winter snows supply much of the water and water power for central Portugal, lies the broad valley of the Tagus. From its fertile alluvial soils come heavy yields of rice, corn, wheat, and fodder crops, while its more arid southern banks support large herds of cattle. Overlooking the vast estuary of the Tagus from its spectacular site high atop several hills is Lisbon, capital and largest city of Portugal (pop. 1,400,000, suburbs included). Almost completely destroyed by an earthquake in 1755, Lisbon was rebuilt in a grand manner, thanks to the wealth it managed to extract from such colonies as Brazil. Even today much of Lisbon's port traffic is entrepôt trade moving between Portugal's African colonies and the markets of western Europe. The commodities shipped include oil seeds, hides and skins, cotton, and copper. From Lisbon's own local hinterland comes cork, wine, and minerals, such as tungsten. Today Lisbon ranks as Portugal's leading industrial center as well, with oil refineries, shipyards, and factories producing fertilizer, textiles, and food products. The economic and transportation hub of the country, Lisbon was joined to the southern provinces of Portugal by Europe's largest suspension bridge in 1966. Internationally, Lisbon has a strategic location athwart commercial air routes to both North and South America; Portugal's mid-Atlantic islands, the Azores, have a similar value militarily.

Beyond the Tagus (indeed, the Portuguese name for it—Alentejo—means just that) the country stretches away in a low monotonous plateau, for the most part devoid of trees and used chiefly for sheep grazing and an occasional harvest of wheat. Like Andalucía, it is a region of large estates worked by tenant farmers and share croppers. Where the countryside does support cork oaks, not only are the trees themselves utilized for bark, charcoal, and as forage for pigs, but the area between them is often cropped in cereals. Once the Serra de Monchique is crossed, the landscape changes dramatically, for this is the Algarve, a garden spot of the Moors. Figs, apricots, and almonds grow on the terraced hillsides, while bananas, citrus, and vegetables are cultivated in the irrigated lowlands. The coast of the Algarve is broken by many small bays, and the region has had a long maritime tradition of fishing, piracy, and exploration. Indeed, it was in this remotest corner of Portugal where the dreams of empire were first dreamed by Europeans; it was at Sagres, on the southwestern tip of the country, that Prince Henry the Navigator erected his famous lighthouse and navigation school.

CONCLUSIONS

Spain. It can perhaps be said, without too much exaggeration, that Spain has been unlucky ever since its misadventure with the Armada. Piece by piece its empire was carved away, with the Americans virtually finishing the process at the end of the nineteenth century. Cut off from its west European markets during World War I, Spain soon found itself caught up in the worldwide Depression—hardly an auspicious time to launch its one real experiment in democracy. The large landowners, the army, and the church rose up to crush the Republic and the ideas it stood for, and in the bloody struggle that ensued, some 300,000 Spaniards died in battle, another 200,000 died from disease and famine, 100,000 escaped into exile, mostly in France, and 10,000 were summarily executed by the victorious Franco, leaving untold thousands more languishing in his prisons or permanently barred from ever holding a respectable job in the Spanish community. Although a generation removed now, these wounds are still deep and sensitive to the Spanish people. They have not forgotten that it was Hitler and Mussolini who put Franco where he is today—even though, it would seem, most Americans have. When America's European allies refused to admit Franco to NATO—despite the fact that he proudly boasts on many of his public buildings that he is "The Conqueror of Communism"—the United States entered into unilateral military agreements with Spain, and thereupon proceeded to erect both air and naval bases in the country. There is little doubt but in American eyes, Franco runs "a tidy little shop", for a major part of his budget, now bolstered with American dollars, goes to his army and various police forces just to "maintain order." Whether such police-state tranquility can be maintained with the passing of Franco, however, remains to be seen.

On the long road back from the Civil War, Spain has made some impressive economic gains, but much remains to be done. One of the major tasks is the rationalization of agriculture through land reform, mechanization, and the introduction of more scientific practices. At the same time there is the problem of absorbing the displaced farm laborers into industry. Spain's balance of payments is very lopsided, for its exports of citrus fruit and olive oil cannot begin to pay for the machinery, petroleum, and iron and steel that constitute its chief imports. Remittances from Spanish laborers abroad help some, and tourism helps much more, but the economic and political problems that lie ahead for Spain remain great and challenging.

As Spain entered the decade of the seventies, it did so with Franco's hand-picked and personally-tutored successor, Prince Juan Carlos legally proclaimed and gradually assuming a more active role in administrative affairs. Within the cabinet, power has shifted out of the hands of old-guard Falangists into those of the Opus Dei, a Roman Catholic lay organization. Conciliatory concessions were being made to the restive intellectual community, and friendly overtures to the Moslem world (with Spain's return of the small territory of Ifni to Morocco). At the same time as Spain was renewing the leases of American military bases, it was clamoring for the return of Gibraltar from Britain and exchanging diplomatic missions with eastern Europe. Industry was growing rapidly and the economy was climbing toward new prosperity. Thus, as the old order showed unmistakable signs of drawing to a close, it seemed that the patience of the Spanish people might at last be rewarded with greater freedom and a higher level of material well-being.

Portugal. Like the rest of Mediterranean Europe, Portugal is basically an agricultural country. Although its farms employ five times as many workers as its factories, Portugal is still unable to feed its people. Not only does it have to import such "luxuries" as coffee and sugar, but it also imports such staples as cereals and fish. With farm holdings in the north reduced to a size that makes it impossible to support a family and those in the south held by absentee landlords, most of Portugal's surplus rural population has had to look to the colonies (Angola and Mozambique) or to former colonies such as Brazil for the opportunities denied them at home. Although the country possesses a few minerals and some hydroelectric power, such industrialization as has taken place to date is based largely on the raw materials supplied by farming, forestry, and fishing. Most Portuguese industries are incapable of meeting foreign competition, however, and must be strongly protected by the government if they are to continue to exist at all. Furthermore, in recent years the sardine has shown signs of abandoning its traditional habitat and moving beyond the range of the refrigeration-less Portuguese fishing fleet, thereby provoking a serious crisis in one of the country's mainstay occupations.

Increasingly Portugal has been looking to tourism to help balance its budget, but the Salazar government, the longest lived dictatorship in western Europe, also counted heavily on the retention of its African colonies to help pay its way in the world, as does its successor today. Ironically, Portugal was the first colonial power in Europe and it is also the last; and, because it was the poorest of them, it has done the least to develop it colonies and extracted the most. Refusing to "read the hand-writing on the wall", Portugal has expended about 8 per cent of its gross national product, 40 per cent of its national budget, and the lives of almost 2,000 of its sons in the last decade to retain its foothold in Africa, and is continuing blithely to plan—in league with the Republic of South Africa—for the economic development of areas now held by antigovernment guerilla forces. What straw it will clutch for when Angola and Mozambique one day win their independence, Portugal does not even contemplate—because it cannot conceive of such a world. And, as long as the Portuguese government uses "geographic blackmail" in negotiating for the continuance of American military bases in the Azores, little pressure against its repressive colonial policies is likely to be forthcoming from Washington.

Table 1.   The Mediterranean South, Selected Statistics (1968)

	Greece	Italy	Spain	Portugal
Area (000's sq. mi.)	50.5	116.3	194.9	34.3
Population (millions)	8.9	53.1	32.7	9.6
Birth rate (per 1000)	18.7	18.1	21.1	21.1
Death rate (per 1000)	8.3	9.7	8.7	10.0
Natural increase (per 1000)	10.4	8.4	12.4	11.1
Infant mortality (per 1000)	34.3	34.3	33.2	59.3
Land use (%)				
Cultivated	29.2	51.0	41.3	46.5
Meadows-Pastures	39.0	16.9	28.4	—
Forest	19.7	20.2	22.2	28.1
Other land	12.1	11.9	8.1	25.4
Pop. density per sq. mi.				
cultivated land	600	910	420	570
Gross national product				
per capita	$660	$1,030	$640	$380
Exports (millions)	$468	$10,183	$1,589	$761
Imports (millions)	$1,393	$10,243	$3,502	$1,178
Trade balance (millions)	−$925	−$70	−$1,913	−$417

Sources: *U.N. Demographical Yearbook, Yearbook of International Trade Statistics, FAO Yearbook of Food and Agricultural Statistics,* and *U.N. Statistical Yearbook.*

CHAPTER **3** *the western fringe*

Lying on the western edge of the European subcontinent are three countries whose location not only put them within the orbit of classical Roman civilization but also permitted them to take part in the colonial expansion initiated by Portugal and Spain. Despite their basic similarities in location, however, the varied paths of evolution they have followed have given them each a distinctive personality today.

France, the largest of the three, is not only the largest European country in area but also its most sparsely populated major state. The Netherlands and Belgium, on the contrary, are among Europe's smallest sovereign states (overlooking for the moment such "postage-stamp" relicts as Andorra, Liechtenstein, Luxembourg, Monaco, and San Marino) and rank as the subcontinent's most densely populated countries. Politically, France was one of the first great nation-states to arise in Europe, whereas the Low Countries have played the role of buffer states through most of their history. Economically, France has entered the latter half of the twentieth century as a largely rural-agricultural country, whereas the Netherlands and Belgium are among the most urban-industrial nations in the world. With the exception of the Mediterranean coastlands of France, all three countries have a climate which is humid throughout the year, and originally the region supported a dense cover of broadleaf deciduous forests. However, two critical warmth boundaries run through this western fringe of Europe; one for such subtropical commodities as citrus and olives in the south of France, and another for such warm-temperate crops as grapes and corn. The latter area extends as far north as the Paris region and includes some of the warmer valleys toward the northeast, notably that of the Rhine, but leaves Belgium and the Netherlands essentially beyond the limits of commercial grape and corn production (see Figure 2). The location of all three countries on the western, maritime fringe of Europe insures them damp and cloudy but mild winters, with snow occurring only over higher elevations and ice a rarity in the rivers and canals.

France

THE REGIONS OF FRANCE. The alert traveler notices many subtle changes in journeying from the Mediterranean South of France to the more maritime North and West. For example, the native building materials no longer consist of only the stone and clay typical of the Mediterranean, but in many areas are joined to an external skeleton of hardwood beams, forming the so-called half-timbered construction. The bridges that span the rivers are designed with lower arches in the North, for the flow of the streams is much more even than in the Mediterranean South. No longer are there louvered shutters on the windows of houses to keep out the sun and still permit the circulation of air; now the sun is welcomed and it is the wind that is to be avoided. As the summer landscape changes from olive drab to lush and green, field crops are increasingly supplemented by pastures for the more demanding forms of livestock, such as cattle and horses, while goats and donkeys almost disappear and the more adaptable sheep inherits both the damper uplands and the drier lowlands. As land uses vary, so do the dietary patterns of the people, who in the northern region depend much more heavily upon animal protein (meat, milk, butter, and cheese) than do residents of the summer drought areas. The problems of agriculture are reversed; it is not the shortage of water that is critical in the North, but rather its surplus. Arid-land cereals such as wheat and barley do best in whatever dry pockets can be found, while oats and rye, which thrive in moister climates, can be extensively grown. The same is true of potatoes and root crops, and beyond the pale of grape cultivation, the native beverages are either cider, as in Normandy, or beer, as over most of the remainder of northern, western, and central Europe. Finally, the dress of the people in the North is warmer and more water repellent, and the umbrella is the companion of the well-dressed urbanite in summer and winter alike.

The Southeast. The Southeast of France is part of the Mediterranean realm, both in its climatic and land use patterns and in its orientation (Figure 10). It consists of four relatively distinct subregions; the Rhone valley, the coast east of the Rhone (Provence), the coast west of the Rhone (Languedoc), and the Maritime Alps.

This was the first region beyond peninsular Italy that the Romans penetrated and, although they recognized it as a separate geographical entity (they called it "the province"—Provence), they also appreciated it for its similarity to Italy. (Loosely translated, they also called it "shirtless Gaul," the distinction being that in the rest of Gaul, they pretty well had to keep their shirts on!) Because most of Provence consists of older, crystalline rocks, it meets the Mediterranean in a series of bold, rocky headlands. In contrast, Languedoc to the west is made up of younger sedimentary rocks, which have been eroded by the waves into long sandy

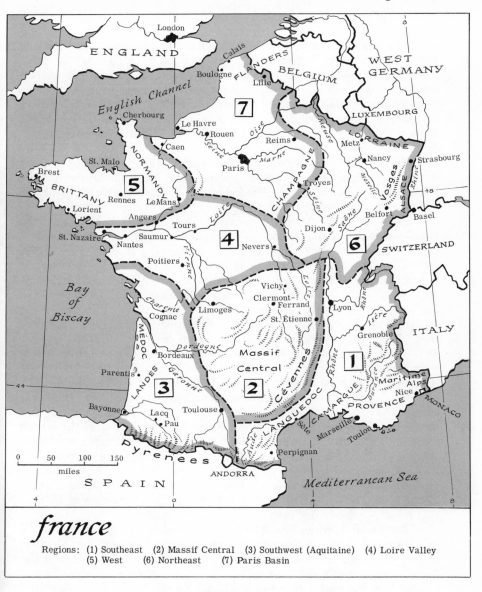

france

Regions: (1) Southeast (2) Massif Central (3) Southwest (Aquitaine) (4) Loire Valley
(5) West (6) Northeast (7) Paris Basin

Figure 10

beaches backed by lagoons. Although olive groves and vineyards dominate the agricultural landscape, in the more well-watered areas there is
intensive cultivation of fruit, vegetable, and nut crops, as well as of
flowers, some of which are used for making perfume. In the marshy
Camargue region at the mouth of the Rhone, some rice is grown, but

many of the deltaic meadows remain pasturelands for herds of semi-wild horses. However, the predominant livestock throughout the Southeast is sheep. Some fishing is carried on out of ports such as Marseille and Sète, but the principal primary products of the region are the table wines of Languedoc. Though they are not distinguished for their quality, the Languedoc wines are produced in such quantity as to make this the most intensive wine-producing region in all of Europe. (Even so, with an average annual per capita consumption in excess of forty gallons, France still finds it necessary to import wine from such countries as Algeria.)

The chief mineral deposit of southeastern France is bauxite; it takes its name, in fact, from Les Baux, inland from Marseille. However, the largest production of the region today comes from the foothills of the Pyrenees back of Perpignan.

Even before the Romans arrived, this region was known to the Greeks, and it was they who laid the foundations of such cities as Marseille (Greek Massilia) and Nice. Today Marseille is a city of 800,000, second in France only to Paris, and also the country's busiest seaport. As the principal gateway to France from its former African colonies, Marseille became the center of such industries as oil refining, petrochemicals, leather processing, sugar refining, and cosmetics. Nice, to the east, is the center of the Riviera resort region, while Toulon, on the coast between them, is France's major Mediterranean naval base.

The ancients were quick to discover that leading out from Mediterranean France there were two lowland corridors, one along the Aude river to the west, and one along the Rhone to the north. The Greeks, and possibly the Phoenicians before them, had no doubt used the Aude corridor to reach the west of France and the tin mines of Cornwall, but for most subsequent peoples, the corridor has simply led in the wrong direction to be of much importance. (However, a canal was constructed between the Mediterranean and the Atlantic through this corridor and it is also traversed by the region's main railway.) By way of illustration, it might be pointed out that the magnificently preserved castle town of Carcassonne, which guards the gap, is magnificently preserved for just that reason—nobody has ever come along to attack it!

The Rhone corridor is another matter entirely, for it constitutes the only lowland route in western Europe leading between the Mediterranean basin and the northern areas of the subcontinent. As such, it has been a major north-south artery of movement ever since Julius Caesar marched up the valley to conquer Gaul. The city of Lyon, strategically situated at the junction of the Rhone and its major tributary, the Saône, was founded by the Romans as the regional capital, and its 530,000 inhabitants give it third rank among the cities of France today. An important communications center, Lyon is also noted for its velvet and silk industries, though tucked into nearby valleys, both to the east and west, are factories producing aircraft, electrical machinery, automobiles, office equipment, chemicals, and plastics. Indeed, the Lyon area demonstrates as well as any other the fact that in France much of the industry is distributed in rural districts, and thus seldom gives rise to the type of urban agglomerations that typify the Low Countries, for example.

Along the floor of the Rhone valley there is some cultivation of specialty crops such as fruit, nuts, and tobacco, while the higher slopes are given over to pasture and forest. The upper reaches of the valley are noted for such vintage wines as Burgundy and Beaujolais, but the region's most valuable export is undoubtedly hydroelectric power. A considerable output is generated on the Rhone itself, but much more comes from its left-bank tributaries, the Isère and the Durance. The bulk of this power is transmitted by high tension lines northward to the Paris Basin. Otherwise the alpine region is chiefly important for its wood industries and its ski resorts, of which Grenoble, the site of the 1968 Winter Olympics, is a major center.

At its upper end, the Rhone-Saône corridor not only opens northwestward through the Dijon gap into the Paris Basin, but also northeastward through the Belfort gap into the Rhine valley. The importance of these routeways has been repeatedly demonstrated all through history, and each advance in the technology of transportation has reinforced their roles still further. Today canals, railways, highways, and pipelines all run side by side through this lowland trough, which may in effect be called the Main Street of France.

The Massif Central. The "obstacle" around which the Aude and Rhône corridors lead is the Massif Central, the most rugged and geologically diverse region within France. It is also the most varied climatically, for its lower western portions have a temperate marine climate, its lower southeastern slopes are mediterranean, much of the higher interior is comparable to the continental climate of southern Sweden, and the highest areas of the Cevennes—the divide between Mediterranean and Atlantic drainage—has an almost tundra-like character. Parts of its western face have 200 days of rain annually, while in the rain shadow to the southeast there are scarcely 60 days a year with measurable precipitation.

Farming in the Massif is restricted to narrow ribbons along the valleys with some wheat, barley, and grapes grown in the lower areas, but with rye and potatoes the chief staples and apples and chestnuts the principal specialty crops. Much of the land is in pasture, but where it is too rugged for dairy cattle, the more nimble sheep and goats are found. A larger proportion of the land is in forest, with conifers dominating the upper slopes.

Scattered throughout the Massif are small pockets of minerals, including coal, iron ore, pyrites, tungsten, lead, zinc, and uranium. Water power, harnessed on the wetter, western side, is transmitted chiefly to Paris. St. Etienne, the largest town of the region, has some 200,000 people and owes its existence to the local occurrence of coal and iron ore. It is a center not only of metal industries, but also of textiles, electronics, and engineering works that produce armaments, bicycles, farm machinery, and locomotives. Down-valley from St. Etienne there are numerous glass and ceramics factories; Clermont-Ferrand is the site of a large rubber factory; and Limoges is synonymous with fine porcelain. Vichy is known as a spa and also served as the puppet capital of France during the Nazi occupation. There are few other towns of any size, however, and the region as a whole is losing population.

The Southwest (Aquitaine).   To the west of the Massif Central lies the Aquitaine Basin, an extensive lowland region floored by sedimentary rocks and drained by the Garonne and Dordogne river systems. Moisture is no problem over most of the Aquitaine and soils, especially along the river valleys, are quite productive, so a wide variety of crops are produced. The cereals include wheat, barley, and corn, and specialty crops such as cauliflower, asparagus, peas, beans, artichokes, and tomatoes are also grown. On the higher valley sides toward the interior, specialization is in fruit and nut crops, including peaches, plums, apples, walnuts, and chestnuts. Some tobacco is grown in the Medoc area and both potatoes and sugar beets are found around Toulouse, but the Aquitaine is by far best known and appreciated for its vintage wines, including those of Cognac, Medoc, and Bordeaux.

One district of the Aquitaine which stands out in sharp contrast to the rest of the region is Landes, south of Bordeaux. Here, the persistent winds off the Bay of Biscay were drifting sand inland to the point where the moving dunes were beginning to threaten cultivated areas. As a result, during Napoleon's time, the entire region was planted to pine trees. Not only did they fix the dunes in place, but they have also subsequently given France the largest naval stores industry in Europe, and today Bordeaux is a major exporter of turpentine and resin, as well as choice wines.

Although Bordeaux is the region's chief port and a center for diversified industries ranging from food processing to foundries, its quarter of a million inhabitants no longer qualify it as the metropolis of Aquitaine. That distinction now goes to Toulouse, a city of 325,000 people, many of whom are employed by the giant Sud Aviation Company. This aircraft company not only produces the famous Caravelle jet but also is making most of the French contribution to the cooperative venture with the British on the supersonic Concorde. Much of the aluminum used in the aircraft industry is produced in large refineries at the foot of the Pyrenees, where there is abundant and cheap hydroelectric power to smelt the bauxite coming from Mediterranean France.

Aquitaine also makes an important contribution to the French energy budget, thanks to the fact that it has the country's largest oil field at Parentis, in the Landes district, and its largest natural gas field at Lacq, near the foothills of the Pyrenees. It should be emphasized, however, that the importance of this contribution is only relative, for France already consumes about twenty times as much oil as the Parentis field is capable of producing.

The Loire Valley.   The Loire Valley, north of the Aquitaine, is also primarily an agricultural lowland, but it is enough different from the Aquitaine to set off as a separate region. For one thing it is cooler and damper, more of the land is in pasture and forest, and oats are a more common cereal than either corn or barley. Otherwise, the Loire also concentrates in the specialty production of vegetables and fruits, as well as in flowers and vintage wines. Some of the better known of the latter include Muscadet, Anjou, Vouvray, and Touraine types. In earlier times the Loire was also noted for its assemblage of stately country residences, or chateaux, many of which are open to the public today as private or public museums.

Industrialization in the Loire has been hampered by the lack of both raw materials and power. Until recently, coal and oil brought to the Loire estuary meant that most of the valley's industrial development has been concentrated in the cities of Nantes (pop. 250,000) and St. Nazaire. Here such heavy industries as steel, oil refining, shipbuilding, lead smelting, petrochemicals, and the manufacturing of railway equipment are located. In the upper valley one finds food processing, textiles, leather goods, ceramics, and farm machinery. The occurrence of uranium in the hills southeast of Nantes and the region's lack of conventional energy resources have prompted the French government to build a nuclear power station on the Loire just above Saumur.

The West. Beyond the mouth of the Loire to the north and west are the ancient crystalline hills of Brittany and Normandy. Rising to elevations of 1200 to 1300 feet, these hills not only form the backbone of two rocky peninsulas jutting out into the sea but are also high enough to intercept about twice as much precipitation as the lower lying Paris Basin to the east. (Indeed, the latter may be thought of as lying in the rain shadow of these western hills.) The result is that Brittany and Normandy have the most pronouncedly maritime climate of any part of France, with winter temperatures considerably milder than those of Paris but also markedly cooler summers, because of the constant onshore winds. The soils derived from the crystalline bedrock are not particularly fertile, and much more of the land is in pasture than in crops. Some wheat and barley are grown, but the best yields are definitely of rye and oats. Other crops include potatoes, carrots, cabbages, and apples, the latter used in making cider, which is the regional beverage because grapes cannot be ripened. Dairy cattle and pigs are the dominant forms of livestock, and butter and cheese making are locally important. Even so, the population densities are heavy enough and the farm land scarce enough to have early encouraged the Bretons, in particular, to look to fishing to supplement their diet. Lorient, which takes its name from the days when it served as a French colonial port trading with the Far East, is the chief fishing port today, while Brest, at the peninsula's outer end, is France's principal Atlantic naval base.

The West of France is notably deficient in power for industry, for it has no coal, no oil, and no hydroelectricity of any importance. This is one reason that the harnessing of tidal energy at La Rance estuary near St. Malo is considered so feasible; the other is that the tidal range in that constricted river mouth is over forty feet. Such industry as is found in the region consists of food processing, textiles, electronic equipment, and shipbuilding at Brest and at Cherbourg. The latter is a frequent port of call for transatlantic passenger liners, although the rather unlikely river port of Caen is the busiest in the region.

Although the West ranks as the poorest region in northern France in per capita income (there are poorer districts in parts of the Massif Central), it does provide a striking illustration of the fact that poverty, like beauty, lies in the eye of the beholder. To the Romans, coming from the sunny climes of the Mediterranean, damp and cloudy Brittany was an extremely unattractive place—so unattractive that they hardly bothered with it, leaving the Celtic-speaking Bretons much to themselves. The result has been that the Bretons have managed to survive as a linguistic minority to this day, for much the same reasons that the Welsh and Scottish Celts have in Great Britain. On the other hand, the rolling green hills of Normandy looked so good to the Vikings that they moved in and appropriated the entire region. Their presence has been perpetuated not only in numerous place names, including that of Normandy itself, but in the high frequency of blue eyes and blond hair one finds in this part of France.

The Northeast. The only other region of France with a major linguistic minority is the Northeast, but for quite different reasons. When the empire of Charlemagne was divided among his three sons (in A.D. 843), one received essentially what is now France, the second received what now is Germany, and the third, Lothar, received a rather nebulous no-man's land (undefined by "natural" boundaries) in between. This buffer zone between regions where French and German (or Latin and Germanic) were spoken had its precedent in the boundary of the Roman Empire that followed the Rhine, but then it was a "line" and not a "zone." Lothar's kingdom was an ambiguous strip of land running from the North Sea to the Alps, and it was out of this zone that four of Europe's small buffer states ultimately came into existence; the Netherlands, Belgium, Luxembourg, and Switzerland. However, in the gap between Luxembourg and Switzerland, the French and Germans directly faced one another across the regions of Alsace and Lorraine (the latter taking its name from the unhappy Lothar).

Germany, or more properly Prussia, did not become a unified political power until 1870. One of the means that Bismarck, Germany's chancellor at that time, used to achieve unity was to wage war on the largest land power in Europe, which then was France. In the ensuing Franco-Prussian War, Bismarck very quickly demonstrated that the Germans had come of age, for the French defeat was both complete and humiliating. A major prize of the war was the acquisition of Alsace and Lorraine, the former known to have large deposits of potash, used in making fertilizer and explosives, and the latter containing some of the largest reserves of low-grade iron ore in Europe. The so-called *minette* iron ores of Lorraine did have a serious drawback, however, for they contained a high content of phosphorus, which made the iron produced from them brittle and of poor quality. Ironically, it was only half a dozen years later that two amateur English chemists, an apothecary and his cousin, stumbled onto a technique for removing the phosphorus, thereby turning the Lorraine iron ores into one of the great natural resources of Europe—and incidentally paving the way for the phenomenal industrial growth of Germany, which was to become Britain's foremost rival.

In 1914, Germany and France were at it again, this time involving much of the rest of the world as well. Were it not for its allies, France would quite likely have gone down to quick and ignominious defeat once again, but the British, Americans, and Canadians finally managed to help France emerge "victorious." By the terms of the Versailles Treaty that followed, France regained possession of Alsace and Lorraine, together with their largely German-speaking inhabitants. France had hardly twenty years of peace in which to develop its own industrial structure around the resources of Alsace and Lorraine, however, for in 1939 World War II broke out. Determined not to be taken by surprise, the French had built an elaborate fortifications system, the Maginot Line, extending from Switzerland all the way to Luxembourg. Whether it seriously deterred the Nazis is difficult to say, for they merely proceeded to "sweep around end," overrunning France in six weeks by way of Belgium. (The French, however, are neither the first nor the last peoples to be beguiled by "Maginot-Line thinking". Both the Great Wall of China and the DEW Line are cases in point.)

In addition to its iron ore and potash, the Northeast also produces about one-fourth of France's coal, primarily from mines in the Metz area. As a result, a number of metallurgical and engineering industries have been developed in and around the cities of Metz and Nancy. These include the manufacture of steel, automobiles, railway equipment, and electrical machinery. Strasbourg, France's major river port on the Rhine, is today the region's largest city, with a population of some 230,000. It handles large tonnages of imported coal from the Ruhr region in Germany and is also a major oil refining center. Crude oil reaches it both by barge from Rotterdam and by pipeline from Marseille. Other industries scattered through the Northeast include clock and watch making, glass, ceramics, textiles, food processing, plastics, brewing, cigarettes, paper, and optical and musical instruments.

Apart from the flat-floored Rhine valley, the Northeast is essentially an upland region, which reaches its highest elevations (over 4800 feet) in the Vosges Mountains of Alsace. Because of its elevation, the Northeast is considerably damper and cooler than the Paris Basin to the west, and its land use patterns faithfully reflect this climate. Oats produce the best yields of the cereals, and specialty crops include potatoes, hops, apples, plums, and cherries. Cattle and pigs are the principal forms of livestock, and much of the region's milk is converted to butter and cheese. All told, however, there is more land in pasture and forest than there is in field crops.

The Paris Basin. Even since the emergence of France as a nation-state, the core of the country has been the lowland basin centered on the Seine River and its tributaries. Here, near the center of the basin where an island in the Seine provided a convenient bridging point, the Roman settlement of Lutetia arose. For the Romans, however, it was scarcely more than a way station en route to Calais and the island of Britain. It remained for the Frankish kings, long after the fall of Rome and the Germanic migrations, to recognize it as any kind of a "natural" center. The growth of Paris was favored, however, by the fact that it lay in the warmest and driest part of France outside of the Mediterranean South, and consequently in the heart of its most productive agricultural region. To this day the Paris Basin is the granary of France, for it produces the highest yields of wheat in the country—in some years even a surplus for export. Barley is relegated to the poorer soils but there is also a diversified production of such crops as sugar beets, oil seeds, flax, mushrooms, and potatoes, to name a few. The region's livestock includes both beef and dairy cattle, but sheep predominate on the drier cuestas— the asymmetrical ridges of limestone and sandstone that form concentric areas around the center of the basin. Some of the ridges are in orchards as well, producing cherries and pears, but many of the higher and steeper ridges have been left in forest.

The Paris Basin itself is devoid of minerals of any importance, though on its northern edge lies the Nord coal field—a continuation, indeed, a termination, of the coal-bearing strata that run through the Sambre-Meuse Valley of Belgium and on into the Ruhr region of Germany. The mines of the Nord field produce about 60 per cent of France's coal and have given rise to a concentration of industries on the Belgian border focused on the city of Lille (pop. 300,000). Otherwise, apart from Paris, the region's largest city is the port of Rouen (pop. 200,000) on the lower Seine.

It is, however, the city of Paris that dominates not only the Basin itself, but all of France. Today, with a population of nearly 7,500,000 including suburbs, the French capital is the home of one out of every seven Frenchmen. It is not only the country's political and administrative center, but the commercial, cultural, communications, and industrial heart of France as well. It is the hub of the rail and road network and the country's busiest air traffic center. The intellectual and artistic life of France finds its focus here, and its multitude of attractions make it the country's largest tourist center. Its industries are so diverse that no one or group of them predominates. Best known, however, are those dealing in fashions and accessories, knitwear, hosiery, shoes, gloves, furs, jewelry, and cosmetics, but also important are automobiles, aircraft, precision instruments, chemicals, and food processing.

As we have already noted, much of the power consumed in the Paris Basin is generated in the Alps and the Massif Central, but there are also large oil refineries at Le Havre near the mouth of the Seine. The latter is the country's second ranking port, exceeding upstream Rouen in volume of imports (but not exports). Boulogne, to the north, ranks as France's chief fishing port, with many of its trawlers working in both the North Sea and the English Channel. Calais is the principal ferry terminus for rail and road traffic to Britain.

CONCLUSION.   Few countries in Europe—indeed, few countries in the world—have so diversified and balanced a resource base as has France.

Moreover few countries in the world have seen their populations grow so slowly in the past century and a half as has France. In Napoleon's day France was the largest country in Europe not only in terms of area, but also in terms of population. Today it ranks fourth in population, in part because it has suffered so grievously in the three major wars of the last century, and in part also because it has lacked enough of the vital ingredients (especially coal), and the peace, to become heavily industrialized. The bane of French existence in the last hundred years has been Germany; thus it is not surprising that most of France's statesmanship, both positive and negative, has been directed toward that country. It was the French who conceived the European Steel and Coal Community, out of which the Common Market eventually developed. But it was also the French who in 1944 signed a secret alliance with the Soviet Union against a re-emergent Germany (only to have it revoked by the Russians in 1955, after the French had voted, albeit reluctantly, to admit West Germany to NATO) and who obstreperously blocked all Four Power attempts to unify Berlin. And it was Charles de Gaulle who attempted to keep the West Germans off balance by renegotiating a "treaty of friendship" with the Soviet Union and "recognizing" Poland's claims to the Oder-Neisse boundary, while at the same time going through the motions of reconciliation with his Common Market partner (West Germany). To be sure, in the person of Charles de Gaulle, French ambitions went much farther than just checkmating her eastern adversary. As leader of the "Free French" forces during World War II, de Gaulle was painfully aware of the debt France owed to the "Anglo-Saxon" powers for its liberation and subsequent rehabilitation. (Over $10 billion in American aid alone was given to the French in the postwar period.) After taking office as premier in 1958, he made a secret proposal to the United States and Britain for a three-power directorate of the western world, but their rejection of the plan led him to initiate France's withdrawal from NATO, which was finally accomplished in 1967. De Gaulle in turn rejected the idea of a supranational European community, and strove instead to make France the leader of a loose association he preferred to call "the Europe of the Fatherlands" stretching from "the Atlantic to the Urals," a "third force" independent of both American and Soviet domination. His veto of British entry into the Common Market was not wholly—or even chiefly— out of spite, but out of the very real recognition that the *relative* importance of France would decline even farther if Europe's *two* largest industrial powers were members. De Gaulle's sensitivity on this score may be judged by the secret proposal he made to Britain early in 1969 in which he envisioned a broadened free trade area to supersede the Common Market in which the United Kingdom, West Germany, Italy, and France would form a four-power directorate. (Obviously when the British revealed this plan to the smaller member states of the EEC, it neither endeared de Gaulle to them—nor the British to de Gaulle!) Astute and capable a statesman as he was (he had the courage, after all, to overrule his generals and terminate a senseless war in Algeria, thereby enhancing France's esteem among her former African colonies), de Gaulle seemed more concerned with restoring the grandeur of France in the international arena than he did with solving some of the country's more pressing internal problems. When his scheme for economic regionalization failed to win the support of the French electorate in a popular referendum on April 24, 1969, he precipitately resigned the following day. There is little doubt but that de Gaulle will be remembered as one of the great figures of the twentieth century for having given France new confidence, stability, and self-respect when she needed them most. On the other hand, such qualities, while important, do not in themselves make France a world power and if de Gaulle thought that they did, he must be excused for having been a more serious student of nineteenth century political history than he was of twentieth century economic geography!

The Low Countries

THE REGIONS OF BELGIUM.   Belgium is one of the more recent countries to appear on the map of Europe, having been created in the wake of the Napoleonic Wars in 1830 (Figure 11). It was from the very outset an artificial state, designed primarily to fulfill the functions of a buffer. Although it had an essential unity of religion (Roman Catholicism), it was divided linguistically between the Flemings on the north, speaking a dialect of Dutch, and the Walloons in the south, speaking a dialect of French. (This division, occurring as it does on a flat plain, traces its origins to a geographic feature no longer in existence, a dense forest that has long since been cut down.) As though this linguistic division were not a serious enough problem in itself, it has been further complicated and intensified by the subsequent economic evolution of the country. By an accident of geography most of the best agricultural land and all of the coal mines lie in the Walloon-speaking area. So today the internal struggles of Belgium are as much between farmers and industrial workers as they are between Fleming and Walloon.

The Ardennes.   Small though Belgium is (11,781 square miles), a large part of it consists of a sparsely populated upland region with poor, sandy soils and a damp, cool climate. This is the Ardennes, which makes up the southeastern two-fifths of Belgium's area. The farms in this region are small and scattered, and their chief crops are rye, oats, and potatoes. Most of the land is in pasture and forest and the few industries in the region are concerned with woolen textiles, leather goods, and paper. With the lowest per capita income in the country and few prospects for improving it, the region is constantly losing population.

The Ardennes is defined on its northwestern edge by the valleys of the Meuse and Sambre rivers, along which coal deposits outcrop almost through their entire length. These have given rise to a line of industrial cities, beginning with Charleroi near the French border and including Namur and Liège, the latter being by far the largest and most important. Aligned along this industrial belt are steel mills; lead and zinc smelters; glass, ceramic, and chemical factories; cement plants; and engineering works.

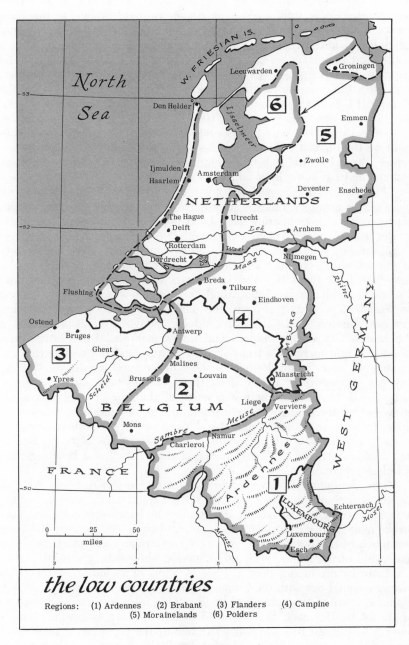

the low countries

Regions: (1) Ardennes   (2) Brabant   (3) Flanders   (4) Campine
          (5) Morainelands   (6) Polders

Figure 11

Brabant. On the left banks of the Sambre and Meuse, the hills give way to the rolling lowland of Brabant, a region of extremely fertile, water-sorted loess soils, known as *limon*. Brabant is by far the most prosperous agricultural area in Belgium, and also its most densely populated. Farms in this region are not only small but also fragmented. Wheat is the most important cereal crop, but vegetables, fruit, sugar beets, and hops are likewise grown. (The latter crop has a particular importance, it would seem, because Belgians drink more beer than anyone else in the world.) It is in Brabant that the country's capital and commercial center, the city of Brussels (pop. 1,000,000, suburbs included) is located, chosen as capital not only for its central location but also because it lies right on the linguistic divide. Besides being the country's administrative center, Brussels is the hub of Belgium's rail, road and air transportation systems and has some light consumer industries.

Flanders. To the west and north of Brabant, the North European plain curves away with hardly so much as a topographic clue that significant geographic boundaries have been crossed. To the west the plain grades into Flanders, a region of essentially sandy soils, whose access to the North Sea is in large part impeded by sand dunes. Here the sterility of the soil is reflected not only in the greater proportion of land in pasture than in Brabant but also in the fact that rye, oats, potatoes, and flax are the chief crops. Interestingly enough, it was the sheep grazing on Flanders' poor pastures and the flax grown on its sandy soils that first put Flanders on the map, and indeed, brought it great prosperity in the Middle Ages. The woolens and linens marketed from Bruges and Ghent brought merchants from all over Europe and the wealth that accumulated later financed great schools of art and music, as well as voyages of discovery. For a time, these two Flemish cities were the largest and most important towns north of the Alps, but like so many cities before them, they became less and less accessible to the sea as their rivers grew shallower and the ships grew larger. Both have canals to the sea today, and while Ghent still has a smattering of trade, Bruges has become virtually a museum piece of stately medieval buildings and cobblestone streets.

The Campine. Today, Belgium's greatest port is Antwerp, located on the estuary of the Schelde River. With a quarter of a million people, it is the second largest city in the country and the second busiest port on the mainland of Europe, for its hinterland embraces not only Belgium, but much of northern France and western Germany as well. It is also a major industrial center, with oil refineries, shipyards, chemical plants, and factories producing electrical goods. Many of its industries reflect its former colonial ties with the Congo, for among them are copper smelting, diamond cutting, the extraction of vegetable oils, and the manufacture of chocolate. However, the region in which Antwerp is located is itself one of the poorest in the country. Known as the Campine, it consists of sandy outwash materials from the Ice Age. Some rye and oats are grown, but by far the greater proportion of the land is in pasture and forest.

THE REGIONS OF THE NETHERLANDS

The Campine. The sterile outwash plain of the Campine continues into the Netherlands as far as the Rhine. By heavy fertilization and intensive cultivation, the Dutch have managed to support a fairly dense population in the region, and in addition to such staples as rye and oats they grow such specialty crops as strawberries, sugar beets, and hops. Even so, much of the land is fit only for grazing and forestry.

During World War I, as the fighting raged all around them and they were cut off from their normal coal supplies in Germany, the Dutch took a hard look at their country's geological map and decided that if there was coal to the west in Belgium and coal to the east in Germany, then there also must be coal in the middle—in the Limburg district near the city of Maastricht. They began digging, and were still digging when the war was over, but they did find coal about 3000 feet down. In 1919 the Netherlands opened some of the deepest and most modern coal mines in Europe, and today the Dutch are efficiently producing about half as much coal a year as all the antiquated mines of Belgium put together. It is still not adequate to their needs, but the Limburg mines play a large and important role in the modern industrial life of the nation. However, the largest industrial center of the Campine itself is the city of Eindhoven. Its chief attraction lies not in any raw material or power resource, but in the pool of intelligent labor it can draw upon. Today Eindhoven is not only the center of the Philips electronics firm, one of the largest manufacturers in Europe of light bulbs, television sets, radios, and tape recorders, but it is also the home of the Netherlands' own automobile, the DAF.

The Rhine essentially marks the northern boundary of the old outwash plain and the southern boundary of the morainic hills that were formed at the time of the glacier's farthest advance. But the Rhine is more than just a physical boundary; it is a cultural boundary as well, for south of the river the Dutch are predominantly Catholics and north of the river chiefly Protestants. Thus, like the Belgians, the Dutch are a divided people. Ever since Holland's long and bloody struggle with the Spanish Hapsburgs, the Netherlands has been keenly conscious of its Protestant heritage, and the ruling family is required by law to belong to the Dutch Reformed Church. (Riots broke out in 1968 when it was announced that one of the Dutch princesses was to marry a Catholic—and a Spanish Catholic at that!) Since the Reformation, Dutch Protestants have constituted a clear majority of the population, and consequently they have ruled quite comfortably in Parliament. But in recent decades, the Catholic minority has been rapidly narrowing the gap, for while the Protestants have been practicing birth control, the Catholics have not. Seeing the handwriting on the wall, Protestant politicians have exhorted their coreligionists to have more children. Thus, ironically, in the most densely populated country in Europe a procreation race is going on, giving the urban-industrialized Netherlands a birth rate far higher than that of the basically rural-agricultural countries in southeastern Europe. Because the Netherlands cannot possibly absorb these additional people, there is a steady out-migration—not of unskilled laborers as in southern Europe, but largely of well-educated, ambitious younger persons.

The Morainelands. The Morainelands of the eastern interior of the Netherlands have scarcely been more attractive than the outwash plain of the Campine, and in fact, their overall population density is considerably lower. Rye, oats, and potatoes are the chief crops, and pasture and woodland make up the largest proportion of the area. Until 1960, the region was considered to be devoid of minerals, but in that year exploratory borings near Groningen struck a pocket of natural gas. Further explorations quickly outlined what is now believed to be the second largest gas field in the world, and this discovery is already beginning to revolutionize the whole energy pattern of northwestern Europe. Dutch dependence on imported coal and oil has been sharply reduced, the specter of depression is looming large over the German Ruhr, and other European nations are intensifying their efforts to find gas, or oil, or both beneath the North Sea. In fact, one of the largest questions raised by the Dutch discovery is, "Who owns what in the North Sea?"

The Polders. Although the Romans reached the Rhine more than fifteen centuries ago and built a fort near its mouth, the physical landscape they surveyed and that which the traveler sees today bear little resemblance to one another. Owing to the constantly accumulating sediments brought down by the Rhine, the Meuse and the Schelde, the block of the earth's crust beneath their common delta has been submerging— at the rate of about one foot a century, in fact, for the foundations of the old Roman fort are now about fifteen feet below sea level. At the same time that the block has been submerging, it has been tilting toward the south, so through the centuries the Rhine has abandoned one channel after another as the main flow of the river has shifted ever southward. Thus, when Utrecht was founded, it lay on the main course of the river. Somewhat later, when Rotterdam was founded, the main stream flowed past it, but today it lies south of Rotterdam as well.

The principal transformation that a reincarnated Roman would notice today is that dry land, covered by a dense pattern of prosperous farms and bustling cities, exists where only tidal marshes were found before. Through centuries of laborious diking and drainage the Dutch have pushed back the North Sea to reclaim the fertile silts and clays of the delta. These rich alluvial soils now support the heaviest density of population anywhere in western Europe. From them Dutch farmers extract the highest yields of wheat, sugar beets, potatoes, vegetables, and fruits in the world. On the lush pastures of these polders (as this reclaimed land is called) graze herds of thoroughbred dairy cattle whose yields of milk surpass those of any other country, providing not only a surplus of fluid milk for export, but also large quantities for processing into butter, cheese, and milk chocolate. Another very lucrative specialty that Dutch farmers have developed is the cultivation of flower bulbs, such as tulips, hyacinths, and narcissus, especially in the Haarlem area west of Amsterdam.

Intensive and efficient as it is, Dutch agriculture cannot feed the country's burgeoning population, and so the Dutch also carry on extensive fishing in the North Sea, landing much of their catch at IJmuiden, the Hague, and Haarlem. However, the country's chief efforts to accommodate the growing population are being made in the direction of winning more land from the sea. Currently under way is the reclamation of the IJssel Meer, the fresh water successor to the Zuider Zee, a vast embayment in the north of the country formed by a single catastrophic storm in the thirteenth century. Also in the works is the so-called Delta Plan, a grandiose scheme budgeted for $600 million over twenty-five years to close off and reclaim the entire delta region. If successfully completed, these projects together could almost double the Netherlands' area of high-quality agricultural land.

Although the clay of the delta region has been used for making bricks, tiles, and the famous Delft pottery, there are no other minerals of importance in the region and no sources of power (thus, the Dutch relied on the windmill to pump the water out of the polders in earlier times, but now have largely replaced them with the more efficient but immensely less picturesque gasoline engine). Industrialization in the Netherlands has therefore had to depend largely on imported raw materials and fuels, which in most other countries would make industry a high-cost, noncompetitive operation unless it (1) was extremely efficient (2) exploited cheap labor, or both. Without minimizing Dutch efficiency and categorically denying the cheapness of its labor, it should be pointed out that the excellence of the Netherlands' geographic location plays a major role in the success of its industry. Lying as it does at the mouth of the busiest inland waterway in the world, the Rhine, the Netherlands is in a superb position to "intercept" such items as coal moving downstream from the Ruhr and iron ore and petroleum moving upstream to the Ruhr. This explains, for example, why some of the largest tin smelters in the world are located at Arnhem near the German border. Tin ore comes all the way from Indonesia (the former Dutch East Indies) by cheap water transportation to be smelted with coal brought down from the Ruhr. This also explains why Rotterdam has steel mills and shipyards, and the largest oil refineries in Europe. Indeed, thanks to the Rhine and an excellent network of interconnecting canals, roads, and railways, Rotterdam has become the busiest seaport in continental Europe. In some years it handles even greater tonnages than New York, thereby qualifying it as the greatest port in the world. Its hinterland embraces not only the Netherlands and much of Belgium, but also most of western Germany, eastern France, and Switzerland. Leveled by Nazi dive bombers in 1940, Rotterdam has risen from its ashes with renewed vigor to become *Europoort*—a port for all of western Europe. With a population of three quarters of a million, it ranks as the Netherlands' second largest city.

The country's largest city is its capital and old colonial port, Amsterdam, with some 920,000 inhabitants. Because its approaches to the sea were becoming increasingly difficult, the North Sea Canal was cut through the polders and sand dunes to the west in 1896, and ships of fairly good size are still able to reach the city. Most of Amsterdam's industries trace their origins to the country's colonial ties, as evidenced by its diamond cutters, sugar refineries, and cigar and chocolate factories. (Here might be the place to point out that the Dutch rank as the world's biggest cocoa drinkers!) The city also has shipyards and an aircraft factory, while IJmuiden, at the North Sea end of its canal, has a large iron and steel works. The Hague (pop. 610,000) is, as its name in Dutch implies, a garden city—and the site of the International Court of Justice, a royal residence, and a number of light consumer industries.

CONCLUSIONS.   Although their location as buffer areas has given both the Netherlands and Belgium internal problems of religion and language to resolve, it is chiefly in the international arena that their major challenge lies. Belgium has been "caught in the middle" in both world wars, and the Netherlands suffered extensively in the second of them; therefore their position is not an enviable one as long as they are surrounded on all sides by bellicose neighbors. Accordingly, it is not surprising that the Netherlands and Belgium, in concert with Luxembourg, have been the most outspoken advocates of the Common Market and, ultimately, of a united Europe. In a world at war, their strategic—and indefensible—position is one of the least comfortable on the globe. In a world at peace, they occupy one of the prime pieces of commercial real estate anywhere on the planet.

Table 2.   The Western Fringe, Selected Statistics (1968)

	France	Belguim	Netherlands
Area (000's sq. mi.)	211.2	11.8	13.0
Population (millions)	50.0	9.7	12.9
Birth rate (per 1000)	16.9	15.2	18.9
Death rate (per 1000)	10.9	12.2	7.9
Natural increase (per 1000)	6.0	3.0	11.0
Infant mortality (per 1000)	20.6	23.7	13.4
Land use (%):			
Cultivated	38.1	30.6	30.6
Meadows-pastures	24.3	25.2	38.3
Forest	21.9	19.7	8.0
Other land	15.8	24.4	23.1
Population density per sq. mi.			
cultivated land	635	2750	3540
Gross national product			
per capita	$1,730	$1,630	$1,420
Exports (millions)	$12,675	$8,150	$8,341
Imports (millions)	$13,943	$8,195	$9,293
Trade balance (millions)	−$1,268	−$45	−$952

See Table 1, p. 54, for sources.

CHAPTER 4   *the insular realms*

Despite their common insularity and their generally similar locations, the islands of Britain and Ireland have strikingly different personalities and significance today. As we will see, their locations are different enough to have resulted in quite distinct innovations having reached them. Nevertheless, the contrasts between Britain and Ireland are not cultural alone, for some critical differences in their physical character have colored their development as well.

Geologically, most of Ireland and a large part of western and northern Britain consists of ancient, crystalline bedrock. These areas are thus devoid of fossil fuels, such as coal and oil, but dotted here and there are metals, for example the gold of the Wicklow Mountains of Ireland and the iron ores of the English Lake District. In contrast, most of England, together with small areas of south Wales and central Scotland, are underlain by younger sedimentary rocks. Where these abut on the older crystallines, rich coal measures are exposed. Topographically, the two major geologic areas are quite dissimilar as well, for the older crystallines have proven very resistant to erosion and still stand as mountains in many areas. In Ireland, for example, the highest peaks rise to over 3400 feet, in Wales to 3500, and in Scotland to 4400. The younger sedimentaries, however, are in every instance synonymous with lowlands, though they too have been slightly disturbed, and pronounced scarps, or cuestas, can be traced for miles across the English countryside. Examples of the latter are the famous Downs, which form the chalk cliffs at Dover, the Cotswolds, and the Chiltern Hills. Though almost all of Ireland and most of Britain (south to the Thames) were covered by ice during the maximum advance of the glacier, the effects on the two islands were quite different as well. The crystalline bedrock of Ireland was ground into coarse and generally infertile sandy soils, and over much of the country the drainage pattern was so disordered that countless peat bogs and small lakes were left in the morainic hollows. In lowland Britain, on the other hand, the glacier left a deep mantle of finer grained soils, liberally mixed with lime (a natural fertilizer) from some of the limestone scarps it ground across.

But the physical contrasts between the two islands do not end with their bedrock, landforms, and soils. Climatically, too, there are subtle but important differences between them. Ireland, being more exposed to the open Atlantic, has a more maritime climate than its larger neighbor. Winter temperatures are milder but summer temperatures are cooler, and its precipitation is considerably heavier. Some of the sharpest climatic boundaries in all of Europe can be seen in the inlets of southwestern Ireland. There, where average January temperatures are above 44° F., there is virtually a twelve-month growing season, and the luxuriant vegetation includes palm trees, fuchsia, roses, and holly (A temperature of 43° F. is widely accepted as the threshhold below which most plants will not germinate and grow.) However, July temperatures in the same area average only about 57° F. Because a summer minimum of about 50° F. is required for trees to grow, and because the average decrease in temperature with elevation is about 3.5° F. per 1000 feet, this means that scarcely 2000 feet up the same mountainsides the treeline, or tundra, will be reached. Thus, it is possible to stand on the shore of Bantry Bay, for example, and in one vista to behold the same range of vegetation that one would encounter between the Carolinas and Labrador!

To be sure, palm trees also grow in the sheltered coves of Devon in southwestern England, and the mountains of Wales and Scotland also get above the treeline, but the vegetation zones are not so compressed, for winters become colder and summers warmer the farther east one goes. In like manner, the precipitation, which is excessive over much of Ireland and heavy over highland Britain, is a more moderate twenty to thirty inches per annum over most of lowland Britain. Even so, rainy days are frequent enough in England to cause British weather forecasters to accentuate the positive whenever they can, by speaking of "bright periods" rather than "occasional showers."

The cultural differentiation of the two islands began the day Julius Caesar stepped ashore in Britain. Up until then, Ireland and Britain had been the home of Celtic-speaking peoples, and before their arrival both islands had felt the impact of the Megalithic culture, with its many dolmens and cromlechs and its crowning masterpiece, Stonehenge. But the Romans never reached Ireland, and for that matter, they didn't really bother with the west and north of Britain either. These areas were so unattractive to them that they didn't consider it worth the time and effort to pacify their ferocious inhabitants. Instead they built a series of forts along the Welsh borderlands and erected a wall across the "narrows" of northern England between Solway Firth and the mouth of the Tyne River. Within the perimeter thus defined, they settled down to build roads, bridges, and encampments and to parcel out the land and its inhabitants to the officer class, many of whom took up residence in fine villas.

The main Roman thoroughface led quite naturally from Dover, their point of entry into Britain, along the edge of the North Downs to the lowest bridging point on the River Thames, thence northwestward across the Chilterns and the Cotswolds through a lowland gap between the Pennines and the Welsh foothills to their major encampment *(castra)* on the Irish Sea, the present site of Chester. This route, which later came to be known as Watling Street, is to this day the major axis of movement in Britain. From their bridging point on the Thames—now London—another great highway led north to the Scottish borderlands. Along it, too, several towns arose, chief among them York on the river Ouse. When Christianity reached Roman Britain, York was selected as the major ecclesiastical center of the north, but in the south that distinction went to Canterbury and not to London. But what Rome couldn't or didn't want to do, Christianity did, gradually winning converts amongst the Celtic Welshmen, one of whom, Patrick by name, also carried the message to his brethren in Ireland, according to legend.

About the same time, however, the Romans were beating a hasty retreat back to Rome, as the tide of Germanic tribes began pouring over the ramparts on the Rhine. Ireland, in its splendid isolation, was too far away to be affected, but southeastern Britain soon was engulfed by Angles, Saxons, and Jutes. The Angles settled in the easternmost bulge of Britain, a region now known as East Anglia; it is to these people that England owes its name. The Saxons moved into the Thames region, some to the east (Essex), some to the west (Wessex), and some to the south (Sussex), while the Jutes took up their abode in Kent, the southeasternmost corner of Britain. The coming of the Germanic tribes not only demolished organized society in Britain, with roads, bridges, towns and churches falling into disrepair, but extinguished Christianity itself. The Irish are proud to point out that theirs was the only country in western Europe where the torch of Christianity did not go out during this period, and in fact, the Irish began sending missionaries back to Britain (by way of Scotland) to try to win over the pagan newcomers. Despite their noble efforts, however, when communications were once more reestablished with Rome, the English elected to accept their religion firsthand from the Vatican rather than secondhand from the Irish.

To call the people of lowland Britain "English" is to indicate that out of the melange of Celt, Roman, and Anglo-Saxon a new people were being born. Still the mixture was not yet complete, because beginning in the late eighth century new sails appeared on the horizon. This time it was Danish and Norwegian Vikings, who came first to loot and pillage and later, finding the English so inept at defending themselves, to move in en masse and occupy large areas of the country. The Danes concentrated primarily in lowland England, pushing at times as far west as Watling Street. In fact, by then this once-proud thoroughfare no longer served as a bond linking southeast with northwest, but it had become merely a convenient way to divide the Danish realm from the English. The Norwegians, coming from a more northerly quadrant to begin with, settled in the Shetlands, Orkneys, and coastal areas of northern Scotland. Many of them skirted the west coasts of Britain to occupy the Isle of

Man, Angelsey, and even parts of Ireland. (Dublin, for example, was originally an old Norse settlement.) Place names ending in *-ey, -ay,* or *-ness* are good clues to the Norwegians' presence; those ending in *-by* or *-thorpe* are indicative of Danish origins.

The last major infusion of new blood into Britain came with the Normans (those Gallicized Vikings) in 1066, but even this was not the final chapter in the cultural differentiation of the two islands. Henry VIII, for marital and other reasons, found it expedient to make England Protestant, while Ireland remained true to the faith of St. Patrick. As English power grew, favored as it was by the best land that either of the islands had to offer, the relative importance of the northern and western Celtic fringe declined, until today the original Gaelic tongues are spoken only by a handful of people in the remotest corners of the Welsh mountains, the Hebrides, and the west of Ireland. In the latter country, a defiant but rather meaningless attempt is being made to revive Gaelic in the interests of nationalism. While it is never a happy occasion to witness the passing of a language, it is nevertheless a rather futile endeavor to keep it alive artificially, as the Irish are now trying to do.

In 1801, the first official census of the two islands was taken. In that year, Ireland had about 5,000,000 inhabitants and Britain, with about three times the area, had some 10,000,000 people. When the latest official census was taken in 1961, the island of Ireland had about 4,000,000 residents whereas Great Britain had over 50,000,000. Thus, in the same time that the population of Ireland had shrunk by about 20 per cent, Britains' had increased by over 500 per cent. (Actually, the decrease in Irish population is much more dramatic than these two census figures reveal. By 1841 Ireland had over 8,000,000 people, so the decline since that time has been more than 50 per cent.)

Clearly, the evolution of the two islands has diverged even more widely since the beginning of the nineteenth century than before. By way of explanation, two principal factors may be cited. One has been the industrialization of Britain, favored not only by its vast colonial empire, which provided her with both raw materials and markets, but also by her rich resource endowment at home—chiefly of coal, but likewise of iron ore. Because Ireland lacked the basic ingredients of modern industry, it has remained an essentially agricultural country. When even agriculture failed Ireland, as it did in the exceptionally wet summers of 1846–47, the potato blight wiped out the country's staple crop, thousands of Irishmen died of starvation and thousands more began an exodus from "the old sod" that has hardly ceased since. (How dependent the Irish had become on the potato is recorded by the English historian, Buckle, who states that the average daily consumption was nine pounds per man and seven pounds per woman, washed down with water. On Sundays and feast days, if they could afford it, they'd add a pinch of salt or some pork fat for flavoring.) Thus, with the good farm lands long since occupied and properties already subdivided beyond the point at which they could provide a family with more than a subsistence living, the choice open to any but the first-born son was rather restricted; indeed, usually there was no choice but to get out. But even the first-born son could not inherit the farm until his father died, which usually meant that he could not marry and begin a family of his own until then. As a result, Ireland not only has the dubious distinction of being one of the few countries in the world whose population *decreases* from one census to the next (East Germany is the other notable example), but it also has the lowest marriage rate and the oldest average age at marriage of any country in Europe. So, nostalgic as the old songs are about "coming back to old Erin," most Irish expatriates find them tinged with more than a bit of romantic Blarney.

To be sure, while Britain gained much by the Industrial Revolution, it lost much as well. Because it was, in fact, the very cradle of this innovation, Britain had nobody else's mistakes to profit by, and in the process, it made some atrocious and irreparable blunders. (Perhaps "blunder" is too strong a word, for at the time there didn't seem to be any other way.) In any event, the coming of the Industrial Revolution created for Britain a host of economic, social, and political problems that no other country had been confronted with earlier, and which few other industrialized countries have satisfactorily solved since.

Ireland

THE REGIONS OF IRELAND. Traditionally, the island of Ireland was divided into four kingdoms, or provinces: Ulster in the northeast, Connacht in the northwest, Munster in the southwest, and Leinster in the southeast (Figure 12). Today six counties of Ulster comprise Northern Ireland, a part of the United Kingdom primarily because the majority of its people are of Scottish Protestant background; the remaining twenty-six counties constitute the Republic of Ireland. It might be argued that the political boundary between them is the only real regional boundary of significance on the island today, for elsewhere the distinctions are primarily a matter of degree, rather than of kind.

The Republic of Ireland. Nearly half of the area of the Republic is in pasture which gives Ireland its appellation "the Emerald Isle." The forests were all but destroyed as the land was cleared for farming and the British sought timbers for the Royal Navy and charcoal for smelting iron. Although the Irish have an active program of reforestation underway, chiefly of conifers, with which they eventually hope to make themselves self-sufficient in construction timber and pulp wood, less than 3 per cent of the Republic is in trees today, and most of these are in hedgerows along property lines. Less than one-fifth of the Republic is in field crops, while some 30 per cent of its area is written off as "other" land—chiefly bogs and rocky wastes above the tree line. Geographically, however, the principal distinctions are that the damper regions of Connacht and Munster have a higher proportion of land in pasture and in waste, while the warmer and drier region of Leinster has a larger share of the area in crops. In most parts of the country, hay, oats, and potatoes constitute the chief crops, though root vegetables, cabbage, and sugar beets are also widely grown. Wheat and barley are almost totally restricted to Leinster.

Sheep comprise the most important livestock over much of the west

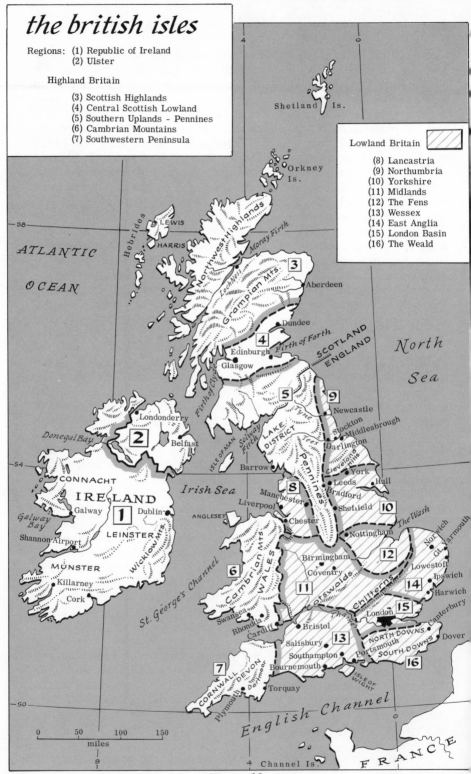

the british isles

Regions: (1) Republic of Ireland
(2) Ulster

Highland Britain

(3) Scottish Highlands
(4) Central Scottish Lowland
(5) Southern Uplands - Pennines
(6) Cambrian Mountains
(7) Southwestern Peninsula

Lowland Britain

(8) Lancastria
(9) Northumbria
(10) Yorkshire
(11) Midlands
(12) The Fens
(13) Wessex
(14) East Anglia
(15) London Basin
(16) The Weald

ATLANTIC OCEAN

Shetland Is.

Orkney Is.

Hebrides

LEWIS

HARRIS

Northwest Highlands

Moray Firth

Loch Ness

Grampian Mts

Aberdeen

Dundee

Edinburgh

Firth of Forth

Glasgow

Firth of Clyde

SCOTLAND

ENGLAND

North Sea

Londonderry

Belfast

Donegal Bay

ISLE OF MAN

Solway Firth

LAKE DISTRICT

Newcastle

Stockton

Middlesbrough

Darlington

Cleveland Hills

Tees

CONNACHT

IRELAND

Galway

Dublin

LEINSTER

Barrow

Irish Sea

Manchester

Liverpool

Chester

York

Leeds

Bradford

Hull

Sheffield

Galway Bay

Shannon Airport

MUNSTER

Killarney

Cork

Wicklow Mts

ANGLESEY

WALES

Cambrian Mts

St. George's Channel

Nottingham

The Wash

Norwich

Gt. Yarmouth

Lowestoft

Ipswich

Harwich

Birmingham

Coventry

Cotswolds

Chilterns

Thames

London

Canterbury

Dover

Swansea

Rhondda

Cardiff

Bristol

Salisbury

Southampton

Bournemouth

NORTH DOWNS

SOUTH DOWNS

Portsmouth

ISLE OF WIGHT

CORNWALL

DEVON

Dartmoor

Plymouth

Torquay

English Channel

Channel Is.

FRANCE

0   50   100   150
miles

Pennines

Figure 12

of the country, while pigs and chickens are rather uniformly distributed. The lush meadows of the Central Lowland are largely given over to beef cattle, though some dairying and the breeding of race horses also goes on here.

The steady rationalization of agriculture, together with the country's declining population, has meant that the Irish cannot only feed themselves well (indeed, measured by caloric intake they're now the best-fed people in the world) but that they have sizable agricultural surpluses for export. These consist chiefly of meat products and live animals, but also include dairy products and processed foods. And, although the Irish would like to have as little to do with the English as possible, fully four-fifths of their trade is with their industrialized neighbor to the east. Indeed, the two countries' economies complement one another perfectly, with Irish foodstuffs moving to Britain in return for British manufactured goods and coal. Thus, despite the fact that Ireland has read itself out of the Commonwealth, it is economically tied to Britain as firmly as ever. In fact, it even retains the British monetary system, but quite understandably has chosen to embellish its coins with cows and pigs rather than kings and queens.

Even so, Ireland's balance of payments is unfavorable, and the country has done whatever it could to make up the difference. In a country of surplus meat, fishing makes little economic sense, as does trying to build a merchant fleet in the shadow of the world's largest one. Tourism has its attractions, at least to second-generation Irishmen scattered about the globe, but also its limitations. (There are few other countries where people go down to the beaches with overcoats and umbrellas!) For a time it looked as though Ireland could finally turn its offside geographic location to good advantage by becoming a way station of the commercial air routes across the North Atlantic. To this end, Shannon Airport was built in the west of the country, and for a decade following World War II it lived up well to its expectations. Since the dawning of the jet age, however, most planes now fly over Shannon on their nonstop flights to London and beyond—a striking example of how the significance of place is constantly being altered by the technology of transportation.

But aside from accepting the hard facts of their geography, the Irish have still had to face up to their problem of trying to diversify the country's economy, especially of its depressed western regions. Like the Italians with their Fund for the South, the Irish have set up a development program for the *Gael-taecht*—the collective name for the western districts of Connacht and Munster. Through tax incentives and a number of other attractive devices, they have managed to entice several foreign firms into building branch plants in the region, but not with entirely positive results. It is said half in jest (thank goodness, the Irish have kept their sense of humor through it all!) that German is now the second language in the streets of Killarney, whereas for an Irishman to go fishing in the famous lake of that name, he literally has to get permission from one of the German villa-owners fronting on the lake. Almost as galling is the realization that a Japanese firm has located in the region to exploit cheap Irish labor—which, in the final analysis, is the only real advantage the region has to offer.

This is not to say that Ireland is completely lacking in industrial potential, for she does have some hydroelectric power (although the major river, the Shannon, flows chiefly through the Central Lowland and has little fall-height) and it is using the vast peat deposits to generate thermal electricity in the Dublin area. Raw materials are almost exclusively of agricultural origin, so most industries found in Dublin and the larger towns are primarily of the food processing variety (flour milling, sugar refining, slaughtering, and brewing). Dublin is the only city of any size (575,000), and owes its importance to its political and communications functions fully as much or more than to what industry it has. It is also the country's principal seaport, handling the bulk of both its exports and imports. Cork, on the south coast, has some metal foundries in addition to its food industries, and is also a port of call for trans-Atlantic passenger liners.

Ulster.   The six counties of Ulster have little more resource potential than the Republic, but the British have seen to it that they derive as much benefit as possible from their continued association with the United Kingdom. (The Republic continues to nurture the idea that it's only a question of time before the six counties are "returned," much as the Germans go on publishing maps of their country with its 1937 boundaries.) Although the division of the island of Ireland stemmed originally from religious differences, few Protestant Ulstermen today seriously fear that they would be discriminated against were they to join the Republic. Their real reluctance is economic, for few of them can imagine being any better off as part of an already poor and struggling country. At least now they enjoy certain advantages by being an integral part of the United Kingdom. The shipyards and linen mills of Belfast and the textile factories of Londonderry are geographically more peripheral than those in Newcastle or Lancashire, to be sure, but yet they are within the national market. As a result, Northern Ireland is far more industrialized and has a higher per capita income than most of the Republic. Moreover, with a population just half the size of the Republic it boasts a city (Belfast) that is little smaller than Dublin.

On the other hand, the contention of the Catholic minority resident in Northern Ireland that they are discriminated against both in terms of employment and housing has led to repeated outbreaks of violence since 1968. British troops have been airlifted in to maintain order and the Irish Republic has called for United Nations intervention. In addition to renewed promises of social and political reform, the central government in London has responded with increased transfusions of economic aid.

Britain

THE REGIONS OF BRITAIN

Highland Britain.   Much of Highland Britain has little more potential than Ireland: indeed, most of it probably has less, because larger areas of it lie above both the limit of crop cultivation and the treeline.

As a result, throughout Highland Britain, whether in the Grampians of Scotland, the Cambrians of Wales, or the Pennines of England, most of the land is in rough pasture, fit only for the grazing of sheep. In the Shetland, Orkney, and Hebrides islands, as well as in the coastal areas of the Scottish mainland, fishing forms an important adjunct to pastoralism. However, apart from smoked and salted herring and some home-spun woolens, notably Harris Tweed, these areas contribute little to the commercial economy of Britain. To the tourist willing to brave wind and rain, the western isles of Scotland offer both grand scenery and much of cultural interest, for this region is the last real Gaelic stronghold in Britain. One further attraction that the rugged and rainy west of Scotland holds is hydroelectric power, and several electrometallurgical in-dustries—chiefly aluminum refineries—have been located there for that reason.

Fortunately, *the Scottish Highlands* are higher in the west and fall off gradually toward the east. While one can hardly speak of a coastal plain in the east, at least the land is more gently rolling on this warmer and drier side of the country and the soils are deeper and more fertile. Small wonder, then, that the east of Scotland was always that country's economic heart and population center as long as agriculture remained the principal means of livelihood. Here arose its capital and cultural center, the city of Edinburgh, as well as such market towns and sea-ports as Dundee and Aberdeen. The former is known today as a center of the marmalade and burlap industries, while Aberdeen is the site of a famous university and major fish processing plants. Although even in this region most of the land is in hay and pasture, here the emphasis is on beef and dairy cattle, such as the Aberdeen Angus breed, which was developed here. Oats is the principal cereal, but both wheat and barley are grown as well, with potatoes, sugar beets, and root vegetables round-ing out the picture.

Breaking across the "wasp waist" of Scotland between the Firths of Forth and Clyde is a structural valley known as the *Central Scottish Lowland.* In a sense it can be thought of as a detached portion of Low-land Britain, for topographically and geologically it is more akin to much of England than it is to the uplands on either side of it. Until the Industrial Revolution, it could probably be said that the major difference between the western side of the lowland and the eastern area around Edinburgh was that more of the former's land was in pasture and less of it was in crops and consequently, that it supported fewer people. However, with the coming of industry, all this changed, for the western end of the valley, in particular, has large coal deposits. A number of heavy industries based on coal developed, including metal working, chemicals, and shipbuilding. In the process, Glasgow quickly surpassed staid old Edinburgh to become not only the largest city in Scotland but the second-ranking city in all of Britain, with over 2,000,000 inhabitants today. Thus, of Scotland's total population, some two-fifths live in the greater Glasgow area alone.

In Wales, much the same sort of population redistribution took place with the rise of industry. It was only in the south, along the shores of

Bristol Channel, that coal was found, and as mines and factories sprang up there, many of the mountain valleys were almost depopulated by the exodus of young people to Cardiff, Swansea, and Rhondda. Today the one southern county of Montgomeryshire has half the total population of Wales. Because of their high quality and seaside location, Welsh coals became a major export to supply bunkering stations around the world. Because of its proximity to the tin mines of Cornwall, South Wales also became a center of heavy metallurgy, of smelting and refining, and tin-plate manufacture.

In the volcanic mountains of the *English Lake District*, the impetus to industrialization came not from coal, but from small pockets of high-grade iron ore. The main industrial center today is the port city of Bar-row, which has not only steel mills but also shipyards. It is in a region such as the Lake District, however, that one realizes how providential it is that "all places were *not* created equal," for had they been, many of its jagged peaks, forested valleys and deep, still lakes would no doubt have borne the scars of industry as well. Perhaps Wordsworth, who found much of his inspiration here, would not have called it providential, but rather poetic justice.

The "lowest" part of Highland Britain is *the Southwestern Peninsula* of Cornwall and Devon. It is composed of a rolling, crystalline plateau, which reaches its highest elevation (just over 2000 feet) in the bleak and windswept expanses of Dartmoor and Exmoor. Where the plateau falls off to the sea, there are many picturesque fishing villages tucked into pleasant little coves, and the region has deservedly been called the "English Riviera." Torquay is no doubt its most fashionable resort, while Plymouth is its largest seaport and commercial center and neighboring Devonport is an important naval base. The region's early spring, long growing season, and mild climate have enabled it to specialize in vege-tables and cut flowers, but more important commercially are its butter, cream, bacon, and cider apples. Since the days of the Phoenicians, how-ever, Cornwall has been known chiefly for its tin and copper mines, but these are now so deep that they can no longer compete with those of Malaysia or Indonesia. Today the principal mineral industry of the re-gion is the mining of kaolin, the raw material for porcelain.

Lowland Britain. If one had to pinpoint the birthplace of the In-dustrial Revolution, there is perhaps no place more deserving of that title than the Lancashire district of northwestern England. Together with Cheshire to the South, it comprises the old Roman region of *Lancastria,* an extensive plain stretching from the Pennines to the Irish Sea. Its rural landscape is one of meadows and pastures, with dairying a primary emphasis of its agriculture and cheese a well-known specialty of Cheshire. Chester, the old Roman campsite, was long the major town and seaport of the region, but its harbor gradually silted up. Esconced within its medieval walls, it has largely been bypassed by the dynamic changes of the last 200 years.

As early as the twelfth century, sheep grazing on the slopes of the Pennines had given Lancashire the basis of a textile industry, but the re-gion's most rapid development began about the middle of the eighteenth century. By this time the demand for textiles, especially cotton cloth, had grown to such a point in Britain's colonies that their production by conventional means (by distributing the work amongst cottagers) was no longer adequate. Then it was that experimentation began with machines, one of the first of which was capable of spinning as much thread as eight women working spinning wheels. This in turn led to the demand for a machine that could weave eight times faster, but one of the early looms proved to be 100 times faster, and so the tempo of spinning had to be increased further. Every invention and improvement triggered another, until the machines were far too expensive to be owned by rural housewives and too large to be housed in their cottages or operated by their muscles. The concentration of these machines in factories and the geographic concentration of factories at water power sites, of which the rainy, western slopes of the Pennines afforded many, came next. Soon whole towns of factory workers grew up around the factories, the houses crowded in as close to the mills as possible, for the only way to get to work was on foot. But before long, virtually every usable water power site had been developed, and it almost seemed as though the further expansion of industry would be precluded by the lack of power.

About this time, however, a machine appeared whose primary purpose was to pump water out of coal mines. If this steam engine, which itself consumed coal to perform its work, could pump water, it was reasoned that it could also turn factory wheels. No longer was industry dependent on rapids and waterfalls; it could be located wherever one found coal or could bring it. Of course, the less one had to move it the better, so when it was discovered that much of Lancashire was underlain by coal, new factories sprang up next to the mines, and again, workers' houses clustered close to both.

When coal did have to be moved any distance, the easiest and cheapest way was by water, and soon canals were being built where nature had provided no rivers. However, between Stockton and Darlington in the northeast of England, an experiment was carried out in 1825 pulling coal cars with a steam engine on wheels. It worked so well that soon people were transported as well as coal, and so the railway was born. From then on, it took no great leap of the imagination to harness the steam engine to paddle wheels and screw propellers as well.

Through all of this development, however, one major problem remained: of what material could these machines, locomotives, and ships be built that was at once strong and durable and also relatively inexpensive? Iron was not the answer, for although the British had learned to smelt it with coke as early as 1709, it could not stand the strain it was required to bear, whether in cast, wrought, or "puddled" form. Steel *was* the answer, but not until Bessemer managed to mass produce it by means of his blast furnace in 1856 could it be made cheaply enough or abundantly enough to be considered seriously. Nevertheless, within a few decades, Britain had initiated a chain reaction of economic and social transformation that has been going on at an accelerated tempo ever since.

In addition to its initial advantages of water power and later coal,

Lancashire was blessed with soft water, essential to the dyeing process, and humid air. Before the days when the humidity of the air could be controlled artificially, static electricity tended to build up in the spinning process if the air became too dry, snapping the threads and causing frequent shutdowns while they were being retied. Furthermore, the region was oriented toward the Atlantic, across which the cotton was brought from the southern United States and unloaded at Liverpool. The latter had been only a minor fishing port up until then, but soon its strategic location as the gateway to Lancashire made it the second largest seaport in the country. Indeed, as its hinterland expanded with the improvement of transportation, it became Britain's most important export port, sending into world trade not only the cotton textiles of Lancashire but a host of manufactures from the growing industrial centers of the Midlands and Yorkshire as well. In addition to its port activities, Liverpool found itself situated on some large salt deposits, which together with coal and limestone laid the foundations for a heavy chemical industry. Today, with 750,000 inhabitants, Liverpool ranks as the fourth largest city in Britain.

The real business and commercial center of Lancashire, however, is Manchester, Britain's fifth city in size (pop. 650,000). Centrally located within the Lancashire plain, Manchester does little manufacturing itself, but did capitalize on its location to become a seaport in its own right with the Manchester Ship Canal, completed in 1894. The actual processes of spinning, weaving, and dyeing are highly specialized among the cities surrounding Manchester, such as Bolton, Oldham, and Stockport, with whole towns performing only a particular function.

During the 1930's Lancashire was not only sorely affected by the worldwide depression but was also becoming painfully aware of foreign competition. It was not just the countries with cheaper labor, such as Japan and India, that hurt, but also those whose industrialization had begun late, with more modern and efficient machinery and more rationally designed production patterns. It was clear that Lancashire's overspecialization and technological obsolescence were beginning to take their toll. In recent decades a diversification into machinery, vehicles, and synthetic fibers has helped ameliorate the crisis somewhat, but the economic gloom, added to the atmospheric pall hanging over the sooty brick factory towns of Lancashire seems destined to continue.

Across the Pennines to the east lies *Yorkshire,* the northernmost area of extensive crop farming in Britain and the site of its largest coalfield. The agricultural heart of the region is the old glacial lake plain in the midst of which the city of York arose. A Roman crossroads, cathedral town, and market center, York has long since been surpassed in size both by Kingston-upon-Hull, the region's principal seaport, and by the industrial towns that developed on the coalfields of the Pennine's lower flank. Hull is today a city of 300,000. Because of its eastward orientation, it is not only a major North Sea fishing port but is also active in the timber trade with Scandinavia, importing pulp and paper as well as pit props for the coal mines.

Like Lancashire's, Yorkshire's location on the slopes of the Pennines provided access to extensive sheep grazing areas, soft water for scouring and dyeing the wool, and numerous water power sites. An eastward orientation, however, largely precluded participation in the cotton trade with America, and Yorkshire continued its specialization in woolen textiles. When the shift to steam power began, Yorkshire found that it was even more bountifully supplied with coal than Lancashire. Furthermore, in the southern areas of the region the local occurrence of iron ores and hard sandstones encouraged the cutlery trade. The latter gradually centered in the city of Sheffield, which now numbers 500,000 inhabitants.

The woolen industry generated two major centers of its own: Bradford, the hub of the manufacturing activities, with a population of 300,000, and Leeds, where most of the industry's distribution, engineering, tailoring, and commercial functions are located. Leeds now has over 510,000 inhabitants. However, due to the exhaustion of the mines along the front of the Pennines, much of the industry's fuel is presently coming from deeper seams farther to the east beneath the plain.

North of Yorkshire, the lowland of eastern Britain grades up into a low, rolling plateau, into which the major rivers, such as the Tees and the Tyne, have incised themselves quite deeply. In so doing, they exposed coal measures that were among the first in the country, if not the world, to be worked. At least as early as the fourteenth century coal was being used as a domestic fuel in England and was regularly being exported from Newcastle to London. Mining by the primitive techniques then available was especially easy in this region, for it was possible to tunnel directly into the side of the valley and to load the coal by gravity into barges waiting in the river below. However, the difficulty in getting coal to the Tees provided the incentive for building the world's first railway, as mentioned earlier. In any case, the construction of barges to haul the coal developed as a natural concomitant of the coal export trade and gradually expanded into full-fledged shipbuilding. At the beginning of the twentieth century it is estimated that one-third of the world's ships were being launched by Tyneside shipyards. Today Newcastle is a city of some 275,000 inhabitants, with glass, chemical, and smelting industries in addition to its shipyards and coal exports.

Middlesbrough and Stockton, at the mouth of the Tees, were likewise coal exporting ports originally, but with iron ore close at hand in the Cleveland Hills, they gradually specialized in steelmaking. Imports of high-grade iron ore from Sweden and Spain now supplement the local iron ores and today this region accounts for about one-third of Britain's total steel output.

Another part of Lowland Britain that got an early industrial start was *The Midlands*, a roughly triangular region bounded on the north by the Pennines, on the west by the Welsh foothills and on the southeast by the Chiltern Hills. Thanks to its central location within England, this region has easy access northwestwards to the Lancastrian plain and the Irish Sea through the Midland Gap; northeastwards to Yorkshire and the North Sea; southwestwards to the Bristol Channel; and southeastwards to the London Basin. Indeed, streams emanate from this region and flow in all four directions. Near the geometric center of the plain lies the city of Birmingham (pop. 1,200,000), much of whose growth and significance can be traced to the excellence of its situation. Originally, local iron ores of the region were smelted with charcoal to give rise to a small iron industry. This industry was greatly expanded with the coming of the Industrial Revolution, for the Midlands were the site of several small coal deposits. However, as the iron ores and the more accessible coal measures have been exhausted, there has been a shift away from heavy metallurgy to lighter, metal-using industries, including hardware, electrical machinery, transport equipment, and jewelry. (For example, the old cathedral town of Coventry, population 330,000, is now so highly specialized in automobile production that it is sometimes called the Detroit of Britain.) Although these industries helped to create the third largest city in Britain, they also produced one of the ugliest landscapes ever fashioned by man—the Black Country, a wasteland of coal pits, slag heaps, smoke, soot, and slums.

Though the Midlands typify some of the most dismal aspects of industrial Britain, they also contain, ironically, some of its most idyllic rural settings as well. Toward the south and east of Birmingham lie the Scarplands, a succession of hills formed by sandstone and valleys floored by limestone. On the drier ridges, such as the Cotswolds and the Chilterns, there is sheep grazing, while in the wet valley bottoms there are lush meadows and orchards in the west and prosperous crop farms in the east. Not only are these meadowlands noted for their ability to fatten cattle (like the Herefords, which are native to the region) without supplementary feed, but they are also the traditional home of English fox-hunting.

South of the Midlands lies a region that has retained much of its rural charm without becoming a Black Country—simply because it had no coal. This is the region of *Wessex*, stretching from the Isle of Wight to the Bristol Channel. The region's natural gateway is through Southampton (pop. 200,000), the most important passenger port in the country. The city is situated in the midst of the Hampshire Basin, which is fringed both to the north and to the south by chalk cuestas. The southern escarpment has been breached by the sea in two places, in the process detaching a portion of the mainland to form the Isle of Wight. As a result, each rise of the tide—which on the south coast of England amounts to several yards, as Julius Caesar, who returned from his initial reconnaissance to find his ships already adrift, learned by experience—reaches Southampton twice, allowing for a considerably longer maneuvering period for ships. Portsmouth (pop. 220,000), at the entrance to Southampton water, is Britain's main naval station on the English Channel, while Bournemouth, to the west, is the most popular residential resort on the south coast.

The chalk ridges of southern England come to a focus in the Salisbury plain. In prehistoric times, when the broad, wet vales between them were heavily forested, early man found his paths along the drier cuestas converging on this natural center. This was the site he chose for the greatest of the Megalithic monuments, Stonehenge. Erected of massive stones rafted and rolled all the way from Pembrokeshire in southwestern Wales, Stonehenge has recently been "deciphered" as a celestial computer, enabling some astronomically astute ancients, circa 1900 B.C., to predict the occurrence of eclipses.

Beyond the chalk belt lie the clayey lowlands of Somerset, which are chiefly used for pasturing dairy cattle. Each town has its "butter cross" (a roofed enclosure, usually surmounted by a cross, under which butter was sold) in the market place, and the caves of Cheddar Gorge have long been used for aging the famous cheese of that name. Somerset is also the site of Bath, a spa popular since the time of the Romans, and of such historic old abbey towns as Glastonbury; its chief city today is Bristol, (pop. 450,000). Because of its location in the west of Britain, Bristol quickly became the country's leading colonial seaport when trans-Atlantic trade began. But, with the coming of the Industrial Revolution, Bristol's westerly situation was not enough to insure its preeminence, for its hinterland embraced no rich coal deposits, and so Liverpool took the lead, which it has maintained ever since. Bristol does have another problem as well, for it is cut off from the sea by a rocky gorge that cannot be dredged but must be blasted to provide access for deep-draught vessels. Such industries as Bristol has depend largely on raw materials from the "colonies"—such as sugar refining, chocolate making, and flour milling, although it is also a center of aircraft construction today.

On the opposite side of Britain, surrounding the shallow inlet known as the Wash, is the region of *The Fens,* a low, marshy area which has largely been reclaimed since the seventeenth century, in part with the assistance of Dutch engineers. Its rich black soils give heavy yields of wheat, oats, potatoes, vegetables, flowers, and fruit; food processing is virtually the region's sole industry.

East of the Fens, beyond the scarp of the Chilterns, is *East Anglia,* a region whose location is decidely apart from the main currents of British life. In earlier times it was almost an island, approachable only along the low chalk ridges from the southwest or from the North Sea. The latter orientation can probably be said to have been the more important, for the primary components of East Anglia's population came from that direction, its earliest commercial contacts consisted of wool exports to Flanders, and much of its present economic life is focused in the fishing ports of Great Yarmouth and Lowestoft. Likewise, the port of Harwich, to the south, serves as a ferry terminus for traffic to and from the Netherlands and Denmark.

After its early start in the wool trade, East Anglia remained Britain's chief center of wool textile manufacturing until the Industrial Revolution. Then, its lack of both water power and coal forced it into reappraising such geographic advantages as it had. Deep soils, combined with dry, sunny summers, made the cultivation of grain the obvious alternative, though today long, sandy beaches have become an added attraction for urbanites on holiday.

Across the Thames estuary from East Anglia lies *The Weald,* a structural basin which forms the heart of the county of Kent. Here the chalk ridges of the North and South Downs meet the sea in the bold white cliffs that gave England its poetic name of Albion. Between the Downs are an alternating series of sandstone ridges and limestone valleys; the latter were originally clothed in heavy forests of oak. Indeed, it was these forests that gave the region its name, for *Weald* is a derivative of German *Wald.* The forests have been largely depleted, however, first for ship construction and later for the making of charcoal for the iron industry, and today the loamy river bottoms are devoted to the cultivation of hops, apples, and cherries. This emphasis on fruit cultivation and horticulture has earned for Kent the title "garden of England," but the region is not all as attractive to farming as its valleys. The sandy ridges are in many places clothed only in heather and in pines, while the grass cover of the chalk Downs is fit only for grazing sheep. However, because of its strategic location on the narrowest crossing to the European mainland, Kent has been a major thoroughfare all through its history.

For several centuries, much of the traffic moving across Kent has either been bound for or coming from the *London Basin.* Always the metropolis of Britain, London has also been one of the great cities of the world since the dawn of the European colonial age. Although it traces its origins to the fact that its site provided the lowest crossing point of the river Thames for the Romans' road system, much of its subsequent growth has been due to its water orientation and its port function. In fact, the port of London, together with its outport, Tilbury (opened in 1886), today handles about half of Britain's import trade, and three-fifths of its entrepôt trade, as against about one-fourth of its export trade.

The nucleus of London was the fortified settlement that the Romans established on two gravelly hills on the north bank of the river, one where St. Paul's Cathedral stands today and the other beneath the Bank of England. This is the part of London now known as the City—the center of commerce, banking, and insurance. To the east lies the Port, and between them, with ready access to imported fuel and raw materials, is the East End, London's industrial district. The political-administrative functions came to be geographically centered in Westminster, upriver to the west, while the West End has become London's most fashionable shopping district and the focal point for its social life. It was not until late in the Middle Ages that London started expanding into the marshy areas south of the river (Southwick), but now almost the entire basin, on both sides of the river, is built up solidly. Interestingly enough, only the sandy patches, which were unattractive to the original agricultural settlers of the basin have remained as green, open areas, such as Hampstead Heath. Today, with some 8,200,000 inhabitants within the circumference of its suburbs, London and its basin contain nearly one-fifth of the entire population of Britain.

CONCLUSIONS.   At the outbreak of World War I, Great Britain was still perhaps to be reckoned as the world's greatest industrial and military power. By the end of World War II, however, it had unmistakably slipped to third place and today probably must be considered a rather precarious fifth. Though it can be argued that Britain's decline is more relative than absolute, the fact remains that the empire is gone, it no longer controls the world's oceans, and its economic and military commitments abroad have undergone a continuous contraction since 1945. This retrenchment has been due not alone to the growing restiveness of colonial subjects but equally, if not more, to the difficult straits in which Britain has found itself at home. The battering taken during the Nazi "blitzes" was in itself enough to have finished off a lesser people, but the war only provided a grim finale to a drama that had long been underway, for most of Britain's fundamental problems had been created by its own economic evolution.

The plight of Lancashire was symptomatic—how was it to meet the increasing challenge posed by more modern and efficient industries elsewhere, while at the same time improving the lot of its long-suffering working masses? How long were the basic industries going to be allowed to go downhill, while the demands of labor for better living and working conditions and the desires of management for continued profits discouraged the owners from renewing their physical plants and equipment? Not that the demands of labor were unreasonable, for few other civilized nations in the world had such abysmal housing conditions and such inadequate welfare provisions. Nor was the desire to make a profit in running the country's coal mines, steel mills, and railways unreasonable; the two could simply not be reconciled, and still permit Britain to meet foreign competition.

Industrialization had not only made Britain the most urbanized country on earth, it had also spurred its growth far beyond the resource base of its own "tight little island." Even with some of the most highly mechanized and scientifically managed farms in the world, Britain was capable of producing only 40 per cent of the foodstuffs it required. And the insatiable demand of its mills and factories for raw materials and fuel (it has no oil at all) had long since made it overwhelmingly dependent on imports of these as well. Great Britain had, in a sense, "painted itself into a corner" by building up an immense industrial machine that must be kept going through the importation of larger quantities of foodstuffs and raw materials. To pay for these, it must constantly export more, at prices that are competitive in the world market; and it must make these prices competitive in the face of long overdue concessions to its labor force, of a long deferred renewal of its obsolescent plants and equipment, of staggering losses in World War II, and of numerous economic and military obligations beyond its borders.

By saddling themselves with some of the highest taxes in the world, by rationing foodstuffs longer than any other country in Europe, by adopting one "austerity budget" after another, by nationalizing ailing basic industries, by trying to launch an all-out export drive, and by devaluing the pound, the British have made as heroic and gallant an effort to solve their problems as any people could have. In the areas of health and welfare, needs were so great that Great Britain may have attempted to do too much, too fast, but the improvements have already been so marked that no Conservative government could conscionably do away with the national health program. Nor has any Conservative government seen fit to de-nationalize the coal mines or public transport, though the question of what to do with steel seems to remain open.

Britain will have to wrestle with these problems for some time to come, but while doing so, it is also taking a new look at its place in the world. Are its primary ties to the Commonwealth, most of which lies half a world away, or are they with Europe, of which it is nominally a part? Certainly, up to now they *have* been with the Commonwealth, above all for reasons of economic complementarity—the exchange of manufactured goods for foodstuffs and raw materials. By preferential arrangements Britain has made it possible for Australia and New Zealand, for example, to put their foodstuffs in British grocers' shops at costs no higher than those of Danish, Dutch, or Irish producers.

Can Britain now afford to give up these ties, as part of the price of admission to the European Economic Community? Can it find enough complementarity within the Common Market to make it advantageous for it to join? Or will high food costs to the working man of Britain increase his demands for higher wages and so reduce Britain's overall competitive position still further? These are just some of the knotty issues that must soon be resolved if Britain is to realistically chart its course. There is little doubt that there will always be a Britain—but its outlines have yet to be discerned.

Table 3. The Insular Realms, Selected Statistics (1968)

	United Kingdom	Ireland
Area (000's sq. mi.)	94.2	27.1
Population (millions)	55.7	2.9
Birth rate (per 1000)	17.5	21.1
Death rate (per 1000)	11.2	10.7
Natural increase (per 1000)	6.3	10.4
Infant mortality (per 1000)	19.6	24.9
Land use (%):		
Cultivated	30.5	18.5
Meadows-pastures	50.1	47.8
Forest	7.3	2.7
Other land	12.1	31.0
Population density per sq. mi.		
cultivated land	1930	630
Gross national product		
per capita	$1,620	$850
Exports (millions)	$14,838	$799
Imports (millions)	$18,410	$1,175
Trade balance (millions)	−$3,572	−$376

See Table 1, p. 54, for sources.

CHAPTER **5** *the germanic core*

Most German-language atlases contain one or more maps depicting *Mitteleuropa* (Central Europe). These maps normally cover the area between the North and Baltic seas and the Po Valley in their north-south extent, reaching from Flanders in the west to Lithuania and the Transylvanian region of Romania in the east. Nevertheless one would have great difficulty in determining the precise boundaries of *Mitteleuropa* from such maps.

From the German geographic literature, a somewhat clearer definition of *Mitteleuropa* emerges. One is quickly given to understand that it is not a physical region that is being described at all, but a cultural one. The unifying bond or theme of that region is *Deutschtum*, "the quality or state of being German." Depending on which source one consults, *Mitteleuropa* could be defined as that area once occupied *or claimed by* German-speaking peoples. Such a definition, of course, raises all kinds of geopolitical connotations, which might be dismissed lightly were it not for the fact that they seem to color many people's thinking even today. However, accepting the basic notion that it is Germanic culture that constitutes the essence of *Mitteleuropa*, it seems far more realistic to define its limits as the political boundaries of those countries where the German language predominates today: namely West and East Germany, Austria, and Switzerland.

The issue of boundaries is fundamental to any discussion of Central Europe, for the region's whole history reflects its lack of precise geographic definition. Division, rather than unity, has been the most prevalent condition of the Germanic peoples. It was in Central Europe, along the Rhine and Danube Rivers, that the northern frontiers of the Roman Empire were reached, but the distinction between 'Roman citizen" and "Teutonic barbarian" had hardly crystallized to any degree before the latter were swarming across the Rhine to escape the thrust of other peoples (notably the Huns) from the east. The Great Migrations not only resulted in a vast westward displacement of the Germanic peoples, but also in the occupation by Slavic-speaking peoples of the areas they abandoned. Again, it would be difficult to pin down a precise boundary between the two linguistic groups, but it probably lay as far west as the Elbe and Saale River valleys (close to the present boundary between East and West Germany), judging from place names. (Slavic suffixes such as -*in* in *Berlin,* -*itz* in the former *Chemnitz,* -*zig* in *Leipzig* and -*au* in *Zwickau* are clues as to their distribution.)

From the wreckage of the Roman Empire, the only impetus to unity that was salvaged was the church, which gradually began sending its missionaries ever farther to the pagan north and east. It was the church that provided the raison d'être of that amorphous and misnamed block of land that occupied Central Europe through much of the Middle Ages, the Holy Roman Empire. It was also the church that provided the now-Christian Germans with the excuse of undertaking a massive "crusade" against the pagan Slavs to the east. This Drang nach Osten, or "Drive to the East," as it has been called, followed two principal arteries of movement, one across the broad front of the North European Plain into what is now Poland, and the other down the Danube Corridor into present-day Hungary. In the wake of the sword and the cross came merchants and settlers, laying the groundwork for towns, industries, and great estates. In most of the areas they reached, the German artisans, landowners and clergy became the economic, social, and political elite. In some places, notably Prussia, they went so far as to reduce the local peasantry to serfdom.

Germany

It was religion that provided the nominal rationale for the Drang nach Osten; it was also religion that split the Germanic center of Europe to its very core at the time of the Reformation. At the end of the Thirty Years' War, the see-saw struggle of Protestant and Catholic armies had left most of Germany in ruins and large parts of it virtually depopulated. It also left the country divided between a Protestant north—with a long wedge extending into Switzerland along the Rhine Valley—and a Catholic south. For the next two centuries Germany was to remain a crazy-quilt of petty kingdoms, and not until a customs union was adopted in the middle of the nineteenth century was there any semblance of unity on even so much as a regional scale.

Politically, the strongest of the kingdoms at the time was unquestionably Prussia, which from its original base in the eastern march lands had managed through deft maneuvering to acquire a foothold closer to the Germanic core in Brandenburg. Indeed, it had even gone so far as to make the Brandenburg town of Berlin its capital. Effective as the customs union was, however, it still fell far short of unifying the German people in any nationalistic sense; in order to accomplish this, Bismarck, the Chancellor of Prussia, came up with a formula well-proven both before and since: the "external threat." In the 1800's, Prussia led the German states in two short and victorious wars against Austria and Denmark, and in 1870, again largely on trumped-up charges, it felt impelled to attack France, then the largest and supposedly strongest continental power. The Germans' easy victory soon dispelled that myth and helped to create a new one—that as long as the Germans were united they were invincible.

With unity coming as late as it did, Germany had all but missed out in the scramble for overseas colonies, but now set to work with a vengeance, picking up whatever pieces of real estate had not yet been claimed. Although Germany managed to acquire four scattered colonies in Africa and some islands in the Southwest Pacific—including one group still known as the Bismarck Archipelago—their overseas empire was a far cry from that of the French or the British. According to the prevailing mercantile philosophy, Germany viewed its colonies as sources of raw materials and as markets for manufactured goods—but acquisitions were hardly adequate in either regard for a state with the potential and ambitions it possessed. By 1914, in alliance with Austria-Hungary and Turkey, Germany felt it was ready not only to redraw the map of Europe but also much of the colonial world as well. If a country wants a war badly enough, it needs little excuse for starting it. Germany found its excuse in the assassination of an Austrian archduke.

Germany launched its attack both to the east, against Czarist Russia, and to the west, against France. The campaign against Russia helped speed the demise of that chaotic country. With the outbreak of the Bolshevik revolution, the Germans saw to it that one Nikolai Lenin was permitted to cross their country in a sealed train to take command of it personally. In March of 1918, the Germans concluded a peace treaty with the new government of Russia, acquiring by cession the rich agricultural and industrial region of the Ukraine. That treaty was signed in behalf of the Bolshevik government by Lenin.

Although Germany had won its goal in the east, the tide of battle was turning against it in the west, and as German troops fell back toward the frontiers of the Reich, the High Command decided that they had had enough. In the peace treaty signed the following year at Versailles it was the Allies who redrew the map of Europe, reducing Austria to an impotent shadow of its former self by creating several new states from its territories, detaching East Prussia from the main body of Germany by giving the newly reconstituted Poland a corridor to the Baltic, forbidding Germany to maintain military forces in the Rhineland (where they could threaten Belgium and France), and prohibiting any form of union between the states of Austria and Germany. In addition, all of Germany's overseas colonies were to come under the control of the Allies as League of Nations trusteeships.

Harsh as the terms of the Versailles Treaty were, Germany's defeat in World War I was as much a psychological shock as it was a physical loss. The myth of German invincibility had evaporated and the great industrial machine the country had built up suddenly had no military orders to fill nor any colonies to produce for. The republican form of government that the Allies had prescribed for Germany soon found itself beset with workers' revolts and runaway inflation—hardly an auspicious environment in which to nurture so fragile a flower as democracy. When the worldwide Depression of the 1930's descended, Germany was ready to look to any savior who promised to rescue it. That "savior" appeared in the form of a neurotic Austrian paperhanger whose explanation of Germany's defeat in World War I was as appealing as it was simple: it was the Jews who had "sold Germany down the river." Apart from removing the German peoples' doubts about their invincibility, Adolf Hitler also had to come up with a formula for getting the wheels of German industry turning again. Once more his solution was simple, and it was effective: rebuild the German military machine, so that Germany could right the "wrongs" perpetrated by the Versailles Treaty. (Again, the idea of using a military buildup to bolster business was not original with Hitler, nor did it die with him.)

Three years after taking office as Germany's Chancellor, Hitler already felt strong enough to make his first move, the remilitarization of the Rhineland in 1936. Already he was being proclaimed Der Führer ("the Leader") of a new, revitalized Germany. Already his secret police were rounding up Jews for deportation to the concentration camps and the gas chambers. And already the swastika had become the symbol not only of his National Socialist Party but also of his master plan of conquest in Europe.

Imagine the swastika as two spiralling scythe blades, cutting down everything in their path. First, Hitler moved west into the Rhineland; next south into Austria, incorporating that country into his Third Reich by "plebiscite" in 1938; now the blades swung north and east, and Czechoslovakia became the next target. His demands for the return of German-speaking Sudetenland prompted a hurried meeting in Munich with the foreign ministers of France and Great Britain. During the course of their discussions, it is said, Hitler escorted his guests to a balcony from which hundreds of tanks could be seen rolling by as hundreds of airplanes flew overhead. Both France's Daladier and Britain's Chamberlain were convinced that Hitler should be given Sudetenland, and both returned home proclaiming "peace in our time." But the Nazi storm troopers that goose-stepped into the Sudetenland kept right on going, until all of Bohemia and Moravia (which had no German-speaking people) were in German hands and Slovakia had been willed to a puppet government in Hungary.

The spiralling swastika now aimed at Poland, and when Hitler's demands were not met, German forces unleashed a *blitzkrieg* against that ill-prepared country, precipitating World War II. Swinging north and west, Denmark and Norway became Hitler's next targets; the former was conquered in three hours, and the latter struggled on valiantly but hopelessly for sixty-seven days. Now the swastika had come one full cycle and was swinging west again, this time in a broader arc.

In May, 1940 the Nazis overran the Netherlands and Belgium and completely crushed French resistance in forty days. The far-southwestern flank was secure, for Hitler's man Franco was firmly in control there, and the same was true in the south, where the other end of the Rome-Berlin axis was anchored in Mussolini. The Italians, however, were not doing too well in their campaign against Albania and Greece—indeed, for a time it looked as though the Greeks might invade Italy!—so Hitler's spiralling swastika went slashing into the Balkans, overrunning Yugoslavia, Greece, Bulgaria, and Rumania. With these areas firmly in hand, his next target was obvious: the Soviet Union. On June 22, 1941, German forces launched a massive assault on the Russians along a 2000-mile front. Despite impressive Nazi gains at first, the Soviet defenses held at Leningrad and Moscow and in the calamitous battle of Stalingrad, the Nazi tide was not only stemmed but turned. About the same time the western Allies invaded North Africa and began pushing northward through Italy. Now, from the island fortress of Britain, which for some inexplicable reason Hitler had left uninvaded, massive Allied air raids against his cities and industries were stepped up and in June, 1944 a new front was opened on the beaches of Normandy.

With the western Allies pushing across the Rhine and the Russians grinding steadily westward across Poland, Hitler killed himself amidst the flaming ruins of Berlin, ringing down the final curtain on his Thousand-Year-Reich—which lasted barely twelve. In those dozen terrible years, some 30,000,000 people had died as a result of Hitler's insane ambitions, 20,000,000 of them in Russia alone. Small wonder, then, that at the end of it all Germany's victims vowed it must never happen again. The country was immediately divided into four occupation zones, representing each of the major powers (the United States, the Soviet Union, Great Britain, and, by courtesy, France). For a time there was talk of turning Germany into an "agrarian state" (as though her geographic potential for industry could be ignored), and the Russians went so far as to dismantle entire factories and ship them to the Soviet Union to replace its own, which had been destroyed.

Already, within a few months of Nazi Germany's collapse, the western Allies were growing suspicious of the Soviet Union's attempts to consolidate its position in Eastern Europe. The victory of the Communists in the 1948 elections in Czechoslovakia and the Russian blockade of Berlin, located some 110 miles within their sector of Germany, caused the Americans in particular to react with vigor. An airlift instituted to keep Berlin supplied, and hurried consultations with America's west European allies led to the creation of the North Atlantic Treaty Organization in April, 1949. Already at that time there was American pressure for including the three western zones of Germany in the pact, but its European allies would not hear of it. Moreover, they pointed out, the three western zones of Germany did not in themselves constitute a sovereign government.

American strategists soon came up with a plan to meet this second objection, for in September, 1949 the establishment of the Federal Republic of Germany was announced to the world. This announcement caught the Russians flat-footed, for while the western areas of the country were now a sovereign state, all the Russians had on their side of the line was a military occupation zone. In what must have been three extremely busy weeks, the Russians prepared "documents" setting up the German Democratic Republic in October, 1949 and the division of Germany was completed.

Because West Germany, as it came to be known, was not permitted to rearm by America's European allies, its defense had to be borne not only by the Americans, but also by the British, French, Dutch, Norwegians, and Danes who maintained military contingents in the country. As a result, West Germany was free to devote all of its energies to rebuilding its industries and communications, and was not required to spend one red *pfennig* on its own "defense." Thus, at a time when Britain and France were struggling along with austerity budgets and rationing, defeated Germany was bounding back with such resilience that its shops were full of such luxuries as nylon stockings, oranges, and chocolate. Indeed, within a few years German business was beginning to reinvest in foreign areas and the country's balance of payments was so favorable that it began building up a surplus of capital. While the western Allies smarted under renewed loans and greater debts, Germany had become the second largest creditor nation in the world after the United States. By 1955, the disparity between "victors" and "vanquished" had grown to such proportions that America's West European Allies were reluctantly convinced to accept West Germany into NATO as a full military partner. Thus, one decade after the fall of Nazi Germany, German military men were sitting in the same counsel chambers as the Britons, Frenchmen, Dutchmen, Danes, and Norwegians who had suffered at their hands.

To be sure, the Germans know why they were invited to join: because they have the money that the others lack. But they have also been very cautious about committing any more of that money to defense than they've had to. One has only to review the discussions between the West Germans and the United States to see how relatively "unmoved" they are by the latter's gold drain, and how reluctant they are to assume any further defense obligations themselves.

Germany not only lies at the geographic crossroads of Europe, it lies also at the subcontinent's economic and political heart. West Germany today is the world's third-ranking industrial power; for this reason, alone, it is perhaps clear why the United States has been so solicitous of its good will and support. For the same reason, the Soviet Union (like all the countries in Eastern Europe) is especially fearful of a rearmed Germany. It was the Russians, after all, who suffered most grievously at the hands of Hitler. East Europeans wonder if the American remilitarization of Germany, coming as it does a little more than a decade after Stalingrad, means that the next time Germans begin eastward invasions, they'll be accompanied by American G.I.'s. As long as there is doubt, the Russians will continue to possess a powerful psychological weapon for keeping their satellites in line. In short, West Germany holds not only much of the economic future of Western Europe in her hands, but also much of the political future of Eastern Europe as well.

THE REGIONS OF GERMANY. From north to south, Germany can be subdivided into four major physical regions: the Northern Plain; the Central Uplands the Rhine graben, or rift valley; and the Alpine Foreland. (Figure 13). Of these, both the Northern Plain and the Alpine Foreland have been glaciated, the former by the continental ice sheets moving out of Scandinavia and the latter by valley glaciers spreading out of the Alps. Consequently, both have soils predominantly composed of unsorted morainic materials, ranging from sands, gravels, and boulders to pockets of finer silts and clays. In both of them the drainage pattern has been disrupted, producing numerous bogs and lakes. Furthermore, in the Northern Plain there are numerous glacial spillways, or what the Germans call *urströmtäler* ("ancient stream valleys") where melt water from the receding ice ran parallel to the glacier's front until it found an opportunity to turn sharply down the natural slope of the land toward the sea. As a result, from a map showing the drainage pattern of northern Germany (and Poland, where the same features are known as *pradoliny*), it is easy to see where the major rivers have all made one or more right-angle bends to the north—the abandoned valleys between them now occupied by lakes or smaller tributaries. The route of the Mittelland Canal, which runs the entire width of the country (East and West Germany alike), follows such east-west valleys through much of its length.

The Northern Plains. Though at the time of the second and maximum glaciation the continental ice sheets pushed right down to the edge of the Central Uplands, the most recent advanced no farther than the peninsula of Jutland and an arc through the northern coastal areas of Germany and Poland known as the Baltic Heights. This band of low hills represents the terminal moraine, out in front of which, to the south and west, the meltwater streams laid down their outwash plains of stratified sand and gravel, These areas comprise some of the most sterile soils in all of Germany, and are for the most part clothed only in heather and pines. One of the most extensive of such areas is the Lüneburg Heath, located just to the southwest of Hamburg.

In sharp contrast to these unproductive heathlands are the loess soils that form an almost continuous belt across the front of the Central Uplands. They represent the accumulation of fine, wind-blown dust whisked off the ice front by glacial winds and deposited where the force of the wind was broken by the obstacle posed by the Central Uplands. These soils are among the most fertile in Germany and early gave rise to a dense agricultural settlement. Indeed, many of the leading towns of medieval Germany grew up as market centers for the rich agricultural hinterlands of the loess belt, including Münster, Hanover, Braunschweig, Magdeburg, Leipzig, and Dresden. It was along the loess belt, too, that medieval Germany's main east-west commercial artery ran (the so-called *Hochstrasse*, or High Street), and the great annual fairs held at Leipzig

central europe

Regions: (1) Northern Plain (2) Loess Belt (3) Central Uplands (4) Rhine Graben
(5) Jura (6) Alpine Foreland (7) Alps (8) Styria (9) Vienna Basin

Figure 13

were a recognition of that city's central location and accessibility from all directions.

The other cities of medieval origin in the Northern Plain were the seaports such as Bremen, Hamburg, Lübeck, and Rostock. In a Germany that was politically splintered, such seaport towns found that individually they lacked the means to protect their shipping and overseas investments, so during the twelfth and thirteenth centuries they gradually collectivized their commercial and paramilitary activities to form the Hanseatic League. This association of German trading towns eventually established "factories," or warehouses, in places as far distant as Lisbon and Novgorod and came to dominate the commerce of large areas of northern Europe. At the time of the League's founding, towns like Bremen, Hamburg, Lübeck, and Rostock were all much the same in size and importance. Although the former two both had religious functions to complement their commerce, the latter two were more advantageously located than the others for Baltic trade. However, after the main currents of European trade shifted to the Atlantic, Bremen, and particularly, Hamburg, capitalized on their westward orientation. Whereas Bremen's hinterland embraced the Weser valley, Hamburg's comprised the much vaster Elbe basin, and it became not only the main port for Berlin, the German capital, but also the country's primary colonial port and the outlet for much of Central Europe (including Czechoslovakia after World War I). However, the solidification of the boundary between West and East Germany, which passes scarcely thirty miles to the east of Hamburg, has cut off much of the port's natural hinterland, and its economic health has distinctly suffered as a result. With a population of nearly 2,000,000, it is nevertheless the largest urban center within contiguous West Germany today and has a host of diversified industries (including shipbuilding, chemicals, and food processing), in addition to its commercial functions. Bremen, with 600,000 people, likewise has a variety of light and heavy industries. Lübeck, virtually on the East German border and long peripheral for most of Germany's trade, now ranks a poor third among the old Hanse towns with 250,000 inhabitants. On the other hand, Rostock has received a new lease on life, for because of the postwar division of the country, it now serves as the principal seaport for East Germany.

The divided city of Berlin is now more of an anomaly than ever. Founded as the political-administrative center of Prussia–Brandenburg, it developed in one of the least auspicious natural settings in Germany. Unlike Paris or London, it was not the spontaneous outgrowth of the country's richest agricultural region; rather, like Madrid, it was virtually created as the largest city in Germany by reinforcement of its governmental functions with transportation and light industries. As the hub of prewar Germany's rail and *autobahn* network, Berlin is still the most central and accessible city in East Germany and an obvious choice for its capital. Within the eastern sector of the city now live 1,100,000 people. Because the Communists assigned higher priorities to other tasks than rebuilding a former enemy capital, East Berlin, apart from one or two main thoroughfares, has a uniformly drab and austere appearance. On the other hand, the West Germans have almost outdone themselves to refurbish West Berlin as a showplace of western democracy, for example by encouraging industries to locate there through subsidies and similar inducements. With a population of 2,200,000, West Berlin probably can be said to have more propaganda value than real economic or political (i.e., military) significance. Its attractions proved so effective that the East zone had to wall itself in August, 1961 in a desperate effort to retain its youthful labor force. Berlin is not only a "listening post" for the West and a center of intelligence activities but it has likewise become an emotionally charged issue in the Cold War, exploited both by West and East. Although the Federal German government never leaves its capital at Bonn otherwise, once each year its parliament makes a point of meeting in Berlin to dramatize the fact the the city *is* an integral part of their country.

Through most of the Northern Plain, hay, rye, and potatoes constitute the chief crops, with wheat, sugar beets, and vegetables being grown on the better loess soils. Mixed farming is the general rule, and milk and meat are the major sources of income for most farmers. In many of the sandy heathlands a sustained yield production of conifers is helping to meet Germany's needs for construction timber and wood plup, and along the northwest coast commercial fishing contributes to the local economy as well.

Apart from a small oil field in the Holstein District north of Hamburg, most of the commercial mineral deposits of the Northern Plain lie along its southern margin, coinciding in large part with the loess belt. Thus, unlike Britain, whose center of population shifted from the more congenial agricultural lowlands of the east to the coalfields of the northwest with the coming of the Industrial Revolution, Germany saw the importance of many of its medieval market towns further reinforced by the presence of industrial fuels and raw materials immediately around them. Along the edge of the Central Uplands in the East German sector there are large deposits of lignite or brown coal, salt, and potash, as well as smaller deposits of bituminous coal. Although the latter are inadequate for East Germany's industrial needs, coal is imported from Silesia in Poland and iron ore is supplied by the Soviet Union. With these critical deficiencies made up by its East bloc partners, East Germany emerges as one of the major industrial powers of the Communist orbit. Indeed, its exports of steel, heavy chemicals, machinery, motor vehicles, machine tools, optical goods, and textiles to East European trading partners give it a healthy balance of payments. Thus, instead of becoming a colonial appendage of the Soviets, East Germany finds itself in much the position of Britain—importing raw materials and exporting manufactured goods. However, there is an important difference as well: Germany is showing a profit. The significant reason, of course, is that the East German consumer has nowhere near the freedom of choice of the English consumer. Most of East Germany's industrial growth has been concentrated in and around her old commercial centers of Leipzig, now a city of 600,000 people, and Dresden, which numbers 510,000 inhabitants. Karl-Marx-Stadt, formerly Chemnitz, has 300,000 people, while Halle and Magdeburg each total about 275,000.

In the West German sector, there are salt, potash, and oil deposits in the Braunschweig-Hanover area, and the former city has a variety of food processing, chemical, and engineering industries. Hanover is a city of 600,000, and among its diversified industries is a major Volkswagen factory. (The main plant of this automobile firm is located at Wolfsburg on the Mittelland Canal, hardly five miles from the East German border.)

The largest industrial concentration in West Germany—and indeed, one of the foremost industrial areas anywhere in the world—is that located in the valley of the Ruhr River, a small right-bank tributary of the Rhine. The Ruhr region owes its industrial preeminence to a combination of factors, primarily to its location on the largest deposit of high-grade coal in Europe, but also to its location adjacent to one of the great navigable rivers of the subcontinent. Through the Rhine and its interconnecting system of canals, as well as by means of a highly developed railway network, the Ruhr has managed to supply large areas of western Europe with coal, while at the same time giving rise to an agglomeration of industries that makes it the economic nerve center of West Germany. Today, within the confines of the Ruhr valley, there are four cities numbering over 500,000 residents, namely Essen, Düsseldorf, Dortmund, and Duisburg; and four others have over 250,000 inhabitants each: Wuppertal, Gelsenkirchen, Bochum, and Oberhausen.

Heavy metallurgy, chemicals, and engineering are the principal industrial emphases of the Ruhr, but all manner of lighter manufacturing is represented as well. Just to the south of the Ruhr lies the commercial center of the entire region, the city of Cologne (Köln), (whose name comes from its origin as a Roman colony), with a population of some 850,000. South of Cologne, in turn, on the very edge of the Central Uplands, is Bonn, the capital of West Germany. The selection of this relatively small university town (pop. 150,000) to be the political center of the Federal Republic was to insure that, if and when the opportunity arose to move back to Berlin, there would be no hesitation to do so. It was anticipated that the location of Germany's capital in a more "favorable" location, such as Frankfurt, might result in the development of regional rivalries and a reluctance to transfer the seat of government once it had become nicely established.

The Central Uplands. The region of Germany we have called the Central Uplands presents a jumbled landscape of low, forested ridges, most of them scarcely reaching 3000 feet elevation, and open, cultivated valleys. Broadleaf decidous trees predominate, but conifers are also found at higher elevations and where reforestation projects are underway. The region's geology is diverse, with older crystalline rocks forming many of the ridges in the west and accounting in part for the narrow and scenic Rhine gorge, but with sedimentaries predominant and a few volcanic areas thrown in for good measure. Technically, the Rhine graben is a part of this varied region, but it is extensive and distinct enough to warrant separate consideration.

The attractions that the Central Uplands hold for agriculture, as compared to those of the Northern Plain, are varied. As a rule, the soils of the valleys and basins are more fertile than those of the Plain (though not of the loess belt, to be sure), for they have largely been derived from the weathering of limestones and shales. On the other hand, the more broken topography means that machinery is more difficult to use, not only because more of the land is in slopes, but also because individual farm properties tend to be smaller. Although the region lies farther south than the Plain, it also lies at a higher elevation, thus offsetting in part the effective warmth of the growing season. Much of the land is in pasture and a mixed livestock-crop economy prevails. Among the cereals, wheat, barley, rye, and oats are all represented, and there is likewise a considerable production of potatoes, vegetables, sugar beets, oil seeds, hops, and fruit.

Most of the forests of the Central Uplands are carefully managed, and a variety of wood-using industries are scattered throughout the region. However, apart from iron ore deposits in the Sieg River valley (near Bonn) and at Salzgitter near Braunschweig, the Central Uplands have only minor deposits of copper and lead. Thus, with no mineral wealth to speak of and few valleys or basins large or productive enough to generate major commercial centers, the Central Uplands can be characterized as an area of small to medium-sized towns and cities. The region's largest urban center is Stuttgart, in the southwest, with 650,000 inhabitants, followed by Nürnberg, to the east, with 475,000. In addition to their roles as regional commercial and transportation centers, both cities have labor-intensive industries such as engineering and electronics. The region's third-ranking city is the road and railway center of Kassel (pop. 220,000) in the north.

The Rhine Graben. The Rhine Graben stands out sharply from the other valleys of Central Germany on account of its origin and its character. It was formed by the buckling of a large segment of the earth's crust, followed by the downfaulting of its center, much as though the keystone had fallen out of an arch. One side of the fault is represented by the Vosges Mountains of France; the other side is composed of the Schwarzwald, (Black Forest). Along these breaks in the earth's crust, magma, or molten rock, flowed to the surface forming such volcanic features as the Hardt on the west side of the valley, Kaiserstuhl near its southern end, Odenwald on its east side, and Vogelsberg at its northern extremity. The flat floor of the valley itself has since been covered with alluvial deposits of the Rhine, and in most areas they are fine-grained and fertile. Also, because most of the valley lies below 500 feet elevation and in the rain shadow of the Vosges it constitutes the warmest and driest region in Germany (see Figure 3). Thus, in terms of terrain, soils and climate, the Rhine graben represents the country's premier agricultural region, an area whose crops include grapes, tobacco, and corn, as well as wheat, sugar beets, stone fruits, hops, and vegetables.

Although the German portion of the valley has no minerals of importance, several large industrial and commercial centers have arisen there, chiefly as strategic communications points where tributary streams open into it. Frankfurt-on-Main is the largest, with 700,000 people, and is situated at the northern end of the graben where roads and railways converge on it both from the north and east. Indeed, with its connections northwestward to the Ruhr and southward along the graben, Frankfurt is without a doubt the natural traffic center of West Germany. This is borne out by the fact that its airport is the busiest in the country; immediately adjacent to the airport is Germany's most heavily trafficked autobahn intersection. Close by to the west are the cities of Wiesbaden and Mainz, both on the Rhine itself, and Darmstadt lies on the edge of the graben to the south. Where the Neckar River joins the Rhine there is another cluster of large cities, with Mannheim and Ludwigshafen at the junction itself, and the old university town of Heidelberg set back on the edge of the valley. Yet farther south, Karlsruhe and Freiburg also occupy valley-edge sites, in locations that were favored by being on the main north-south route of medieval times, the Bergstrasse, or "mountain street."

The Alpine Foreland. The final region of Germany, the Alpine Foreland, can be contrasted in almost every way with the Rhine graben. As we indicated earlier, it has been glaciated and has infertile morainic soils. Its rolling surface varies from less than 700 feet to over 2200 feet in elevation, so despite its location in the far south of Germany its summer temperatures are cool and its winters are cold and snowy. Located at the foot of the Alps, it is a favorite area of tourists in both summer and winter. But agriculture is chiefly based on hay and dairying, and the most important field crops are potatoes, oats, and barley. Large areas of the poorer sandy soils are in conifers, as are the lower slopes of the mountains, so forestry is locally important. The prevalence of soft woods is likewise reflected in the greater frequency of wooden houses than in central and northern Germany, where half-timbered construction is most characteristic. With no minerals of any importance, save sand and gravel, the region's only industrial asset, apart from such raw materials as its agriculture and forestry provide, is hydroelectric power.

It is for good reason, then, that the Alpine Foreland is notably deficient in cities of any size. Through most of the Middle Ages the region's largest urban center was the old Roman town of Augsburg, which was located on the main approach road to the Brenner Pass and was also the seat of the wealthy entrepreneurial Fugger family. The town of Munich (München), however, was chosen as the capital of the Kingdom of Bavaria, and with the dawn of the railway age, it became the transportation and commercial hub of the region rather than Augsburg. Munich's accessibility also attracted such industries as food processing (including brewing), textiles, and light engineering, and it quickly outpaced its older rival. Today Munich ranks as West Germany's third largest city and has 1,200,000 inhabitants, while Augsburg numbers about 220,000.

CONCLUSION. Although West Germany is unable to feed itself and also is critically short on petroleum, it is easily able to pay for such imports with its immense exports of manufactured goods. In effect, Germany's unparalleled prosperity has demonstrated that the great vigor and resourcefulness of the German people has won more for them industrially than they ever could have hoped to achieve militarily. Indeed, it has been said that the Volkswagen has accomplished what Hitler couldn't do—it has conquered the world! In any event, West Germany's booming postwar economy has markedly dampened the more radical revanchist elements (largely headed by Germans evicted from eastern territories after the war) who were militant not only in their notions about reuniting West and East Germany but also in reincorporating the areas lost to Poland and the U.S.S.R. beyond the Oder and Neisse Rivers. Although one still sees signs along the roadsides proclaiming "Drei geteilt —Niemals! ("Divided in Three—Never!), they are now getting rusty and battered.

While it is not politically expedient for them to say so publicly, one wonders if many West German politicans are not quite content to leave well enough alone, for to insist on reunification with East Germany would mean considerable financial outlays to bring that region up to the level of prosperity that the West now enjoys. And certainly life is too good, what with farmers driving to their fields in their Mercedes-Benzes, and junior executives owning villas in the Aegean, to think about upsetting the apple cart to retrieve something as uninspiring as East Prussia! No, the contentment of German affluence in itself militates against a resumption of the "Drang nach Osten." The only danger the East of Europe need fear, and it is a real one, is the specter of economic crisis in Germany. If postwar democracy has flourished thus far, it is largely due to favorable economic conditions. Put the country's pounding industrial machine into neutral, or reverse, and then the real test will begin. (One has only to note the ominous rise in Neo-Nazi activity as the momentum of the "German economic miracle" has been tapering off.) One can only hope that the lessons of peace and prosperity will not be wasted on a new generation of Germans, too young to have known Hitler but old enough to want to forget.

Austria

The Austria that emerged from World War I was an ethnically German but economically unbalanced nation of 6,000,000 people, compared to the multinational empire of well over 40,000,000 inhabitants that had entered the war. Cut off from the sea and otherwise thoroughly dismembered, Austria was left with the imperial capital, Vienna, a city of nearly 2,000,000, and the sparsely inhabited backbone of the Alps from which to support it. At the end of World War II, having been an integral part of Hitler's Third Reich, Austria was divided into four occupation zones, like Germany, and Vienna, like Berlin, became a divided city within the Russian sector. A decade later, however, as NATO was negotiating the inclusion of West Germany, the four occupying powers reached agreement on the withdrawal of their forces from Austria and the reestablishment of that country as a sovereign state. The Soviet price for this agreement was the neutralization of Austria and the continued delivery of oil as reparations for a further ten years.

Neutrality was indeed a new concept for Austria, for like Germany, it had been on the military front lines through most of its history. Vienna, its capital, owes its origins to a Roman strongpoint and Austria owes its very name (Österreich) to its role as one of the eastern kingdoms from which the Germanic thrust eastward began. Lying athwart the Danube Valley, which has been one of Europe's primary arteries of movement since prehistoric times, Austria, by virtue of its location alone, could not fail to be involved in virtually every struggle that affected Central Europe. Owing in large part to its turbulent history, Austria has had little opportunity to assess and develop its own resource potential.

THE REGIONS OF AUSTRIA. Much the largest part of Austria is composed of the Alps, which reach their highest elevation in the Gross Glockner, at 12,457 feet. On either side of their crystalline core, the Alps have lower ranges of sedimentary rock, separated from the former by great longitudinal valleys. (A good map of alpine drainage will reveal how many of the rivers line up with each other, such as the Inn, the Rhine, and the Rhone; or the Salzach and the Ems.) These east-west ridges and valleys not only establish the "grain" of the country but also are in large measure responsible for giving it its shape. The north slope grades down into the basin of Upper Austria, centered on the city of Linz; the southern slope grades down into the basin of Carinthia, centered on the city of Graz; and where the main ranges taper off to the east, reaching the Danube in the low spur of the *Wienerwald* (Vienna Woods), lies the Vienna Basin, centered in the country's capital and largest city.

The Alpine Foreland (Upper Austria). Land use in the Alps is largely a reflection of elevation and exposure. In the valley bottoms and on some of the great glacial-river terraces most of the land has been cleared for fields and hay meadows. This is also the case on the sunny, south-facing slopes of the valleys, whereas the shady, north-facing slopes have been left in forest. Even on the south-facing slopes, however, there is little cultivation above 3000 feet and the treeline seldom gets as high as 6000 feet, leaving the highest areas in alpine meadows and snow fields. The primary emphasis of agriculture is on dairying, but potatoes, barley, and hardy vegetables are grown. There are numerous wood-using industries scattered through the region, but its only mineral deposit of importance is high-grade iron ore located at Erzberg, in the lower ranges to the east. Most of the region's hydroelectric power is transmitted to the adjacent lowlands for use by industries there. Otherwise, the greatest asset of Austria's alpine area is the grandeur of its scenery, which attracts increasing numbers of both summer and winter tourists. The largest city of the region is Innsbruck, strategically located near the northern entrance to the Brenner Pass.

The basin of Upper Austria, on the northern flanks of the Alps, is a continuation of the Alpine Foreland of Germany, but with some important differences. It lies at a lower elevation (generally between 700 and 1200 feet), and the effects of glaciation were limited to a narrow foothill zone; thus, it is not only warmer but also has more fertile soils. Accordingly, more of the land is in crops, such as wheat, sugar beets, and vegetables, though even here hay and dairying are important as well. The region's mineral endowment includes salt, mined in the vicinity of the famous music festival center of Salzburg, and bauxite, in the foothills farther east. The commercial and industrial hub of Upper Austria is the Danube River port of Linz, a city of 210,000 people. Thanks to its coal imports from Germany, it boasts a large steel mill, and also has an aluminum refinery and food processing industries.

Styria. Over the Alps to the south lies the *Styrian Basin,* a region whose sheltered southern exposure permits the cultivation of such warm-temperate crops as corn and grapes, in addition to wheat, sugar beets, and barley. Its commerce and industry are largely focused in the regional capital of Graz, whose 250,000 inhabitants make it Austria's second city. The presence of local coal deposits has permitted the development of metallurgical and engineering industries, in addition to food processing and textiles.

The Vienna Basin. The heart of Austria, however, has always been the Vienna Basin. Not only is it lower and warmer than Styria to the south, but the Danube has also endowed it with fertile alluvial soils and a degree of accessibility that Styria lacks. Intersecting the Danube corridor within sight of the last spurs of the Alps is an historic route from the southwest. Leading up over Semmering Pass (3231 feet elevation), it follows the longitudinal valley of the Mur River and winds through the Julian Alps into Italy. Not only did this route provide the Romans with their easiest access to the northeast frontier of their empire, but its intersection with the Danube likewise provided the site for their border fortress, which later became Vienna.

The significance of Vienna's location was greater than probably even the Romans imagined. Leading northeastward from the city is the valley of the Morava River, which nearly bisects the country of Czechoslovakia and affords a lowland connection through the Moravian Gate (1020 feet elevation) into the North European Plain. Thus, in a Central Europe uncluttered by political boundaries—or rather, in a Central Europe politically dominated by Austria—Vienna again would be as it once was, one of the great natural foci of communications and commerce. As it is, its population of 1,700,000 is still somewhat incongruous for a country whose total population numbers only 7,200,000, especially when industry accounts for so little of its total employment and its political function has been so sharply curtailed. However, the imperial airs it has retained, combined with its many cultural attractions and its relaxed, friendly atmosphere continue to make Vienna one of the great tourist meccas of Europe.

The basin that Vienna dominates is important not only agriculturally, what with its vineyards, corn, wheat, and suger beets, but also because it contains both oil and gas fields northeast of the capital. Although production has levelled off—in part, perhaps, due to overpumping by the Russians when they occupied this sector of the country—these deposits have allowed the Austrians to establish major refineries and petrochemical factories in the area. In a sense, they can also be said to round out Austria's resource picture, for in sum the country will be seen to have one of the most balanced economic endowments of any nation in Europe. In addition to a diversified agriculture, Austria has timber, water power and all the basic ingredients of heavy industry: iron ore, coal, petroleum, and natural gas. Yet, of the three central European countries (overlooking East Germany for the moment, where comparable data are not available), Austria has the lowest per capita income, a figure well below that of West Germany and scarcely half that of Switzerland. It also has the highest suicide rate in Europe (a statistic often erroneously attributed to Sweden), although West Germany and Switzerland are not far behind. Where the explanation lies for such regional differences, the social geographers and psychologists have yet to tell us.

Switzerland

If Austria provides an example of an inverse relationship between diversity of resources and economic well-being, Switzerland provides an even stronger case. The Swiss, along with the Swedes, rank as the most prosperous people in Europe, yet their resource endowment is one of the poorest of any nation on the subcontinent. Of the country's three main regions, its best is the so-called Mittelland Plateau— a continuation of the Alpine Foreland of Germany, one of the *poorest* areas in that country. Sixty per cent of Switzerland's area falls within the Alpine region, and another 10 per cent lies in the Jura Mountains. Switzerland is completely lacking in coal, iron ore, and oil; indeed, apart from its glacial sands and gravels and some limestone, its mineral endowment is nil. Timber and water power it does have, but its soils are generally infertile and its growing season is relatively short and cool. Thus, in the light of the seeming inconsistencies demonstrated by Austria and Switzerland, one might be tempted to ask if a country's economic well-being has anything whatsoever to do with its geography.

If, by natural endowment we mean only such things as minerals, soils, climate, and so on, then the answer must obviously be a qualified no. But if we include location—the very essence of a place's personality, then the answer is decidedly yes. Austria's location, like that of Germany, has given it little option all through history to withdraw from the conflicts that have surged around it. The Danube corridor, like the North European Plain, is a thoroughfare where the collisions of peoples and ideas have almost been continuous. Switzerland, on the other hand, embraces the highest mountain knot on the subcontinent: a region that has been a barrier to movement rather than a funnel to channel it, a region whose relative isolation has made detachment and withdrawal possible for the Swiss. Indeed, it would scarcely be an exaggeration to say that the Swiss state crystallized as a political entity for the exact opposite reasons that Austria arose. Austria, (the "Eastern Kingdom") was a forward-point *for* military expansion; Switzerland evolved as a reaction *to* military expansion, by withdrawal from it. While both Germany and Austria expanded their territories by force of arms, Switzerland grew by peaceful accretion, by the free choice of one valley and region after another to withdraw from the turmoil around them. Such withdrawal began in 1291 when the first three valleys (cantons), Uri, Unterwalden, and Schwyz (the latter eventually giving its name to the country) reacted by joining together to turn back an army of the Austrian Hapsburgs from the approaches to the St. Gotthard Pass. It did not end until 1815, when the last districts along the French border voted themselves out of Napoleon's troubled domains and into the Swiss Confederation. In the same year, the Congress of Vienna granted international recognition to the neutrality of Switzerland, serving, in a sense, to legitimize a condition already of long standing.

The voluntary accretion of Switzerland was not stopped by the physical barriers of the Alps or the Jura, nor was it stopped by the cultural barriers of language and religion. Although Germans and Protestants predominate, Switzerland's boundaries today include French, Italian, and Romansch-speaking peoples (the latter is a dialect of Latin preserved in the most remote areas of eastern Switzerland) and a large minority of Roman Catholics. So, the obvious lesson to be learned from all this is that peoples of differing language and religions *can* live together in harmony (the Netherlands and Belgium, among others, please note!) if the bond that cements them together is a common desire for peace.

THE REGIONS OF SWITZERLAND.

The Alps.   As in Austria, it is the Alps that dominate the country, both physically and areally. In Switzerland, however, they average about 2000 feet higher, with Finsteraarhorn, the highest peak wholly within Switzerland reaching 14,023 feet, and Mont Blanc, whose flanks it shares with France and Italy, topping 15,771 feet. Correspondingly, the passes all lie considerably higher than those in Austria. Compared to the Brenner Pass, which breaks across the Alps at 4,497 feet, the Simplon crosses at 6,578 feet, the St. Gotthard at 6,916 feet, the Splügen at 6,933 feet, and the Great St. Bernard at 8,101 feet. Unlike the Brenner, all the Swiss passes lie above the treeline and are closed by snow in winter. Although road traffic across the Swiss Alps comes to a halt at that season, rail traffic continues by virtue of tunnels bored through the Simplon and St. Gotthard Passes. Of the two, the latter is the more centrally located and thus the more important, for it funnels traffic from Germany, the Low Countries, and Scandinavia, whereas the Simplon chiefly expedites traffic from France and Britain.

As in Austria, the crystalline arc of the Alps is separated from the sedimentary ranges to the north (in Switzerland, the Bernese Alps) by a longitudinal valley in which both the Rhine and the Rhone have their headwaters. Land uses are likewise conditioned by elevation and exposure, and perhaps the chief difference in the economies of the Alpine regions of the two countries is the much greater development of tourism in Switzerland. This can be explained not only by Switzerland's closer proximity to the more affluent lands of northwestern Europe, especially Britain, but also to the fact that political stability has always been a major concern of tourists and is a luxury that Switzerland has been able to guarantee ever since the real dawn of tourism about a century ago.

In contrast, *the Jura* are singularly unimpressive mountains, composed chiefly of folded sedimentary rocks and nowhere reaching an elevation much above 3000 feet. Their sandstone ridges are largely forested and their limestone valleys are so porous that much of the precipitation the area receives quickly disappears underground. Farming is chiefly confined to pastoralism, and there are few towns of any size within the region itself. Woodcarving, especially the making of clocks, has been a craft of long standing in the Jura, just as it has in the adjacent areas of France and in the Black Forest of Germany. Although wooden cuckoo clocks continue to be made as tourist novelties, the skill of clock making has been transferred to a new medium and a new dimension: the wristwatch, with which Switzerland is virtually synonymous today. Most of this labor-intensive industry is concentrated in the Jura, with the cities of Neuchatel and Geneva (pop. 180,000) serving as major marketing outlets.

In addition to watchmaking and watch marketing, Geneva is the European center of the United Nations (occupying the old Palace of the League of Nations) as well as the headquarters of the International Red Cross and several banking and insurance firms. All such functions are, of course, related to the neutrality and stability for which Switzerland is noted. Because Swiss law permits anonymous bank accounts, identified by number only, many businessmen and politicians resident in countries of questionable economic and political stability also find a financial sanctuary in Switzerland.

Alpine Foreland (Mittelland Plateau). Geneva lies at the outlet of the lake of the same name, one of the many finger lakes produced along the base of the Alps by the damming of stream valleys by glacial moraines. Zürich, the country's largest city (pop. 450,000) occupies a similar location near the northern end of the Mittelland Plateau. Zürich is chiefly noted as an industrial center, producing electrical machinery, optical equipment, precision instruments, high-quality art books, and similar products requiring a large input of skilled labor. As in watchmaking, the Swiss capitalize on their human skills rather than on their limited resource base. This can be demonstrated even in their textile industry, which is largely centered in the St. Gallen district to the northeast. Because they cannot possibly hope to compete in the volume production of fabrics, the Swiss concentrate instead on a quality production of such items as lace, embroidery, ribbons, and velvet.

Switzerland's second largest city is its Rhine river port, Basel, which today numbers 220,000 inhabitants. As the country's only access to a navigable waterway, Basel acts as the chief import port of Switzerland, handling large tonnages of the fuels, metals, and foodstuffs for which Switzerland must look to the outside world. Its industries include food processing, metallurgy, engineering, and pharmaceuticals. And, while land locked Switzerland does lack a navy, other than its patrol boats on Lake Constance, it boasts a larger merchant fleet (chiefly of river barges and tugs, but also of smaller, ocean-going vessels) than does Belgium, for example.

The capital of the Swiss confederation is the city of Bern (pop. 175,000), located near the center of the Mittelland Plateau, and close to the linguistic boundary separating the two largest language groups, the Germans and French. In addition to its political function it is also a major center of publishing and finance.

CONCLUSION.   Though Switzerland's neutrality has never been challenged by an invading army, the Swiss maintain their army and air force in a high state of readiness. But though it is said that they can mobilize a force of some 600,000 men, completely armed with up-to-date weapons, in a matter of hours, Switzerland is continuing to rely on its geography to spare it from invasion. Just as the legendary Wilhelm Tell and his colleagues helped turn back the Hapsburgs by catapulting stones down on them from the mountain sides, Swiss defense forces stand ready to dynamite the country's major bridges and tunnels, if necessary. Thus, if the attractiveness of the economic and political sanctuary that Switzerland offers is not inducement enough to spare it from involvement in the troubles of the world around it, perhaps the knowledge that the walls of the Alps could be sealed in a matter of minutes has halted would-be aggressors. However, in a world of nuclear weapons and global strategies, Switzerland counts for little—unless it be the lesson that peace and good ·will among men can become an enduring and profitable way of life.

Table 4. The Germanic Core, Selected Statistics (1968)

	West Germany	East Germany	Austria	Switzerland
Area (000's sq. mi.)	95.3	41.7	32.4	15.9
Population (millions)	58.1	16.0	7.4	6.2
Birth rate (per 1000)	17.2	14.8	17.4	17.7
Death rate (per 10000)	11.2	13.2	13.0	9.1
Natural increase (per 1000)	6.0	1.6	4.4	8.6
Infant mortality (per 1000)	22.8		26.4	17.5
Land use (%):				
Cultivated	34.1	47.4	20.8	10.2
Meadows-pastures	23.1	13.4	27.3	42.2
Forest	28.9	27.8	38.3	23.8
Other land	13.9	13.3	14.9	23.8
Population density per sq. mi.				
cultivated land	1840	840	1140	3980
Gross national product				
per capita	$1,700	$1,220	$1,150	$2,250
Exports (millions)	$24,842	$3,456	$1,989	$3,966
Imports (millions)	$20,150	$3,279	$2,496	$4,513
Trade balance (millions)	+$4,692	+$177	−$507	−$547

See Table 1, p. 54, for sources.

CHAPTER 6

the eastern crush zone

Europe is at its narrowest along a line that might be drawn from the Baltic Sea to the northern end of the Adriatic. East of that imaginary line, Europe also demonstrates its greatest cultural diversity, for every wave of peoples, every surge of ideas coming out of the steppes of Russia or across the land bridge of Asia Minor has left its mark in this region, as has every impulse flowing from western Europe in the opposite directions. Thus, owing to its location, Eastern Europe has found itself almost continuously assailed by forces from both east and west, with the result that economic, social, and political orientations within the region have been in a state of flux all through its history. Small wonder, then, that this region has come to be known as Europe's "shatter-belt" or "crush-zone."

Within Eastern Europe, there are many effective illustrations of the interplay of terrain and culture. Lowlands and open plains tend to be culturally homogeneous, as in Poland, Hungary, and the lower Danube Valley of Romania; mountain regions demonstrate considerable heterogeneity, owing not only to the fact that their rugged terrain is divisive but also because they serve as refuges from lowland invaders (much like Switzerland). Thus, the uplands and plateaus of Czechoslovakia, as the country's name suggests, are inhabited by both Czech and Slovak-speaking peoples, while Yugoslavia (literally, "the land of the South Slavs") embraces no fewer than six related but distinct Slavic peoples: Serbs, Croats, Slovenes, Bosnians, Macedonians, and Montenegrins. Mountainous Albania, the part of Eastern Europe most remote from one of the great lowland corridors, became a refuge area for the ancient Illyrian language, while the region of Transylvania, tucked into the arc of mountains curving through western Romania, became a detached pocket of Szekeli (Magyar) and German-speaking peoples. (The latter, however, have been expelled from all East European countries to prevent

Germany from ever using *Deutschtum* as an excuse for renewing her claims on the areas they inhabited.) Transylvania also has the largest gypsy population of any region in Europe.

Seen in a broader geographic context, the linguistic pattern of Eastern Europe can be said to be composed of two main Slavic groups: the so-called Western Slavs in the north (Poles, Czechs, and Slovaks) and the South Slavs in present-day Yugoslavia. They are separated through the Danube corridor by two non-Slavic peoples, the Romanians, who pride themselves on speaking a Romance language traceable to the Roman garrisons that manned the Empire's eastern outposts on the Danube, and the Magyars, who swept in off the steppes of Russia as late as the ninth century A.D. and came to rest in the Hungarian Plain. Beyond the South Slavs, pushed into Eastern Europe's most rugged and isolated corner, are the Albanians. The Bulgarians offer a curious illustration of a nomad people moving out of the Volga region of Russia into southeastern Europe and giving up their native language altogether, becoming in the process the East European people who are most culturally like the Russians today. This is because they not only speak a Slavic tongue but they were converted to Christianity by the Eastern Orthodox Church and employ the Cyrillic alphabet.

The Bulgarian illustration demonstrates that after language, religion has been the greatest force for cultural diversity within Eastern Europe. Once again a people's location and orientation were all-important in determining whether they became adherents of Latin Christendom or Eastern Orthodoxy. Thus, the German missionaries who paved the way for the *Drang nach Osten* managed to bring the Poles, Czechs, Slovaks, and Hungarians into the domains of the Roman Catholic Church. Penetration from Italy likewise succeeded in annexing the Slovenes and Croats (along the coast and in northwestern Yugoslavia) into the Vatican's fold. On the other hand, missionaries such as St. Cyril, working out of Constantinople, converted the Greeks, Bulgarians, Romanians, Serbians, Bosnians, Macedonians, and Montenegrins to the eastern faith. If any Christian sect ever held sway in Albania, it has since been submerged by the Moslem Turks, for Albania is the only predominantly Islamic country in Europe today.

Normally, it was the religious orientation of a people that determined what alphabet they used for transcribing the Bible, and for written language in general. However, the Romanians accepted Eastern Orthodoxy but chose to retain their Latin alphabet. The peoples of Yugoslavia, on the other hand, were split right down the middle, both linguistically and religiously. The country's bank notes, for example, are printed in four different languages using two different alphabets. The Moslem influence remains strong in the south of the country as well, for there are numerous mosques in evidence, many men wear fezzes, and many women are clad in Moslem costume.

Before the war, another religious minority added diversity to the region's cultural personality. These were the Jews, who found refuge from the persecution they suffered in western Catholic Europe, in eastern Poland and the adjacent areas of White Russia and the Ukraine. Although not immune from persecution even here, they at least found a greater measure of tolerance in this religiously diversified region than they did within the solidly Roman Catholic West. This tolerance was abruptly and brutally terminated by the arrival of Hitler's *Herrenvolk*, who by the time they were finished, had exterminated over 6,000,000 people, most of them East European Jews, in such notorious death camps as Auschwitz and Treblinka in Poland.

The Nazi invasion of Eastern Europe in the early 1940's was simply the latest of a long series of military adventures that have ravaged the region. Merely to list them all would take several pages of this book; here we will point out only those that have been most responsible for the political configuration we find within the region today.

Since the close of the World War II, the dominant presence in Eastern Europe has been that of the Soviet Union—at war's end, the world's second greatest military and industrial power. The Red Army, having "liberated" the countries of Eastern Europe from the Nazis, did not go home, but stayed to help in the establishment of "peoples' democracies" friendly to the Soviet Union. The primary Soviet concern was that an invasion of its territory must never be allowed to happen again, for this was not the first time that an attack had been launched on Russia through Eastern Europe, but the fourth within the last 250 years. [Two other invasions of Russia sponsored by West European powers were launched through the Crimea (British and French in 1854–56) and the Arctic and Pacific coasts of the country (British, Americans, and Japanese in 1918–20).] Charles XII of Sweden, in a desperate last-ditch effort to retain his country's great power status, launched a disastrous invasion of the Ukraine in 1709. Little more than a hundred years later, the French under Napoleon were waiting amid the burning ruins of Moscow to sign a peace treaty with a "vanquished" people—who did not put in an appearance, except to cut his troops to shreds as they limped back toward France. Again, little more than a century later, German troops of the Kaiser's army were thrusting their way eastward into Russia, even managing to win in a limited sense and get a treaty signed for the surrender of the Ukraine.

The chaos within Russia at the time of the Bolshevik Revolution and the end of World War I was so great, however, that any country that had any designs on or claim against it used this opportunity to further its cause. Finland, the Baltic States, and Poland were all detached from Russia as independent states at this time, and both Finland and Poland saw fit to seize additional areas on their eastern frontiers in 1920. Romania followed suit, annexing the region of Bessarabia, while Turkey and Iran did likewise in the Middle Eastern regions of Russia.

World War I had not only redrawn the boundaries of Russia vis-á-vis her East European neighbors, but it had also resulted in dramatic internal changes within the region. The empires of Austria-Hungary and Turkey were no more; older countries such as Hungary, Romania, Bulgaria, and Albania had come back on the map, with much-changed sizes and shapes; and new countries that had never existed previously, such as Czechoslovakia and Yugoslavia, took their places alongside them. (Czechoslovakia, for example, had been "conceived" in Pittsburgh, Pennsylvania, and "sanctified" in Washington, D. C., ten days before it was promulgated in Prague.)[1]

World War II resulted in far vaster destruction and loss of life within Eastern Europe but in far fewer boundary changes. The Soviet Union had reabsorbed the Baltic States in 1940, and when the war ended it saw fit to reclaim the eastern areas of Poland and Romania that these countries had taken from her in 1920. In addition, it detached the easternmost tip of Czechoslovakia and annexed that country's Ruthenian-speaking people into the Ukraine, with which the area has a stronger cultural identity, and it divided the old German area of East Prussia with Poland. However, the latter areas are the only ones not a part of Czarist Russia.

While they were involved in the readjustment of Eastern Europe's boundaries, the Russians saw fit to recompense the Poles for the area they had reclaimed in the east by moving the Polish-German border west to the Oder and Neisse rivers, thus abolishing the old Polish Corridor by giving Poland a broad expanse of the Baltic seacoast. However, apart from rectifying a few boundary changes made by Hitler, who had favored his puppet government in Hungary by allowing it to double its size at the expense of Czechoslovakia and Romania, there were no other major shifts of political areas in Eastern Europe following World War II. There were, nevertheless, mass expulsions of German-speaking people to remove the bone of contention caused by their continued presence, as noted earlier.

Once the Soviet Union felt that the communist-dominated "peoples' domocracies" it had sponsored in Eastern Europe were securely in power, it began withdrawing the major components of the Red Army, while retaining garrisons and air force bases at key points. As early as 1948, Soviet hegemony over the region was given a rude jolt by the defection of Marshal Tito's Yugoslavia from the Moscow orbit. (The pattern of Yugoslavia's "liberation" and postwar evolution had differed from the other East European countries anyway, by having been largely accomplished by local Communist partisans rather than the Red Army.) There were some in the western world who expected the Soviet fist to come down hard on the wayward Yugoslavs, but apart from vitriolic press attacks, no move was made by the Soviet Union to reincorporate them into the Russian sphere. The Soviets were obviously content that, even with an independent Communist government in control in Belgrade, the security of their *cordon sanitaire* was not impaired.

However, it was quite another matter when in the wake of world confusion over the Suez crisis, the Hungarians decided the time was ripe to throw off their Communist government. This the Soviets would not countenance, and their mailed fist did come down hard against the rebels of Budapest. There was also unrest in Poland in 1956, but its goals were reform, not revolution, and the Poles were able to accomplish bloodlessly what many in the West said was impossible—including the unheard-of step in a Communist country of de-collectivizing agriculture.

After Khrushchev's famous speech in 1956 denouncing Stalin, Eastern

1 See *Encyclopedia Americana* (1957), vol. 8, 383 g.

Europe cautiously looked for clues as to what line it should follow. When it became clear that the Khrushchev position *was* accepted by the Soviet party leadership, all of the East European countries quickly joined ranks, except Albania, which denounced Russia and the others as revisionists and continued to espouse the old Stalinist line favored by Red China. There is little doubt that Khrushchev's denunciation of Stalin was an earth-shaking event for the entire Communist movement, for never before had any party member been encouraged to find fault with his party's leadership. If Stalin was fallible, then so might his underlings be. This meant that there might very well be more than one "right" answer to a given question, so debate was engendered within the Communist bloc as never before. That the decisions and policies of their leadership *could* be challenged was the main lesson East Europeans had learned from this episode.

The lesson has not gone unapplied for long. When the Romanians disagreed with the plan that had been worked out for their country in the Council for Mutual Economic Assistance, or COMECON—the East bloc's version of the Common Market—they rejected it and proceeded to draw up plans of their own, which they felt would better serve their nation's needs. Similarly, when Czech leaders felt their country's economic growth was being hampered by the too-rigid and unimaginative policies of their premier, they replaced him with a younger man with "new" ideas. For western observers, accustomed to thinking in terms of intrigue and firing squads as the chief means of removing unwanted party officials, it comes as a welcome sign of political maturation that they are now being retired with pensions instead!

Nonetheless, the Russian invasion of Czechoslovakia in August, 1968 provided the world with a clear indication that nationalism remains a primary force in international affairs, even among states supposedly linked in "socialist brotherhood." Not only were the economic reforms and extensions of freedom permitted by the Dubček regime seen as dangerous precedents for its own internal evolution, but the Soviet Union also viewed a growing Czech-West German rapprochement in the economic and political spheres as particularly ominous. Once more the tragedy of Eastern Europe's crush-zone had been reenacted, for Czechoslovakia became again the victim of its unhappy geographic location between two great powers, each obsessed with fear and distrust of the other.

Poland

Poland is the largest of the East European countries, both in area and in population. (see Figure 14A) Like East Germany, which borders it on the west, Poland lies primarily within the North European Plain, but its southern border with Czechoslovakia is defined by the crests of the Sudeten, Beskid, and Carpathian mountains. In the latter area elevations as high as 5000 to 8000 feet are reached, but except in the far southeast, passes everywhere cross the ranges below 2000 feet. South of Warsaw the Silesian-Polish Plateau extends more than 100 miles out in front of the mountains and reaches an elevation of just over 2000 feet. Otherwise the morainic hills bordering the Baltic are the most pronounced topographic features in the country.

South of the Baltic Heights, much of the land consists of sterile outwash areas and old glacial spillways (*pradoliny*). South of these, in turn, are the rolling till plains of the maximum ice advance and finally, adjacent to the uplands along the border, is the loess belt. In Poland, as in Germany, the earliest urban development took place in this favored agricultural region, with the city of Krakow becoming Poland's first commercial, cultural, and religious center. It now ranks third in size with 520,000 people. Warsaw was later selected as the country's capital by virtue of its more central location. Today, as the political, commercial and transportation hub of Poland, Warsaw numbers 1,300,000 inhabitants. When the Industrial Revolution reached Poland, a host of new cities arose on the rich Silesian coalfields, of which the largest today is Katowice (population 290,000).

Following its independence from czarist Russia and the creation of a corridor to the Baltic after World War I, Poland developed the seaport of Gdynia. However, as a result of the boundary changes of World War II, Poland acquired the ports of Gdansk (formerly Danzig), with a population of 320,000, and Szczecin (formerly Stettin, pop. 310,000), both of which are larger and more advantageously situated than Gdynia. Another acquisition from Germany was Wroclaw, formerly Breslau, whose inhabitants now number 470,000. Two of its other major cities occupy strategic locations in the glacial spillways: Poznan, with 440,000 people, on the Warta River with connections to the Oder (Odra), and Bydgoszcz, with 250,000 people, near the Vistula with connections to the Notec, Warta, and Oder. Lodz, the country's second-ranking city (pop. 750,000) lies on the edge of the Silesian-Polish plateau, where water power gave it an early start in textile manufacturing.

Over half of Poland's total area is under cultivation, with its chief crops being potatoes, rye, oats, and flax in the morainic soils of the north and center and wheat and sugar beets more strongly concentrated in the loess soils of the south. Poland not only can supply most of its own food requirements but also exports a considerable amount of butter, cheese, and meat products. Indeed, the agricultural sector of the Polish economy is about the only one in Eastern Europe that normally meets its production quotas. It is said that even the Russian minister of agriculture was impressed enough by Polish results to have been quoted as saying, "Maybe the Poles have got something here"—meaning the idea of the private ownership of farmland!

Since the war, the Poles have also gone in strongly for large-scale commercial fishing. However, because the Baltic is relatively poor in marine life, they have constructed a long-range fishing fleet that operates chiefly in the North Sea and in the waters between Scotland and Norway, being out for many weeks at a time and doing all the processing on board.

Fully a quarter of the Polish countryside is in forest, and because it is chiefly coniferous, the Poles cover most of their own needs for timber

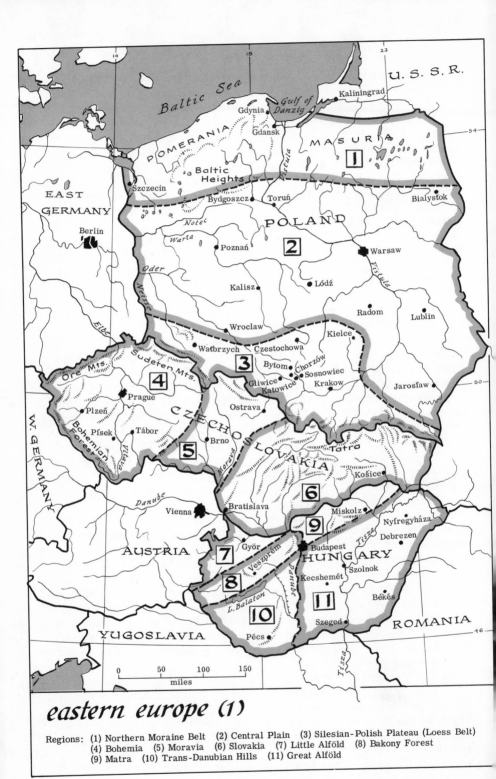

eastern europe (1)

Regions: (1) Northern Moraine Belt (2) Central Plain (3) Silesian-Polish Plateau (Loess Belt)
(4) Bohemia (5) Moravia (6) Slovakia (7) Little Alföld (8) Bakony Forest
(9) Matra (10) Trans-Danubian Hills (11) Great Alföld

Figure 14A

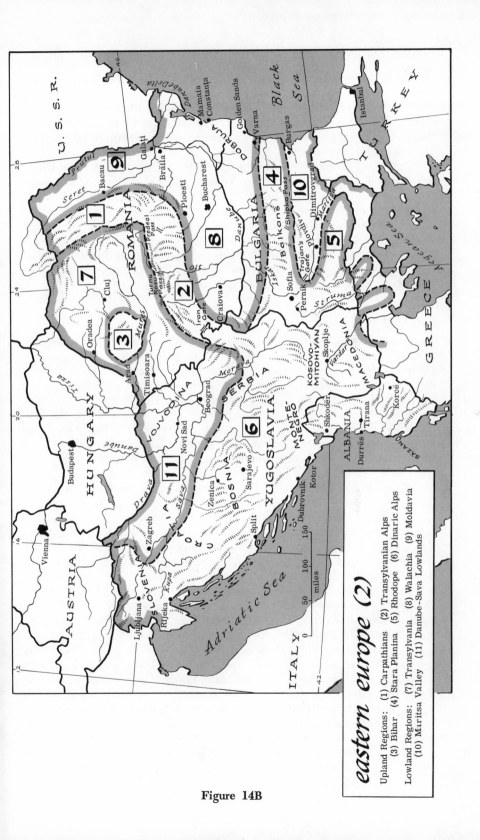

eastern europe (2)

Upland Regions: (1) Carpathians (2) Transylvanian Alps
(3) Bihar (4) Stara Planina (5) Rhodope (6) Dinaric Alps

Lowland Regions: (7) Transylvania (8) Walachia (9) Moldavia
(10) Maritsa Valley (11) Danube-Sava Lowlands

Figure 14B

and wood pulp. The country's mineral endowment is fairly varied, and like East Germany's, most of its commercial deposits are concentrated in the foothill zone of the south. The Silesian-Polish Plateau has lead and zinc, and a fairly sizable deposit of iron ore, and there are major salt mines near Krakow. The country's most important mineral resource, however, is coal, mined in the Upper Silesian field west of Krakow. Ranking as the second largest deposit of high-grade coal in Europe, the Upper Silesian field has spawned a little "Ruhr" region of its own, with several industrial cities engaged in heavy metallurgy, chemicals, and engineering clustered around Katowice. Polish coal has also been a major item of export since the war, moving largely by rail to its east bloc neighbors and to the Baltic ports of Gdansk and Szczecin. Though Poland has a minor output of petroleum from its own fields in the southeast, the Soviets have built a pipeline across the width of the country and are now supplying oil to both the Poles and the East Germans.

Czechoslovakia

Czechoslovakia's elongated east-west configuration is, like Austria's, a reflection of the alignment of its major topographic features. The western half, or Czech-speaking part, of the country is composed of two distinct regions: Bohemia, a roughly diamond-shaped area centered on the basin of the Elbe River and its tributaries and surrounded by uplands on all sides; and Moravia, the broad lowland that breaks across the center of the country along the axis of the Morava River. The eastern, or Slovak-speaking, region is dominated by the Beskid, Carpathian, and Tatra mountains, with the country's highest peak (Gerlachovka, 8711 feet) being found in the latter range.

Bohemia's boundary with Poland runs through the Sudeten Mountains, its boundary with East Germany follows the crests of the Erz Gebirge, or Ore Mountains, and its boundary with West Germany largely coincides with the water divide of the Böhmer Wald, or Bohemian Forest. All of these ranges reach elevations of 4000 to 5000 feet, are chiefly composed of crystalline rocks, and are largely in forest. The Bohemian Basin is a rolling region, varying from about 500 to 1200 feet in elevation, and its best farm lands are the rich alluvial valleys that converge in the basin's center. It was here that the region's—and the country's—greatest city arose, the venerable old religious, cultural, and commercial center of Praha (Prague), chosen as the country's capital in 1918 and now boasting a population of 1,100,000. The only other city of any size in Bohemia is the great industrial center of Plzen (Pilsen), famous not only for pilsener beer, but also as the home of the Skoda armaments works and automobile factory. In the mountains ringing Bohemia, and especially in the Ore Mountains, which take their name from the fact, are sizable deposits of a number of metallic minerals, including iron ore, copper, lead, and zinc, and also some of the more exotic ones, such as silver, gold, radium, and uranium. Indeed, Czechoslovakia is a major supplier of uranium for the Soviet Union's nuclear arsenal. Most of it comes from

Jachymov (German, Soviet Joachimsthal), which in the Middle Ages was noted for the production of silver coins called *Joachimsthaler,* from which our word "dollar" is derived.

The agriculture of the Bohemian Basin emphasizes chiefly field crops such as wheat, barley, sugar beets, hops, vegetables, and corn, while much of the sloping land is in orchards. Much the same is true in the warm and relatively dry *Moravian lowland,* which is centered on the commercial and industrial city of Brno (pop. 330,000). However, near the northern end of the valley the presence of coal has given rise to a large heavy-industrial complex focussed on the city of Ostrava (pop. 260,000).

By comparison, the rugged *Slovakian* region is largely in forest and pasture, with a greater emphasis on animal husbandry and crops such as potatoes, oats, and rye. The regional capital of Slovakia is Bratislava on the Danube, a city of 270,000, which is located in the part of Slovakia by far the most congenial to agriculture. Here, adjacent to the Vienna Basin, both corn and grapes are grown, in addition to wheat, sugar beets, and oil seeds. The bulk of Slovakia, however, is agriculturally marginal and supports the lowest population density in the country. In an effort to spur the region's economy, COMECON planners decided to utilize some local iron ores and develop a large integrated steel mill at Košice, in the eastern end of the country. The Soviet Union has also built an oil pipeline across the Carpathians, with one branch going to Hungary and another terminating in Bratislava.

Hungary

The Magyars who arrived in the Hungarian Basin in the tenth century found themselves in the westernmost tongue of grassland accessible from the Asian steppes whence they had come. Surrounded by forested mountains on every side, they settled down to the pastoral pursuits with which they were familiar. Cattle, sheep, and horse breeding remained the dominant aspect of the economy until well into the nineteenth century when the introduction of steel plows for breaking the heavy sod coincided with the growing demand for bread grains in the industrializing west of Europe. Few more congenial areas for agriculture could be imagined: broad, rolling plains, and deep chernozem soils, supplemented by the alluvium of two great rivers, the Danube and its tributary, the Tisza. Today over 60 per cent of Hungary's area is under cultivation, while its pastures and meadows have shrunk to hardly 15 per cent of the total. Among the chief crops are wheat, barley, corn, sunflowers, sugar beets, peppers, and tomatoes, and in the more rolling areas of the northern foothills there are extensive vineyards, famous for their production of Tokay wine. Large herds of cattle, sheep, and pigs are common in the drier eastern areas where the soils are sandier. These so-called *puszta* regions (the largest of which is the Hortobagy) constitute the principal grazing areas of the country today, apart from places where the animals are pastured in fallow fields.

About 15 per cent of Hungary is in forest, and these wooded areas largely correspond to the range of low mountains that strikes diagonally across the country from southwest to northeast. West of the Danube the range is known as the Bakony Forest, and it reaches its highest point (2339 feet) just back of Lake Balaton. The latter ranks as Hungary's premium resort area, and its wooded shores are lined by swank hotels and plush villas. Where the spurs of the Bakony come down to the Danube, the Romans had located their chief settlement in the region. This is now the site of Buda, the west bank section of Budapest. Buda's commanding position on the hills overlooking the Danube was an ideal defensive location, and it gradually developed as the country's political, cultural, and religious center. However, the commercial and industrial functions took hold on the east bank, where a separate city of Pest grew up, and not until the late nineteenth century, when the two were linked by bridges, did the combined city of Budapest emerge. Today, with a population of some 2,000,000, it is the only major urban center in Hungary.

East of the Danube the low mountains continue as the *Matra*. Although the Matra does contain some iron ore, the principal mineral resources of Hungary lie west of the Danube. There are large bauxite deposits in the foothills of the Bakony Forest and an oil field southwest of Lake Balaton. A range of low hills in the south of the country contains coal and also some uranium.

Industrialization had gotten off to a slow start in Hungary before the war, but since 1945 it has been greatly accelerated. To such prewar industries as food processing and textiles, heavy metallurgy and petrochemicals have now been added, especially in the Dunaujvaros area south of Budapest. With oil and iron ore coming in from the Soviet Union and coal from Poland and Czechoslovakia, Hungary has been firmly integrated into the broader regional pattern of economic development now well underway in eastern Europe.

Romania

The arc described by the *Carpathians* and the *Transylvanian Alps* through the center of Romania helps to set off the country's three main regions (see Figure 14B). Within the arc to the northwest lies the upland basin of *Transylvania*, a region composed largely of rolling, grass-covered hills. Although much of the land is in crops such as wheat, corn, and grapes, more of it is used for pasturing sheep, cattle, horses, and water buffalo. The region also contains a variety of minerals, including natural gas in the north; zinc, gold, and manganese in the west; and iron ore in the southwest. Near the sites of the latter deposits, at Hundeoara and Reşita, steel mills have been built, with coal being brought in from the foothills of the Transylvanian Alps. The latter, like the Carpathians, are mostly in forest and reach over 8000 feet elevation at their highest points. Passes through the mountains are generally lowest in the west, where the Danube breaks through in the famous Iron Gates (now the site of a great power dam), and become higher to the east and north. Thus, the Predeal

Pass (3445 feet) is about three times higher than the Turnu Roşu Pass to the west, but because of its more central location, it is the more important route.

East of the Carpathians lies the rolling lowland of *Moldavia,* a region of rich, chernozem soils devoted largely to the cultivation of wheat, corn, sugar beets, hemp, tobacco, and fruit, including grapes. Its principal mineral deposit is oil, and the main center of production is Bacau near the front of the mountains.

The plain of *Walachia,* to the south of the Transylvanian Alps, is the core area of Romania, for it occupies a strategic location athwart the lower Danube Valley. Like Moldavia, it has rich chernozem soils that are extensively used for the cultivation of wheat, corn, sugar beets, and tobacco, as well as the grazing of cattle and sheep. Adjacent to the mountains, centered on the city of Ploesti, are the largest oil fields in Europe. Pipelines carry the oil not only to the western areas of Romania and east to the port of Constanţa, but also to Bulgaria and to Odessa in the Soviet Union. Besides oil refineries, Ploesti is the site of large petrochemical industries.

At the bend of the Danube, just before it turns east into its delta, are the cities of Galati and Brǎila. A complex of heavy industries has grown up around them, thanks to their central location for the assembly of raw materials and the distribution of finished products. Iron ore is shipped in from the Ukraine and coal is brought down from the mountains by rail. Although Galati and Brǎila are Romania's principal river ports, Constanţa on the Black Sea is the country's only seaport. Oil and agricultural products constitute the bulk of its traffic. The coast on either side of Constanţa is low and sandy, and the development of swank seaside resorts has given the area the flavor of a communist-style Miami Beach.

The capital and largest city of Romania is Bucharest (Bucuresti), which today numbers 1,300,000 inhabitants. Although its site is undistinguished, it occupies a situation from which it can dominate the Walachian Plain, as well as the routeways that skirt the Carpathians into Moldavia and cross the Transylvanian Alps (through the Predeal Pass) into Transylvania. In addition to its political function, it is the country's commercial, cultural, and transportation center and has a variety of light industries, including food processing, engineering, and publishing.

Bulgaria

The south bank of the Danube—on the Bulgarian side of the river— is high and hilly, compared to the low, marshy Romanian side. These rolling hills comprise the approaches to the *Stara Planina,* the main range of the Balkan Mountains, which at their highest point reach almost 7800 feet elevation. The lower valleys are devoted to the cultivation of such crops as wheat, corn, and grapes, but the mountains themselves are in forest, especially the north-facing slopes where the evaporation rate is lower. Apart from the Isker River, which has cut a gorge through the western end of the mountains, there are no passes across the Stara

Planina below 3600 feet, and the most central pass, the Shipka, crosses at 4,376 feet, scarcely 100 feet lower than the Brenner Pass. The southern slopes of the mountains drain into the Maritsa Valley, the largest and most productive lowland of Bulgaria. Here roses are cultivated as a base for perfume oils, as well as cotton, hemp, tobacco, grapes, and cereals, including rice. Plovdiv is the region's largest market town but Dimitrovgrad, at the junction of the main east-west and north-south rail lines, has been selected as the site of some of Bulgaria's heaviest industries, including steel and chemicals. The Rhodope Mountains to the south have lead and zinc, and coal is mined on the north slopes of the Stara Planina.

Bulgaria has two ports on the Black Sea: Varna, north of the Balkan Mountains, and Burgas, to the south. The former is the larger and more important, for it has more direct connections with Sofia, the country's capital and largest city. The coast in the vicinity of the two ports is being increasingly developed as a tourist area, of which the center is the so-called Golden Sands (Zlatni Pjasăci) resort.

Though the city of Sofia is located near the far western border of Bulgaria, it nevertheless occupies the most "central" situation in the country, because several river valleys radiate out from the low mountain basin in which it is nestled. The Isker, as we noted earlier, cuts through the Balkan Mountains to the north, while the Struma Valley opens southward to the Aegean, and the Maritsa serves as the country's main east-west axis. Sofia has connection with the latter through a low pass, 'Trajan's Gate (elevation 2765 feet), and because a tributary of the Morava (not the Morava of central Czechoslovakia, but that of eastern Yugoslavia) also provides access to the northwest, the city occupies a true crossroads position. Sofia's political function is thus enhanced by the city's role as the hub of the country's transportation system, and as its chief commercial and cultural center. With a population of 800,000, Sofia also has a variety of light consumer industries. Most heavy industries in the basin are concentrated at nearby Pernik, or Dimitrovo.

Yugoslavia

No other country in Europe is as culturally diverse as Yugoslavia and few demonstrate so wide a variety of physical landscapes. As has been pointed out, the two facts are interrelated, for the rugged mountains that form the backbone of the country have divided its people into a full spectrum of linguistic and religious variations. The *Dinaric Alps* are high enough (7–8000 feet elevation) to intercept the heaviest precipitation in Eastern Europe (over 180 inches annually in some places) and to reach through the zones of Mediterranean, broadleaf, and coniferous forest into that of the Alpine meadows. In contrast, some of the eastern basins and valleys in the rain shadow are so dry that they support only a steppe-like grass cover. Soils run the gamut from thin, stony podsols in the higher mountains to deep, rich alluviums along such river valleys as the Drava, Sava, and Danube. Virtually every variety of crop grown in Europe can be found somewhere within its territory, and its mountains contain a great diversity of mineral wealth, including gold, silver, copper, lead, zinc, bauxite, mercury, iron ore, coal, and manganese. In addition there is a small oil field in the Drava Valley adjacent to Hungary. Not least important economically is its long, scenic coast fronting on the Adriatic, with its picturesque medieval cities, such as Dubrovnik and Kotor, and its many beach resorts.

The most sparsely inhabited parts of the country are the mountainous interior regions of Bosnia, Hercegovina, and Montenegro. However, the occurrence of iron ore and coal in Bosnia has led to the establishment of the country's largest steel mill at Zenica, down-valley from Sarajevo, which is the political and commercial center of the Bosnian republic. Access to the coast is difficult, and the region's orientation is decidedly down-slope to the eastern valleys. This explains why virtually the entire coastal region of Yugoslavia belongs to the Croatian republic, whose primary approach to the Adriatic is by way of the Sava and Kupa River valleys in the north. This also explains why the country's principal seaport is Rijeka, which is situated on the coast nearest to the Kupa Valley. The capital and largest city of Croatia, however, lies over the mountains to the east in the broad and productive Sava River Valley. This is Zagreb, which, with 475,000 inhabitants ranks as Yugoslavia's second city today. A communications and commercial center, it also has a variety of lighter consumer industries.

Tucked into the far northwestern corner of Yugoslavia, in the more mountainous headwaters region of the Sava, is the Slovenian republic. Its capital, Ljubljana, is also a communications hub in the upper Sava Valley, having access both southward to the coast and northward into Austria, and is the republic's commercial and cultural center. It ranks third among the cities of Yugoslavia and has a variety of industries including food processing, textiles, and woodworking and metal working.

Yugoslavia's largest and most populous constituent republic is Serbia, the core of which lies in the eastern lowland where the great rivers of the country meet the Danube. The Morava Valley forms the primary axis of Serbia, but the flat, alluvial plains surrounding the confluences of the Sava, Drava and Tisza rivers with the Danube are also part of it. The fact that a portion of the latter area is inhabited by Magyar-speaking peoples has led the Yugoslav government to set it off as an autonomous region known as Vojvodina. Similarly, an isolated mountain basin in the southwest of Serbia, which is inhabited by an Albanian-speaking group, has been granted recognition as the autonomous region of Kosovo-Mitohiyan.

Belgrade, the capital of Serbia, is also the capital of the Federal People's Republic of Yugoslavia. From its hillside site overlooking the junction of the Sava and the Danube, Belgrade is in a position to command the crossroads of the country, for here the north-south corridor of the Morava-Vardar and Tisza valleys intersects the east-west corridor of the Sava-Danube valleys. Its central location insured its growth as a communications and commercial center and also made it the most logical choice for the country's political center. Today, a sizable proportion of its 600,000 people likewise earn their living in industry, mostly of the lighter consumer variety.

Yugoslavia's southernmost region is Macedonia, an ill-defined area basically centered on the Vardar Valley. Its capital, Skopje, was severely damaged by earthquakes in 1963 but has largely been rebuilt and is again functioning as southern Yugoslavia's major communications and commercial center.

Albania

Apart from a couple of isolated peaks in the Rhodope range of southern Bulgaria, the highest mountains in Eastern Europe are those which form the border between Yugoslavia and Albania. Beyond these peaks, a half dozen good-sized rivers wind their way to the coast, combining to produce along their lower courses the most extensive lowland area on the eastern shore of the Adriatic. Though the coast itself is low and marshy, the inner valleys form the nucleus of the state of Albania. Agriculture and grazing have always been the country's main economic support, with wheat, corn, and tobacco among its major crops (although some rice is grown in the coastal lowlands) and the weaving of woolen rugs one of its chief handicraft industries. Albania is not without minerals, however, for there is a small oil field in the north, and it also produces some chrome ore. The capital, Tirana, is a city of nearly 160,000 inhabitants located inland in one of the central river valleys. It is linked by road and railway to the port of Durrës (pop. 45,000), which is located on somewhat hillier ground between two river mouths. Before the parting of their ideological ways, Albania had permitted the Soviet Union to build a submarine base on the strategic island of Sazan, but this seems to have been a casualty of their rift, along with such economic support as the U.S.S.R. was supplying.

Conclusions

Each of the East European countries is confronted by its own distinctive array of economic, social, and political problems, but because of the basic similarities of their geographic locations (as buffers between great powers lying to the east and west) and also because for the first time in their history they share the same ideologies and forms of government, they also have a number of problems in common. Among the latter, one of the more conspicuous is the consistent failure of the agricultural sector of the economy to measure up to the goals set for it by the central planners (Poland, of course, being the exception here). This phenomenon can be attributed both to the generally low priority that agriculture receives in terms of the allocation of national resources and also to the obvious diminution of incentive when the title to the land, tools, and produce all passes from the hands of the individual to the state. At the moment, Yugoslavia is engaged in an interesting experiment to demonstrate to its farmers that state-owned, state-operated farms can actually outproduce privately owned farms, and thereby guarantee the average farm worker a greater measure of security and material well-being. Whether Yugoslav peasants will be sufficiently impressed by this demonstration to give up their grumbling about collectivization remains to be seen. In any case, it should be pointed out that while the idea of collectivization might conceivably have some merit in lowlands, where farm properties are contiguous to begin with, in a mountain environment, such as that of Yugoslavia (or parts of Czechoslovakia, Romania, and Bulgaria, as well as in most of Albania) it would seem largely fruitless to attempt to draw together farms and farm laborers who are—and must be (because of soils, terrain, etc.)—geographically dispersed.

Characteristic of most communist economic planning is its pronounced emphasis on industrialization. There can be little doubt that the rapid strides that Eastern Europe has made in industrialization since the end of World War II are unlikely to have been made under the free enterprise system, because no capitalist country would so singlemindedly invest its energies to that end. Nor would any capitalist country so consciously restrain the development of its consumer goods industries, while devoting the lion's share of its investment to the production of capital goods. In other words, what Eastern Europe has achieved in the last twenty years has been accomplished by an enforced degree of discipline that "free" societies seldom attain, even in times of national emergency.

As one examines the industrial scene in Eastern Europe today, the signs are unmistakable that the first "great push"—the development of basic industries under forced draft—is now reaching its final stages, and that the long-suffering consumer will at last have his day. Inevitably, this will mean that the consumer will decide what kind of clothes, shoes, or appliances he wants, and not some central planner; thus quality and style will become the primary determinants of consumption and not availability, as heretofore. Gone are the days when Bulgarian raincoats will be offered to the prospective customer with arms of differing lengths and the buttons sewed on the back—just because production quotas had to be met! To be sure, the East European consumer will not get all that he wants exactly the *way* he wants it for some time to come, but there are hopeful signs that his patience will soon be rewarded.

Lest the mistaken impression arise that the East European consumer has been unhappy all this time because the state has been discriminating against him, it should be pointed out that, by and large, the peoples of East Europe have never been as prosperous as they have during the last decades. Some of these countries have experienced responsible government—a government that cared enough about its people to do something for *them*—for the first time in their histories. Remote rural villages have been provided with safe drinking water, the main streets have been paved, and street lighting has been installed. Schools have been built, working conditions improved, and housing standards sharply upgraded, though much yet remains to be done in all these areas. Improved medical facilities have materially lowered infant mortality rates, but here too, there is a long way still to go before West European levels are reached.

And, whether the East European peoples are enamoured of their governments or not, they can be fairly certain that their officials are, in their own way, accountable to them and that graft and corruption is probably at the lowest level it ever has been in most of these countries.

Obviously, the well-being of the East Europeans is relative. Relative to that of West Europeans, it is not so impressive; relative to what they knew before, for most of these peoples, it is very impressive. But in their striving to improve their well-being, the East Europeans have manifested some very "capitalistic" (or are they merely human?) characteristics. Among younger married couples, both the man and wife will take jobs, and postpone having a family, thereby also limiting its possible size, in order to save enough money for a larger apartment, a television set, a cottage in the country, or a small car. Such "materialist" drives have seriously thrown off the population projections of the central planners, and in some countries, notably Hungary and East Germany, the population is not even reproducing itself. Will raising wages (so only one member of a family need work) be the answer, or will that just heighten the pressures of pent-up consumer demand? This is merely one of the interesting, and vital, side effects that the rising affluence of the east bloc countries is having on their economic evolution.

Some of the political changes afoot in East Europe, especially the tendency to challenge the wisdom of officials, if not of the official policies themselves, has already been noted. This can hardly be construed as synonymous with any great measure of freedom, but in communist society it still constitutes something of a landmark. And, as the relative affluence of Eastern Europe continues to grow, not only will internal antagonisms against the state lessen, but the whole character of the communist movement is bound to mellow. Khrushchev was quite right when he told the Hungarians that "What this world needs is more goulash"; but what he doubtless failed to realize was that once you fill hungry peoples' stomachs, it is difficult to convince them to get out and militantly wave the Red flag. The greater success that communism has in achieving its goals the less likely its success will be in attempting to export it to other areas by force of arms. For the first time in their history, the peoples of Eastern Europe have been unified—unified by an ideology imposed on them from the outside, largely without their consent, but an ideology, which in achieving its goals, is ultimately self-defeating. Given the peace to attain prosperity, Eastern Europe can only use its prosperity to perpetuate peace.

Within the framework of its unifying ideology, Eastern Europe has managed to work together on a regional economic scale to a degree scarcely conceivable before the war. COMECON has clearly not worked out as the Russians anticipated; by exporting raw materials to its East European satellites and buying back finished manufactured goods, Russia has run into a serious balance of payments problem itself. Some trading partners, notably the Poles, are pressing for more payments in gold rather than in rubles, so that a greater volume of trade can be developed with the West. (The Poles have enough nonconvertible rubles on hand, and Russian industry is hardly prepared to meet the Polish consumer demand,

much less its own, so Poland is at a loss to know where to spend them.)
If more West European industrial firms sign contracts with East European governments, and the tide of West European tourists to these countries continues to swell, the more quickly the myth of the "Iron Curtain"
will vanish.

The unifying ideology of communism in Eastern Europe has also set
the stage for an era of political cooperation between these states that in a
sense has put them on their best behavior. Since it is a basic tenet of
communism that only capitalist states wage wars amongst themselves,
and that within the "rational" brotherhood of communism, war between
their countries is unthinkable, one wonders how much such dogma has
contributed to the peaceful adjustment of boundary and minority problems within the region since World War II. A case in point is Romania's
recognition of the Magyar-speaking Szekelis as an autonomous group,
an issue that was long a point of serious friction with Hungary. Whether
the same reasonable spirit will be evidenced in Bulgaria's claim against
Yugoslavia regarding Macedonia is yet to be seen. Moreover, although
Marshal Tito is publicly on record as having denounced Albania as "the
little trouble-maker of the Balkans," it is doubtful that he, or any other
Communist, will ever find cause to attack Mao Tse-tung's sole non-Asian
puppet.

On the other hand, the Soviet Union's occupation of Czechoslovakia
in August, 1968 not only raised anew the specter of "militant communism"
in many western eyes, but it also had grave repercussions within the communist world itself. What Russia had failed to achieve by reason at con-
ferences in Cierna and Bratislava it felt it must achieve by tanks in the
streets of Prague. Yet, how hollow and Pyrrhic a victory it won, time
alone will reveal. Motivated by its obsession with the growing economic
and political influence of West Germany, especially in one of its key
satellites, the Soviet Union, in its desperate quest for security, only
managed to heighten the sense of insecurity in Western and Eastern
Europe alike.

Thus, Eastern Europe's only cause for political disquietude regarding the future remains the "German question," and the Soviet Union's
reaction to it. As explained earlier, as long as Germany's own economy
prospers, one has little reason to look for trouble from that quarter. But
many East Europeans, especially Poles, would rest more comfortably if
a straightforward answer were forthcoming to the inquiry the Polish
foreign minister has repeated at every regular session of the United Nations since its founding: "Will the United Nations guarantee the western
frontiers of Poland?" As long as he is met with silence, doubts are bound
to remain. Nor has the same foreign minister's plan for a neutralized Central Europe ever been considered seriously in the West. In that, Comrade
Rapacki has proposed that both West and East Germany, his own country, and Czechoslovakia be declared a neutral zone, and all foreign
military bases and personnel be withdrawn. For Poles, this solution would
not only remove the German threat, but would require the Soviet Union
to loosen its grip over Poland. Seen through Western eyes, the Rapacki
plan seems to represent an unfair bargain, for the importance of West

Germany to NATO is far greater than that of East Germany, Poland, and Czechoslovakia to the Warsaw Pact. When and if the time ever comes that Moscow finds it in its interest to permit the reunification of Germany —in other words, the surrender of the East to the West—we may be certain that the price will be high. But inasmuch as no solution to the German question is yet in sight, it behooves the east bloc to hold their East German hostage a while longer. It is also apparent, however, that it is in the interests of the Soviet Union to keep the fear of a German threat alive as long as possible, for the day this disappears, Soviet hegemony over Eastern Europe will quickly begin to crumble. Clearly, the rapid strides toward rapprochement taken by Willy Brandt's government (including the signing of a nonaggression treaty with Moscow and preliminary discussions with the Poles on the Oder-Neisse boundary) are already taking the backbone out of the Soviet argument, and one seriously wonders how long the Soviet's East European brotherhood can be held together by raising the spectre of more distant 'threats' such as the United States and China.

Table 5.   The Eastern Crush-Zone, Selected Statistics (1968)

	Poland	Czechoslovakia	Hungary	Romania	Bulgaria	Yugoslavia	Albania
Area (000's sq. mi.)	120.4	49.4	35.9	91.7	42.8	98.8	11.1
Population (millions)	32.5	14.4	10.3	20.0	8.4	20.4	
Birth rate (per 1000)	16.3	15.6	14.5	27.1	15.0	19.5	
Death rate (per 1000)	7.7	10.0	10.7	9.3	9.0	8.7	
Natural increase (per 1000)		5.6	3.8	17.8	6.0	10.8	
Infant mortality (per 1000)		23.7	38.4	46.8	33.1	61.3	
Land use (%):							
Cultivated	51.1	40.0	60.6	44.2	41.2	32.6	
Meadows-pastures	13.4	14.2	14.4	17.9	10.8	25.1	
Forest	25.5	35.3	15.1	26.9	32.5	34.0	
Other land	9.9	12.1	9.9	11.0	15.4	8.3	
Population density per sq. mi cultivated land	540	700	480	500	480	640	
Gross national product per capita	$730	$1,010	$800	$650	$620	$570	
Exports (millions)	$2,527	$3,031	$1,702	$1,469	$1,458	$1,264	$60
Imports (millions)	$2,654	$2,680	$1,776	$1,609	$1,572	$1,797	$98
Trade balance (millions)	−$118	+$333	−$74	−$140	−$114	−$533	−$38

See Table 1, p. 54, for sources.

CHAPTER 7

the northern frontier

By virtue of its having been the center from which the great glacial ice sheets emanated, Northern Europe was the last major region of the subcontinent to be occupied by man. By virtue of its out-of-the-way location, it was also the last major region to be reached by the innovations of agriculture and stock raising, as well as (much later) by Christianity. Although it was a region dimly known to the Romans, its contacts with their classical civilization were marginal at best. In no part of Europe, save perhaps the higher areas of the Alps, had man found himself in a more challenging environment, for he discovered that one after another the crops he had come to depend on for the sustenance of civilized society gave way to the onslaught of cold as they reached the northern limits of their cultivation. It was here on the northern frontiers of Europe that civilized man made his first, and perhaps his most enduring, penetration of the sub-Arctic.

History, in the sense of a written record, did not really begin in Northern Europe much before the year 800 A.D. Before that time, the story of the Scandinavian peoples must be read chiefly from archeological remains. However, about the end of the eighth century, sleek square-sailed ships adorned with dragon's head and manned by fierce blue-eyed, blond barbarians began raiding the coasts of England, Scotland, and the Low Countries. These raiders, coming out of the general area of the Skagerrak and Kattegat—an arm of the North Sea known to them as Viken ("the bay")—at first confined their forays to the summer, usually returning home with their loot and captives to spend the winter. However, as they ranged farther afield and discovered how completely the mere mention of their coming demoralized the inhabitants of Latin Christendom, the more they were tempted to remain in these more attractive climes and appropriate the riches of the land. (During this time, the Lord's Prayer was usually recited with an additional petition, "Deliver us from the fury of the Northmen!") Danish and Norwegian Vikings ranged up and down the coasts of western Europe, attacking any city accessible to their shallow draft vessels: London, Paris, Lisbon, Seville, and on into the Mediterranean, where they held Sicily and some of the Balearic Islands for a time. In the east, Swedish Vikings, coming chiefly from *Roslagen* (literally "the district of the Ros people"), an area north of Stockholm, moved across the Baltic into the coastal areas of present-day Finland (where Swedes are still referred to as *Ruotsi*), Estonia, Latvia, and Lithuania and up the rivers of western Russia. Portaging from one stream to another, they floated down the Volga to the Caspian Sea, on the shores of which they traded with the Persians, and down the Dnepr to the Black Sea and on to Constantinople. In fact, after they had attacked Constantinople several times, the Metropolitan (the head of the Eastern Church) decided it would be cheaper to put them on the payroll, and for several centuries Swedish Vikings constituted the core of the elite Varangian Guard. In the interior of Russia itself, the Swedes founded several trading posts, some of which later grew into towns, among them Novgorod in the north and Kiev in the south. To them, this vast country was known as *Det stora svithjod,* or "Greater Sweden," but to the local inhabitants it gradually became known as *Russia,* "the land of the Ros."

What initiated this outburst of northern peoples has been variously explained as overpopulation with respect to the level of technology then prevailing; political disaffection, especially in Norway; and sheer love of adventure. In any event, what ended it was the slow but inexorable conversion of the Scandinavians to Christianity—a process largely completed in Denmark by the tenth century A.D., in Norway and Iceland in the year 1000, and in Sweden in the twelfth century, making it the last great nation in Europe to bow to the authority of Rome. Once Christianized, however, the Swedes felt impelled to carry the gospel to Finland, and the "crusade" they launched in 1154 did not end until the latter country had been firmly annexed to the Swedish crown.

Norway's orientation toward the Atlantic quite naturally focused its ambitions of statehood to the west, and shortly after the middle of the thirteenth century all the far-flung areas occupied by Norwegian Vikings had given their allegiance to the Norwegian king, including the Shetlands, Orkneys, Faeroes, Iceland, and Greenland. Denmark, on the other hand, looked east to the Baltic, where it soon ran afoul of Swedish ambitions in the same region. However, all three countries found themselves challenged by the Hanse, with Norway and Sweden coming under its sway first and Denmark coming to terms with it later. Indeed, for a time it looked as though Denmark would emerge as the region's dominant political power, for following the extinction of Norway's royal family in 1380, that country and all its Atlantic dependencies were joined to Denmark. By 1397, Danish control over Sweden had grown to such a point that the Kalmar Union was proclaimed, signaling the first and only time in the history of Scandinavia that the three states were politically united.

Gradually, however, the economic growth of Sweden—particularly of its mining and forest industries—led to an increasing divergence in the interests of the two countries and in 1523, Sweden broke away from Denmark. From then on, there was almost an incessant struggle between the two for mastery of the Baltic. By 1660, Swedish power had succeeded in driving the Danes off the Swedish mainland in the south (the provinces of Skåne, Blekinge and Halland having always been an integral part of Denmark until then) and in converting the Baltic into virtually a "Swedish lake." Shortly thereafter, however, the rise of Russia under Peter the Great spelled the beginning of the end for Sweden's role as a great power. One after another her trans-Baltic possessions were plucked away from her until finally, in 1809, the crowning blow came with the loss of Finland to the Russians. Seeking to salvage something out of the chaos of Napoleonic Europe, Sweden belatedly joined the war against Denmark, which had allied itself to the French emperor, and demanded and received Norway as its prize in 1814. But, within less than a century, Norway's own economic development had caused its interests to diverge so widely from those of Sweden that it proclaimed its independence in 1905. During the chaos of the Bolshevik Revolution Finland managed to shake itself free of czarist Russia, and in 1944 the political evolution of the North was completed with the abrogation of the union between Denmark and Iceland, the latter country regaining its sovereignty for the first time since 1262. (However, World War II had other, less desirable consequences within Northern Europe as well, for Finland was attacked by the Soviet Union in 1939 and forced to cede the latter some territory for the defense of Leningrad; in 1940 Denmark and Norway were occupied by the Nazis; in 1941 Finland joined Hitler against the Russians, but was forced to sign a separate peace treaty in 1944, with large reparations now added to the territorial cessions. Because Iceland had been occupied first by the British and later by the Americans, only Sweden escaped direct involvement in the war.)

Within Northern Europe today, it is literally possible to see the boundaries of the successive waves of economic innovation that have spread over the region since the arrival of man. The first and most primitive form of economic activity was hunting and fishing, which is now practiced commercially, in those areas which lie beyond the physical limits of agriculture, chiefly in North Norway and in Iceland. Where the climate, soil, or vegetation have permitted a more advanced form of land use, animal husbandry is carried on in the marginal areas, and crop farming becomes the primary emphasis of agriculture only in those southern lowlands with the most congenial combination of physical factors. However, even the practice of animal husbandry reveals a hierarchical adjustment to the environment, with domesticated reindeer being pastured on the low, alpine plant forms of the far north, goats and sheep inheriting the poorer mountain pastures of the south, and cattle becoming the dominant form of livestock in the lusher meadows of the southern valleys and lowlands. Obviously, the innovation of industrialization has not been restricted by such factors as climate, soils, and vegetation as have animal husbandry and farming, at least to nowhere near the same degree; but the fact remains that any primarily market-oriented manufacturing enterprise automatically finds itself in the more densely populated southern areas of the region, where communications and commerce are also the most highly developed. Perhaps of all the northern countries, Norway exemplifies this transition from fishing through animal husbandry and crop farming to industry best of all, for it embraces the widest range of environmental settings.

From Denmark through Sweden, Finland, and Norway to Iceland, one can also see an interesting pattern of transition in architectural styles and building materials. In Denmark and the adjacent areas of southern Sweden, broadleaf deciduous forests, in which the beech and oak are common, are the prevailing vegetation type; therefore, as in western and central Europe, these areas are characterized by half-timbered houses in which brick and fieldstone constitute the chief construction materials. The houses and barns are all under one roof, forming an enclosed square around a source of water. As one gets into the mixed forest region of southern Sweden, one finds a combined use of wood, brick, and stone, but there, because of the colder winters and the increased danger of fire, the house and outbuildings are somewhat separated, but still usually grouped around a central courtyard. Farther north, where wood becomes all-important (and fire a potential hazard), houses and outbuildings are detached and more widely separated, with no attempt to group them in any set pattern. Virtually every function is allocated to a separate structure, of which there may be as many as twenty or thirty.

When the Vikings moved to Iceland, it was just as though they had moved above the treeline in the mountains of Norway, for there the highest forms of plant life were scrub birch trees, willows, and mountain ash. The only real source of construction timber that the island possessed was the driftwood rafted into its northern and eastern coasts by currents coming out of the Arctic Ocean from Siberia. As a result, the original houses in Iceland consisted of sod, with the scarce timber used only where necessary for doors, rafters, and window frames. Since fuel wood was also in short supply, heat had to be conserved in every way possible. Usually only the so-called *badhstofa*, or bathing room, was heated, and the sleeping areas were immediately above the cattle pens, so that the warmth of the animals' bodies could be utilized to the best advantage. With wood such a precious commodity, it can perhaps be understood why Iceland was willing to give up its independence and acknowledge the King of Norway as its sovereign in 1262 in return for the promise of one shipload of timber a year!

In the urban centers of Northern Europe the use of wood as a building material frequently had disastrous consequences, for in these congested areas the spread of fire was extremely rapid. Most Scandinavian cities experienced repeated conflagrations, one of the most recent wiping out the center of the Norwegian west coast port of Bergen in 1916. As a result, "urban renewal" was an oft-recurring phenomenon until more substantial building materials were made mandatory. Consequently, few Scandinavian cities have preserved much of their medieval character.

Although the mineral endowment of Northern Europe is fairly varied, there is a notable lack of fossil fuels in all the countries. The absence of coal meant that industrialization in the north begain late and proceeded slowly—so slowly that many a nineteenth century Scandinavian felt he had as little prospect of making a decent living as many a contemporary Irishman. The good farmlands had long since been occupied, and by law they could not be further subdivided. Therefore, a young rural person either became a hired hand on an existing farm or left. Since there were few industrial jobs to employ these surplus rural folk, leaving meant going to America. Out-migration began in Norway in the 1820's, Denmark in the 1840's, Sweden in the late 1860's, and Finland in the late 1880's. At its peak in the 1880's, the exodus to America was viewed as a national calamity in most of the countries, the numbers leaving were greater in proportion to their total populations than in any other European nation, save Ireland. By 1920, some 300,000 Danes, 800,000 Norwegians and 1,200,000 Swedes had left. In retrospect, however, it can now be seen that this wave of out-migration served as a safety-valve in releasing these countries from a burden of surplus population just as the Industrial Revolution was dawning for them. As a result, the pace of economic growth has been more rapid and it has proceeded much further than it could have had they remained at home, simply because there have been fewer people among whom to divide the pie.

Denmark

Within the area of present-day Denmark, even early man could distinguish two distinct regions (see Figure 15). To him, they were seen in the obvious differences of vegetation: extensive, open heathlands in the west of the peninsula of Jutland, as opposed to the heavy forests of beech and oak that clothed the rest of the country. It was not until the advent of agriculture, however, that man became aware of the subtler distinction between these two regions—the soil. Then he discovered that the Heath of Jutland was composed of virtually sterile sands (the outwash materials from the last advance of the glacier), while the remainder of Denmark consisted of deep loamy soils rich in lime (the rolling, morainic deposits of the last glaciation). The lime had come from the great chalk beds that underlie much of the country and that outcrop in spectacular cliffs in the east of the island of Møn, among other places. Through the centuries, therefore, virtually all of the great beech and oak woods were removed to make way for fields and pastures, while the barren heath remained a rough grazing land.

The agriculture was mixed farming, by means of which the Danish peasant produced as great a variety of crops and livestock products as he could to insure self-sufficiency. This meant the cultivation of wheat and rye for bread grains, oats and hay for his livestock, and barley for making his beer. However, early in the second half of the nineteenth century, this age-old pattern of farming received a couple of rude jolts. One came from Denmark's defeat at the hands of Bismarck and the Germans in

northern europe

Norway: (1) North Norway (2) Tröndelag (3) West Country (4) East Country

Sweden: (5) Norrland (6) Central Swedish Lowland (7) South Swedish Highland
(8) Skåne Lowland (9) Baltic Islands

Denmark: (10) Eastern Morainelands   (11) Heath of Jutland

Finland: (12) Coastal Plain   (13) Lake Plateau   (14) Lappland

Iceland: (15) West Basalt Region (16) Southern Lowlands   (17) Central Plateau
(18) East Basalt Region

Figure 15

1864, for the terms of the peace treaty that followed it forced Denmark to surrender about one-third of its area and crop land (the old provinces of Schlesvig-Holstein, as well as the base of the peninsula of Jutland as far north as Kolding). This increased the population pressure on the remaining farm land of Denmark and led to the formation of the so-called "Heath Society," which proceeded to initiate the reclamation of the still largely barren region of western Jutland.

Another jolt, which was to have even wider repercussions in Danish agriculture, was the realization that the prairies of the American Great Plains and the steppes of the Ukraine could produce grain more cheaply than the Danish farmers could market it themselves. It soon became clear that general farming would not be able to meet the competition of foreign areas, and that Denmark itself must specialize in that form of agricultural production for which she was geographically most suited. Because of Denmark's relatively cool, damp climate and short growing season, the natural choice seemed to be animal husbandry; and since the 1880's, Danish agriculture has increasingly specialized in the production of livestock products—milk, butter, cheese, eggs, and meat.

Helping to effect this radical economic and social transformation have been the so-called "peoples' high schools," which gave instruction in scientific farming practices and management, and the development of the cooperative movement. The latter made it possible for groups of Danish farmers to pool their limited resources and to purchase collectively the fertilizer, seeds, and machinery they needed. Producer cooperatives were also formed to oversee efficiently the inspection, grading, and marketing of agricultural products. Illustrative of the degree to which this specialization has proceeded is the fact that Danish agricultural scientists have produced a "streamlined pig" having a bare minimum of waste, and that the inspection and control system is so elaborate that if an English housewife complains that she got a "bad" Danish egg, it can literally be traced right back to the farm whence it came and to the chicken that laid it! To some, these may seem like extreme lengths to which to go to insure peak productivity and performance, but for a country with little else than its soil as a resource, Denmark has every reason to want to assure its reputation as a producer of quality farm products.

Not only have the changes of the last century given Danish agriculture a new orientation, but, in a sense, they have also given the country a new geographic orientation. The formerly barren heath of Jutland has largely been taken under cultivation, and even those areas too poor to grow crops now support extensive plantations of conifers. Furthermore, to expedite its export trade with Britain—a principal buyer of Danish foodstuffs—Denmark laid the foundations for a new seaport on the west coast of Jutland in 1868. The resultant city of Esbjerg is now the fourth largest in the country. In addition to its export functions, it has likewise become the country's leading fishing port, inasmuch as most of the latter activity is concentrated in the North Sea. Before the founding of Esbjerg, the lack of good harbors on the west coast of Jutland meant that Skagen, at the peninsula's northern tip, provided the closest sheltered anchorage to the fishing grounds; even now it ranks as the country's second most important fishing port.

Denmark's mineral endowment is not particularly diverse, but it has given rise to several specialized industries. The chalk and clay deposits that occur in close proximity in the northeastern areas of Jutland have encouraged the development of several large cement plants in the Aalborg region. Danish specialization in the making and use of cement is reflected in the fact that the Danes not only manufacture and export much of the heavy machinery for this industry but also "export" their engineering skills for building dams, bridges, and highways in many parts of the world. The northern half of the island of Bornholm is the only part of Denmark where crystalline rock is exposed. As a result, the granites of this area have long been used to pave the streets of Danish cities and the kaolin deposit which occurs within them has given rise to an important production of both quality and utility porcelain.

The industries that have developed within Denmark are totally dependent on imported energy, for the country has no coal, oil, or hydroelectric potential. As a result, port cities have been the favored sites for industry, because of their access to incoming fuel and raw materials. Food processing, textiles, and other light consumer industries predominate, but metal working, engineering, and shipbuilding are also found in some of the larger cities. Indeed, Denmark's largest single industrial enterprise is the Burmeister and Wain shipyard in Copenhagen. This firm bought the patent for the diesel engine from its inventor and launched the first ocean-going motor ship in the world in 1912. Since that time, Denmark has built motor ships not only for its own sizable merchant fleet, but also under contract to foreign countries.

In 1967, Copenhagen celebrated the 800th anniversary of its founding. Starting as a small fishing harbor ("havn") on the shores of the Öresund, it attracted an increasing volume of commerce after a castle was built there in 1167, and gradually became known as "the merchants' harbor," from which title its present name, København, is derived. Because of its strategic location at the entrance to the Baltic Sea, it soon aroused the envy of the Hanse, especially Lübeck, which sent one expedition after another to destroy it. But Copenhagen occupied too vital a situation not to spring back, and in the fifteenth century its importance was enhanced by its being made the capital of Denmark and the seat of the country's first university. As Denmark's commercial, political, and cultural center, it quickly outpaced other Danish towns, and the advent of industry in the nineteenth century spurred its growth even further. Today Copenhagen, with its population of 1,200,000, is the largest city not only in Denmark but in all of Northern Europe. To its strategic location on the water route between the North and Baltic seas can now be added its role as a major land and air gateway to Scandinavia from the rest of Europe. Truly, Denmark is the "crossroads of Northern Europe," and Copenhagen is right on the main intersection!

Sweden

THE REGIONS OF SWEDEN. To the earliest Danish settlers, the Öresund was just another channel between the country's many scattered islands, and not the widest one at that. To them, the land on its eastern shore looked no different than that to the west, and indeed it wasn't, for it too was composed of rolling, lime-rich morainic soils covered by dense forests of beech and oak. However, farther inland to the north and east they encountered rocky hills dotted with lakes and swamps; thin, sandy soils supported a mixed forest of conifers and birch, with only a scattering of beech and oak. The differences they discovered were ultimately the differences that make the regional personality of the so-called *Skåne Lowland* (taken from the name of Sweden's southernmost province) and that of the South Swedish Highland so distinct. The former is Sweden's primary agricultural region, for in addition to its lowland terrain and rich soils, it also has the longest and warmest growing season in the country. Here, much of Sweden's wheat, vegetables, and oil seeds are produced, as well as most of her sugar beets. But, as in Denmark, even here the primary emphasis is on livestock products, such as milk and meat. Skåne's commercial and industrial center is the city of Malmö (pop. 250,000), the third largest in Sweden.

The *South Swedish Highland*, on the other hand, owing to its ancient crystalline bedrock and higher elevation, has some of the country's poorest soils and a relatively cool, damp climate with a short growing season. As a result, it has remained largely in forest, and the farms found within the region are mostly small and marginal. Hay, oats, rye, and potatoes are the chief crops here, and there is an even greater emphasis on dairying. The mixed forests provide raw materials for a variety of wood-working industries, including matches, furniture, and carpentry goods. The sterile sands, especially of the southeast, also provided the original raw material for the Swedish glass industry, centered in such places as Kosta and Orrefors. Today, however, the famous Swedish crystal is made primarily of white beach sands imported from the Netherlands.

The South Swedish Highland long served as a buffer between the Danes in the south and the Swedes, whose original core area lay in the eastern end of the *Central Swedish Lowland.* The latter is a structural depression that breaks across the country from the Kattegat to the Baltic, and which in early postglacial times was occupied by an interconnecting channel between the two water bodies. Today the region is occupied by four large lakes: Vänern, Vättern, Hjälmaren, and Mälaren, but the intervening clay lowlands constitute Sweden's second most important agricultural region. The moister western half of the lowland is largely in hay and fodder crops, whereas the drier eastern half is mostly in cereals.

The main religious center of Viking Sweden was Uppsala, on an arm of Lake Mälaren. Because of the close association of temporal and religious authority, Uppsala was also, in effect, the country's capital. It was chosen, as the site of the archepiscopal see of Sweden by the Church and also became the seat of the country's first university. Its political function, however, gradually devolved upon Stockholm, which had been founded about the middle of the thirteenth century to guard the entrance to the Mälaren from the incursions of Wendish pirates. Indeed, its name comes from the fact that logs (Swedish *stokk*) were chained together between the small rocky islands (Swedish *holm*) to prevent the passage of pirate ships. Stockholm owed its early commercial importance to the export of iron and copper from the *Bergslagen,* a mining district about 100 miles to the northwest. Today, in addition to its political and commercial functions, it is Sweden's largest industrial center and the hub of the country's communications system. Among its diversified industries are food processing, textiles and apparel, engineering, electrical machinery and apparatus, and publishing. A city of 800,000, Stockholm has long since spilled over onto the mainland, to both the north and south of its original island site.

Scattered over the *Central Swedish Lowland* to the south and west of Stockholm are a number of other industrial centers, such as Västerås, which produces high-voltage electrical machinery; Eskilstuna, with its tools, cutlery, and hardware; and Linköping, with its aircraft and automobile factories. At the western end of the Lowland, at the mouth of the Göta River, lies Göteborg, Sweden's principal seaport and second largest city (pop. 425,000). Founded as a fortified "window to the west," Göteborg (from Swedish *borg* "castle") not only handles the bulk of Sweden's export trade and much of its imports, but is also an industrial center in its own right. Sweden's automated shipyards have helped to make it the second largest shipbuilding country in the world, and Göteborg is also the home of SKF, internationally known as a producer of ball bearings, and of Volvo automobiles.

North of the Central Swedish Lowland lies *Norrland,* a vast region of ancient crystalline rock mantled with morainic soils and clothed in a dense and almost unbroken stand of spruce and pine. Although Norrland comprises nearly two-thirds of the total area of Sweden, it contains scarcely one-fifth of the country's people. Its southern edge, the Bergslagen, gave rise to a cluster of mining towns early in the Middle Ages, thanks to its deposits of iron ore, copper, and silver. Indeed, it was the wealth of the Bergslagen that financed Sweden's short but dramatic career as Northern Europe's "great power." Today Bergslagen iron ores not only provide the basis for Sweden's production of high quality special steels, but also form a major item of export, moving into commerce through the port of Oxelösund, south of Stockholm.

Over most of Norrland, it is the forest that makes the largest contribution to the region's, and the nation's, economy. Logs are floated down the many large rivers of Norrland to great sawmills and pulp and paper factories at their mouths. Towns such as Karlstad on Lake Vänern, and Gävle, Umeå and Sundsvall on the Gulf of Bothnia owe their existence primarily to such wood industries. Indeed, Sundsvall, thanks to the fact that it can tap the hinterland of three large rivers, ranks as one of the largest wood processing and exporting centers in the world.

The rivers of Norrland are not only used for floating logs, however. Most of them come down off the old crystalline shield area in a series of rapids and waterfalls, so Norrland is responsible for generating over 80 per cent of all the hydroelectric power in Sweden. Because these power sites are so remote from the cities and industries where the electricity is to be used, the Swedes have had to build some of the longest high-tension transmission lines in the world to link them together.

In the north of Norrland, Sweden has two other important mineralized areas. One lies along the Skellefte River and has its main center at Boliden. At a concentrating plant in Boliden, the polymetallic ores of the district are separated into their constituent metals, among them lead, zinc, copper, silver, and gold—no one of them present in commercial quantities by itself, but profitable to exploit only because they all occur together. The enterprise has one unfortunate by-product, however: arsenic, of which Sweden ranks as the world's largest producer. The demand for arsenic being rather limited, the Swedes have to stockpile most of it in an immense warehouse on the coast.

The other great mineral district of northern Norrland is the great iron mining area of Lappland. Here, some of the world's largest deposits of high-grade iron ore are located, and the mining centers of Kiruna and Gällivare have grown up to exploit them. Although the reserves were already known to be vast, in 1967 it was announced that further ore bodies had been discovered that will more than double the longevity of the industry at the present rate of production. Although the Lappland ores were known to exist as far back as the seventeenth century, they could not be commercially exploited until they were made accessible to transportation. This was accomplished through the building of Sweden's first electrified railway in 1903, a line that still has the distinction of carrying the heaviest volume of traffic of any railroad in Northern Europe. Because the northern end of the Gulf of Bothnia is closed by ice from 6 to 7 months of the year, however, the Swedish port of Luleå can be used only in the summer. However, by sending the iron ore north and west over the mountains, the Swedes were able to reach a warm-water harbor in Norway, and this quickly grew into the town of Narvik.

A Swedish region both far removed in distance and in character from Norrland is that composed of *the Baltic islands* of Gotland and Öland. Both islands essentially consist of tabular limestones and sandstones, and because of their porosity, they have no surface drainage to speak of. Moreover, lying on the east side of Sweden they are already climatically dry. (Gotland, in fact, boasts the sunniest climate in Europe north of the Alps.) Therefore, the islands support an almost steppe-like grass cover, dotted here and there with clumps of pines. Where the soils are deep enough to permit cultivation, wheat and sugar beets are grown, but much of the land is used for grazing sheep. Because of Gotland's strategic location near the center of the Baltic, it was long a center of commerce, and its chief city, Visby, once ranked as the busiest seaport in northern Europe. However, after being sacked by the Danes in 1361, Visby never revived, and it sleeps today amidst its picturesque ivy and rose-covered walls.

Finland

THE REGIONS OF FINLAND. The Finland that the Swedish "crusaders" invaded in the middle of the twelfth century was a land of forest-dwelling tribes, who lived chiefly from hunting and fishing but also practiced rudimentary forms of stock raising and farming. Though they had come ostensibly to Christianize the Finns, the Swedes stayed to subjugate and exploit them as well. They built their first church (later to become a cathedral) and fortress on the banks of the Aura River in the southwest of the country, and around this a settlement gradually grew up, which the Swedes called Åbo (literally "river settlement"). To the Finns, however, it became known as Turku, from the Swedish word *torg*, meaning "market place." When this district was firmly in hand, the Swedes launched their second campaign against the tribes of the interior, a group they called the Tavasts and who called themselves the Häme. Here they built a second fortified point known as "the fortress of the Tavasts"— Tavastehus or Hämeelinna. Finally, late in the fourteenth century a third campaign subdued the Karelians in the east, and there the fortress of Vyborg, or Viipuri, was founded. Thus, the Swedes initiated the urbanization and commercialization of Finland, as well as Christianizing the country and profoundly influencing its ethnic and linguistic development.

Turku was made the Swedish capital of Finland, and because its dialect was used in the translation of the Bible, this became the national standard of the Finnish language. Turku also became the seat of the country's first university, so its commercial, political, religious, and cultural functions assured its preeminence as the country's largest city throughout the Swedish period of occupation. After the Russians took over, however, they felt that Turku was too close to Sweden, so in 1812 they transferred the seat of government to Helsinki, where a more watchful eye could be kept on it from St. Petersburg. A conflagration in Turku in 1827 gave them further excuse to move the university to Helsinki, and when the railway age dawned, it was natural that the new capital should become the center of the country's transportation network as well. (Because the railway age dawned while Finland was a part of czarist Russia, all of its main lines were built with the broad Russian gauge, so Finland today can interchange rail traffic directly only with the Soviet Union.) Within a few decades Helsinki edged ahead of Turku in population and today, as the country's chief seaport and industrial center, in addition to its other functions, it numbers some 615,000 inhabitants, suburbs included. Turku's population of 140,000 has just recently been exceeded by that of Tampere, an industrial town in the southwestern interior founded on one of Finland's largest water power sites. Starting with cotton textiles, Tampere has since branched out into metal working, engineering, and a host of consumer industries as well.

The Swedish settlers that flocked into Finland following the "crusade" quite naturally appropriated the best clay lowlands (the *Coastal Plain*) along the coasts of the Gulf of Bothnia and the Gulf of Finland for themselves. The Finns, in turn, were pushed into the morainic soils of the *Lake Plateau* region of the interior. This resulted not only in a geographic separation of the two peoples, but in economic, social, and political separation as well. (Swedish was the country's only official language, and, besides learning the language, any Finn seeking to improve his station in life usually found it expedient to adopt a Swedish name. At the time, Latin endings were much in vogue, so names like Sibelius and Wallenius were popular.) In the early nineteenth century Swedes made up one-fifth of the total population, comprising the bulk of the urban dwellers and large landowners. But because these were precisely the classes that had the lowest reproduction rates—and also because Finland's greatest emigration took place from the Swedish-speaking coastal districts—the Finns have gradually narrowed the Swedish minority down to some 8 per cent. However, the Swedes have been very reluctant to learn Finnish, not only because of its difficulty as a language, but also because they feel it draws them into a "blind alley" culturally. At least, by retaining Swedish, they have a tie to the rest of Scandinavia and the Germanic languages. Finnish, on the other hand, apart from its similarity to Estonian and a very distant connection with Hungarian, is without significant ties to any other language or culture.

It is only in the coastal lowlands that cleared land comprises any significant proportion of the total area of Finland, for north of the great recessional moraines of the Salpausselkä, most of the land is in forest. Despite its approximately 60,000 lakes and innumerable swamps, Finland has the greatest area of productive forest per capita in the world. Indeed, it is the "green gold" of its woodlands that has allowed Finland to achieve its high standard of living, for fully three-fourths of Finnish exports are wood products in one form or another: construction timber, pulp, paper, newsprint, prefabricated houses, plywood, and veneer. Most of the large wood industries are located at the ends of inland lake systems or at the mouths of rivers, where the timber can be assembled most easily, and, in the latter situations, the finished products exported. Thus, coastal cities such as Kotka, Pori, Oulu and Kemi are all major wood processing and export centers.

Apart from timber, Finland has little in the way of natural resources for industry. There is a deposit of low-grade copper ore at Outukumpu in the east and some low-grade iron ore in the north, and unlike Sweden's, Finland's hydroelectric potential is rather limited. The Vuoksi River in the east was Finland's most accessible major water power source, but with the exception of one large generating station at Imatra, most of the river's potential who lost with the postwar cessions to the Soviet Union.

As a result, Finland has had to look to the far north to utilize the Oulu and Kemi rivers, and now that these have largely been developed, there is little future expansion that is economically feasible.

Norway

THE REGIONS OF NORWAY. The area where Sweden, Finland, and Norway come together in the north is the region of *Lappland*, the refuge of a docile hunting and herding people pushed into this remote and unproductive extremity by the northward advance of the Scandinavians from the southwest and of the Finns from the southeast. Although Norway has the smallest proportion of Lappland's area (it calls the region Finnmark, or "land of the Finns," because the Lapps speak a dialect of Finnish), it has the largest proportion of the Lapps, or *Samer*, as they prefer to be called. This is because the barren Finnmark Plateau was even less attractive to penetration by the Scandinavians and Finns than were the lower, forested Swedish and Finnish areas, and so the Lapps gained the area by default. Although the herding of reindeer is still carried on by a small number of Lapps, most of them have settled down to other occupations: some are engaged in fishing, farming, and forestry, and not a few are employed as miners in the Swedish iron mines. Gradually, another of man's colorful and individualistic cultures is succumbing to the homogenization process, which is going on virtually everywhere today.

The Finnmark Plateau is but one part of the much vaster region of *North Norway*, which curves in an arc along the Arctic Ocean and Norwegian Sea from the Soviet border to well south of the Arctic Circle. This is a region whose cool, maritime climate leaves all but the most sheltered interior lowlands beyond both the limit of crop cultivation and the treeline. Along its windswept tundra coast, fishing provides virtually the sole source of livelihood, and not until one comes as far south as the Vesterålen and Lofoten Islands do hay, potatoes, and dairying assume any real importance. Even though farming and forestry are distinctly marginal within the region, North Norway does have some of the country's most important mineral deposits, as well as bountiful supplies of hydroelectric power. For example, Norway's largest iron ore deposits are in the far northeast, within sight of the Soviet border. Although they contain only 33 per cent iron, they are beneficiated and shipped as briquets of 65 per cent purity from the port of Kirkenes, both to Norway's own steel industries and abroad. One of Norway's largest steel mills is the government-owned plant at *Mo i Rana*, just south of the Arctic Circle, which began operation in 1955. It was designed to use local ores as well as those from Kirkenes, and it has both limestone and large amounts of hydroelectric power close at hand. Coal for the plant is brought in from mines in the Norwegian Arctic dependency of Svalbard.

The steel mill at *Mo i Rana* is merely one of several ventures sponsored by the Norwegian government to help develop and diversify the economy of North Norway. A large aluminum refinery has been built at Mosjöen, and a railroad has been pushed north as far as Bodö, now the largest town in the region. Before the "North Norway Plan" was initiated, a large electrochemical plant and pyrite mines were among the enterprises already in existence, and production has been expanded in those industries. In number of persons employed, however, fishing is still the region's principal livelihood; half of Norway's fishermen live in this area. The famous Lofoten cod fisheries, which are conducted every February and March when the cod swarm into the funnel-shaped Vestfjord to spawn, still attract some 10,000 fishermen and 3,000 fishing craft, but over-fishing and alternative forms of employment are gradually reducing the magnetism that this great annual event has exercised on the people of Norway for over 1,000 years.

About halfway along the coast of Norway, a large fjord breaks into the heart of a rolling lowland district, the climate of which is warmer and drier than the exposed coastal areas. Moreover, its clay soils support extensive farms and productive forests. This is Trondheimsfjord, upon which the region of *Tröndelag* is centered. Tröndelag is not only Norway's second largest agricultural area, but also its second most important forestry region. Dairying is the primary emphasis of farming, and crops include hay, oats, barley, and potatoes. In addition to a variety of wood industries, Tröndelag also has iron ore deposits in the north and copper pyrite deposits in the south. Its ice-free fjord and a low pass into the Jämtland district of Swedish Norrland have likewise prompted the Swedes to build a transit port on an inner arm of the fjord.

Tröndelag was the historical heart of Norway, for its chief town—Nidaros, now Trondheim—was one of the first residences of the king. Following the battle of Stiklestad, a few miles to the north, Nidaros also became the resting place of St. Olav, the patron saint of Norway, and thus the country's most important religious center. Every monarch of Norway, whether Norwegian, Dane, or Swede, has had to journey to the great Nidaros Cathedral for his formal coronation. Long the third-ranking city of Norway, Trondheim has just recently edged into second place with a population of 120,000.

South of Tröndelag, the mountains of the *West Country* of Norway become higher and more rugged and the fjords that cut back into them become longer, deeper, and more precipitous. Settlement sites are restricted to a narrow, rocky brim along the outer coast (the strandflat) or to little patches of flat land at the heads of the fjords. The mountains themselves support little in the way of tree growth, and the higher areas are occupied by the largest ice fields on the mainland of Europe. The hundreds of waterfalls that hurl themselves down the fjord sides testify to the region's greatest resource—hydroelectric power—and at the inner end of several of the fjords there are large electrometallurgical and electrochemical plants (for example, aluminum at Årdal in Sognefjord, carbide at Odda in Hardangerfjord, and ferro-alloys at Sauda in Boknafjord). Otherwise, the West Country of Norway has looked to the sea for its livelihood, through both fishing and shipping. In the Kristiansund district, the flat rocks along the coast have long been used for drying split and salted codfish (the so-called *klipfisk,* which once was the principal form in which the fish was preserved and marketed). Today klipfisk finds a market only among the poorer countries of southern Europe, Africa, and Latin America. In the Ålesund district, herring is "king," and during the annual herring run each January and February, the catch is usually so enormous that three-fourths of it must be ground into oil or meat if it is to have any economic value at all. In the Stavanger district, the brisling provides the basic raw material for the Norwegian sardine industry. However, the chief commercial center for the Norwegian fishing industry has always been Bergen, and from Hanseatic times until as recently as the 1820's, Bergen was also Norway's largest city. Tucked into the end of a fjord and surrounded by mountains, Bergen has been little more than a land base for a far-flung sea-oriented economy that at times embraced much of the North Atlantic. With its old Hanseatic warehouses and narrow cobblestone streets, Bergen is truly one of the cities of Europe with distinctive personality and charm. A center of culture as well as of commerce (it was the home of Edvard Grieg, the composer, Ole Bull, the concert violinist, and Wilhelm Bjerknes, the father of modern weather forecasting, among others), Bergen today is Norway's third largest city and has a population of 118,000.

Stavanger, near the southwestern corner of Norway, is one of the few west Norwegian cities with a strong landward orientation. This is because just to the south of Stavanger there is a rolling morainic lowland called Jaeren, whose mild climate and good transport facilities have allowed it to become a center of early vegetables, fruit, and livestock products for eastern markets of Norway as well as for local ones. As a result, Jaeren ranks as one of the most prosperous agricultural areas in Norway and the third most important farming region in the country.

The distinction of being Norway's most productive agricultural region, and also its leading forestry, commercial, and industrial area, belongs to the *East Country*—the part of Norway that tends to focus on Oslofjord, a sixty-mile-long arm of the Skagerrak. The East Country is a region of broad, open valleys, rushing rivers, and large lakes. Its landscape is a patchwork of crop land, pasture, and forest, for it is not only the most extensive area of Norway at low to moderate elevations, but it also has the warmest, driest summers of any region in the country and its most productive soils. Cereals, vegetables, and potatoes are all grown, but most of the cultivated land is used for hay and fodder crops.

As in Sweden and Finland, the rivers constitute the chief arteries of movement for getting timber from the interior valleys to the coast. Near their mouths such wood processing centers as Sarpsborg, Drammen, Larvik and Skien have grown up. The East Country also has easy access to the bulk of Norway's hydroelectric power, 80 per cent of which is concentrated in the mountains between the East and West Countries. With the greatest hydroelectric potential of any country in Europe, Norway has scarcely developed one-third of her reserves as yet and is already the greatest per capita consumer of electricity in the world. A major consumer of electric power in the Telemark district, southwest of Oslo, is the famous Norsk Hydro concern, which produces nitrate fertilizers by extracting nitrogen from the air. A by-product of its operation is deuterium, or heavy water, which Nazi scientists sought unsuccessfully (thanks to Norwegian saboteurs!) to obtain for their atomic bomb experiments during World War II. At Kristiansand, in the far south of Norway, cheap hydroelectricity is used to refine nickel shipped in from Canada, and about half of the country's rail traffic is also moved by electricity.

Nestled in a ring of forested mountains at the inner end of Oslofjord is the capital and largest city of Norway, Oslo (population 485,000). Just as the valleys of the East Country converge on Oslofjord, so the political, cultural and economic life of Norway comes to a focus in Oslo. It is the hub of the country's transportation system, its busiest seaport, and the home port of the greater part of the vast Norwegian merchant fleet, the fourth largest in the world. For Norway, three-fourths of which consists of unproductive mountains, its merchant fleet has spelled the difference between affluence and poverty, for its earnings permit the Norwegians to import consistently goods more valuable than those they export.

Iceland

THE REGIONS OF ICELAND. In a sense, Iceland—Norway's daughter country in the middle of the North Atlantic—can be thought of as having much the same basic problem as Norway itself. More than three-fourths of the area of Iceland is unproductive wasteland, consisting of the largest glaciers in Europe, vast lava fields, and bleak Arctic deserts. However, Iceland has no forests, as Norway does (the few scrub-birch copses protected by law constitute hardly 1 per cent of its area), and its climate is too cool to permit the cultivation of much besides potatoes and turnips (so less than 1 per cent of its area can be called crop land). Indeed, were it not for the fact that a little over one-fifth of the island will support a grass cover, there would be no means of sustaining any form of advanced land use in the country. As it is, Icelandic agriculture is based primarily on sheep grazing in the more remote areas, and dairying in the more productive lowlands having access to local marketing centers.

In the modern economic life of Iceland, however, the land makes only a minor contribution compared to the sea. Beginning in the 1880's, when steam trawlers permitted them to fish farther afield than in their own bays and fjords, the Icelanders began reorienting their life to the sea, with the result that today over 90 per cent of the country's population resides on the coast and a similar proportion of the country's exports are derived from fishing. Along the south and west coasts, the chief species caught is cod, most of which is landed at such ports as Reykjavík and Keflavík. Along the north and east coasts herring is the principal variety caught, and in recent years the main port of landing has been Raufarhöfn.

Apart from food processing (fish, meat, and milk products) and textiles (wool), Iceland has no raw material basis for industrialization. It does have power, however, not only hydroelectric power but also geothermal power, or "earth heat." Such industries as Iceland has managed to develop to date are based on a limited development of hydro-electric power, chiefly in the Reykjavík and Akureyri areas. A large nitrate fertilizer plant has been built near the capital, and across the bay to the north, at Akranes, a cement plant is in operation. Because Iceland has no limestone, the plant derives its lime from seashells dredged up off the floor of Faxaflói. A large aluminum factory, financed by Swiss capital, began operations near Hafnarfjördhur in 1970 and derives its power from a new hydroelectric plant located at Burfell near Mount Hekla. A diatomite plant started production at Lake Myvatn in the northeastern interior in 1969, using a nearby steam field for energy. Otherwise, the earth heat has not yet been utilized industrially, but most of the city of Reykjavík is heated by water piped from hot springs eleven miles north-east of the city, as are many swimming pools and hothouses in scattered areas of the country. The largest cultivated area under glass is at Hveragerdhi, in the Southern Lowlands, where tomatoes and cut flowers are the chief crops, but where experimentation is also going on with grapes and bananas. Altogether, it is estimated that Iceland saves im-porting some 75,000 tons of coal a year, thanks to its geothermal energy.

In a country as small as Iceland (200,000 people), the presence of a foreign military contingent at times composed of 5000 men and more has a sizable impact on its economy. From 1941 on, with the exception of the years 1947–51, Iceland has been the site of an American air base, located at Keflavík, some thirty miles west of the capital. The money invested in the base's construction, maintenance, and operation has had a markedly inflationary effect on the Icelandic economy. It has, moreover, created such a dependence that if it were withdrawn (as for a time the Icelanders thought they wanted), there are serious doubts as to whether the island could maintain the same level of economy it now enjoys. The Icelanders are disturbed by the base's presence, but they might be more disturbed by its absence.

There is little doubt that the rapid growth of Reykjavík since 1940 is in large part attributable to the money poured into the country since that time by the Americans. Today it is a modern city of 80,000 inhabi-tants, or more than 40 per cent of the country's total population. It is in every respect "the" city in Iceland, for the country's second largest town is Akureyri, the regional capital of the north, with 10,000 inhabitants.

Conclusion

Though the events of World War II forcefully demonstrated that "Europe's quiet corner" is not immune from involvement in the intrigues and conflicts of the Great Powers that surround it, the problems con-fronting the Northern countries today are primarily the result of their own respective economic evolutions. Because all of the countries of the North have strong trade ties with the United Kingdom, the three Scan-dinavian states joined with Britain in the founding of the European Free Trade Association, or the Outer Seven as it is sometimes called (Switzer-land, Austria, and Portugal are the other members), and Finland, with a nod of approval from the Soviet Union, became an associate member. In

1970, Iceland likewise joined EFTA, making the region's economic association complete. Like Britain, however, the Northern countries realize that the division of Western Europe into two trading blocs is not a satisfactory situation, and are looking forward to the time when they, along with Britain, will become members of an expanded Common Market. At the moment, it is probably Denmark that feels the awkwardness of the two-fold division of the West most acutely, for although Britain is Denmark's principal customer, West Germany ranks a close second. As tariffs on agricultural products within the Common Market come down, to the benefit of France, they go up on farm produce from the "outside," to the detriment of Denmark's competitive position.

Economically, Sweden has no qualms about joining EEC, but politically it is apprehensive as to how membership in the Common Market would affect its neutrality. (Of course, both Switzerland and Austria have similar misgivings.) As long as de Gaulle seemed intent on recasting Europe in France's image and West German intentions vis-à-vis the East remained in doubt, there was good reason for proceeding with some caution. Even now, however, with "le grand Charles" gone and a new era of amity beginning between West Germany and the East Bloc countries, Sweden is hesitant to compromise her neutrality by casting her lot too wholeheartedly with "the West."

Similarly, Finland must keep an ear open to the East, for any course of action it might choose to pursue is bound to be closely scrutinized by the Soviet Union. One has only to recall how Khrushchev gave all of the North the jitters in 1958 when he called the Finnish president to Siberia to renew for 20 years a treaty of friendship and mutual assistance. One paragraph in the treaty, which points up the Soviets' overriding concern, stipulates that Finland shall not allow its territory to be used as a springboard of attack against the Soviet Union (as it did in 1941). So, any grouping of nations that includes both West Germany and Finland is likely to be viewed with great reservation, if not blanket disapproval. Sweden is, of course, sensitive to Finland's delicate position as well, and is not about to make any move that would put its Finnish buffer in a more precarious situation.

Although Norway may likewise have some questions of a political nature regarding EEC membership, its chief concern is economic. Significantly, when the Norwegian delegation went to Brussels to initiate preliminary discussions, it included two economic geographers whose function it was to explain Norway's special geographic problems, by way of background for their country's requests for certain economic concessions. Not only is much of Norway's farming marginal, but even her fisheries, especially in remote areas such as the North, will find it difficult to meet the competition of more advantageously located Dutch and Danish fishermen, for example. For Iceland, the problems will be similar but even more exaggerated, for that country's inflation has pushed its wage rates to uncompetitive heights as it is.

In terms of their domestic economies, the Scandinavian countries in particular are fast approaching the saturation point. Poverty has been abolished, slums are nonexistent, the individual's welfare is looked after from the cradle to the grave, the trains run on time, a month's paid vacation is guaranteed by the government, and the family's major issue for debate becomes where to spend it—at their cottage in the mountains, at a seaside resort, or in Rhodes, the Balearics, or the Canary Islands? In the Scandinavian countries, life is so well ordered that politics has lost most of its dramatic flavor; the issues most likely to engender passion are integration in the United States, *apartheid* in South Africa, and the war in Vietnam. The Scandinavians have lived under socialism so long and prospered so well that they now find themselves voting "conservative," to retain the status quo. In Sweden, which was spared from the war and where the affluence is the greatest, perhaps as "perfect" a society as man is capable of creating is in existence. The frequently heard charges of Swedish "decadence" have their basis in part because of the Swedes' propensity for openness, in that they assiduously collect and publish statistics on such things as illegitimacy, alcohol consumption, and crime, which other countries either ignore or try to cover up. But where comparisons are possible, it will be seen that socialist Sweden has far lower rates of illegitimacy (about 4 per cent), of alcohol consumption (half that of the U.S.) and of crime (murder rate one-seventh that of the U.S.) than most other countries, and we have already noted that capitalist countries such as Austria, West Germany, and Switzerland have higher suicide rates. If Sweden is not perfect, it is only because man is not perfect.

Table 6.   The Northern Frontier, Selected Statistics (1968)

	Denmark	Sweden	Finland	Norway	Iceland
Area (000's sq. mi.)	16.6	173.7	130.1	125.2	39.7
Population (millions)	4.9	8.0	4.7	3.8	0.2
Birth rate (per 1000)	16.0	15.4	16.5	27.6	22.4
Death rate (per 1000)	9.9	10.1	9.4	9.6	7.0
Natural increase (per 1000)	6.9	5.3	7.1	8.0	15.4
Infant mortality (per 1000)	15.8	12.9	14.2	14.8	13.3
Land use (%):					
Cultivated	63.7	7.3	8.1	2.6	0.9
Meadows-pastures	7.6	1.2	0.3	0.5	21.4
Forest	10.2	50.0	64.6	21.7	1.0
Other land	18.5	41.5	27.1	75.2	76.7
Population density per sq. mi.					
cultivated land	470	670	450	1170	630
Gross national product					
per capita	$1,830	$2,270	$1,600	$1,710	$2,235
Exports (millions)	$2,368	$4,941	$1,637	$1,938	$82
Imports (millions)	$3,224	$5,126	$1,598	$2,706	$138
Trade balance (millions)	−$856	−$185	+$39	−$768	−$56

See Table 1, p. 54, for sources.

CHAPTER 8

europe: summary and prospects

Like the deeply lined face of a weatherbeaten sailor, the physiognomy of Europe has a fineness of detail which, as has been seen, can be appreciated only through careful study. Yet, unlike the wrinkled brow of the "old salt" which is but a superficial manifestation of his age and experience, the lineaments of Europe were in large part *responsible* for molding its character and personality. Plain and plateau, mountain and sea have all played their part in influencing the location and orientation of man's multifarious innovations as they spread over the subcontinent through the ages. Indeed, Europe's richness and depth of cultural diversity can be attributed in no small measure to its kaleidoscopic melange of physical landscapes.

Because Europe was settled at a time when the technology of transport encompassed little more than the use of man's own feet, the horse, or the sailboat (in contrast to the United States or the Soviet Union, for example, which are largely products of the railway and automotive ages), the range and scope of interaction between peoples remained so limited for so long that strong regional differentiation developed. Apart from the occasional merchant, soldier, or religious pilgrim, the effective range of movement of most people was probably little more than twenty or thirty miles from the town or village of their birth. Travel was slow, arduous, and often fraught with danger; therefore it was usually undertaken only for the compelling reasons of profit, conquest, or salvation.

With contacts between peoples and places so restricted, it is small wonder that parochialism, intolerance, suspicion, fear, superstition, and antagonism all flourished as part of the "European way of life" for centuries. Nor is it any great surprise that the ideas of the nation-state and nationalism should have been spawned in Europe, for it was there that the correspondence between given patterns of culture (especially language and religion) and certain fairly well defined physical landscapes became apparent to man at a relatively early date. Probably in few parts of the world could the distinctions between "us" and "them" be more clearly associated in the human mind with natural regions, whether defined by topography, vegetation, or both. Moreover, it was in Europe that the city-state reached its ultimate form of development (i.e., Rome) and that the march of communications technology first made possible the broader radius of spatial interaction implicit in the nation-state. Thus, for reasons of geography and history alike, the consciousness of national identities and of national territories has persisted longer and more intensely in Europe than in any other major region of the world.

Although many far vaster regions of less diversified physical character had managed to achieve unities of an economic, social, or political nature by the late nineteenth century (among them Australia, Brazil, Russia, and the United States), Europe entered the twentieth century as a collection of small, ambitious, and vengeful competitors. By the end of the century's second decade a disastrous war had fragmented Europe even further along nationalistic lines, and it was not until midcentury, after a second and bloodier holocaust, that the subcontinent had essentially crystallized into two supranational groupings. These were the ideological blocs, loosely refered to as the West and East respectively, or as the Free World and the Communist World, neither of which had its power base within Europe, however. It has subsequently taken a whole generation to revitalize Europe to the point where it is once again able to reassert its significance as a major center of world power. At the same time, there have been unmistakable signs in both West and East (especially in France and Romania) that nationalism continues to remain a force not only to be reckoned with but, as de Gaulle's visit to Romania in the spring of 1968 illustrated, also one to be exploited in the broader ideological struggle currently under way.

The dawn of the second half of the twentieth century found Europe asking itself how its two dozen sovereign political entities could function effectively in a world shrunk by jet aircraft travel, living in the shadow of nuclear annihilation, and witnessing an ominous increase in population. Against such a sobering backdrop, Europe has for the first time in its history begun to recognize the emergence of a "European" identity—to realize that the differences separating Belgian from Bulgarian and Spaniard from Finn are far less that those setting Europe apart from Asia, Africa, or Latin America, for example. Though substantial differences in wealth continue to exist within countries and between countries in Europe (see Figure 16), far greater disparities separate Europe from the so-called underdeveloped regions of the world. Europeans are increasingly becoming aware that they not only constitute a "racial" minority in the world, but an economic, social, and political minority as well. Whether they live under capitalist, socialist, or communist systems of government, Europeans realize that they enjoy a way of life that allows them a measure of personal participation and material reward which few peoples in other cultures even remotely approach.

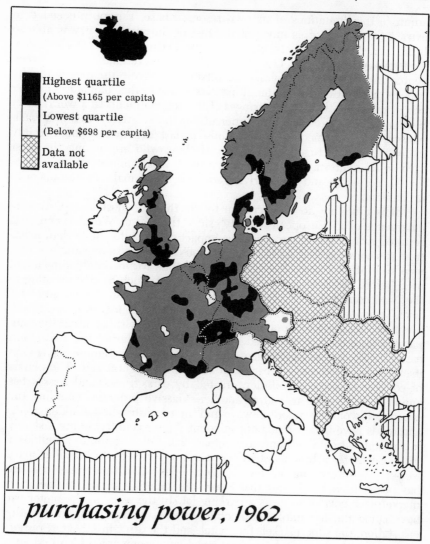

Figure 16

Data issued by Chase-Manhattan Bank, 1964

To be sure, Europe did not develop its institutions or achieve its affluence in a vacuum. Indeed, it is hardly an exaggeration to say that Europe owes its uniqueness to the fact that it was able for so long to defer its problems, passing them on to other regions by trading space for time. For example, rather than succumb to the burden of its own burgeoning population, Europe exported millions of its sons and daughters to overseas areas, especially in the Americas and Oceania. Rather than admit to the limitations of its own resource base, Europe proceeded to extract the wealth of as much of the rest of the world as it was able to bring under its control. In effect, Europe became the "center"; Africa, Asia, the Americas, and Oceania became its "hinterland"; and between center and hinterland a symbiotic relationship grew up that gradually concentrated most of its material manifestations in the colonialist "mother countries" along the Atlantic fringes of the subcontinent. In a world beset by hunger, disease, fear, and superstition, the relatively well-fed, well-housed, well-informed Europeans must at last demonstrate their ability to live and work together in peace. If they, who are among the most favored residents of this planet, cannot do it, what glimmer of hope exists for the desperate and underprivileged masses that make up the majority of mankind?

It is probably no exaggeration to say that for most Europeans, the emergence of a "European identity" since the end of World War II has resulted more from the unconscious impact of the automobile than it has from the conscious impact of the repetition of the phrase by various statesmen and intellectuals. Although the automobile was certainly known and used before and during the war (indeed, it did much to give meaning to the Nazi concept of *blitzkrieg*, or "lightning war"), it was essentially a "class" phenomenon rather than a "mass" phenomenon. During the 1950's, however, the automobile age dawned in Europe with an intensity comparable only to that witnessed in Anglo-America during the 1920's and early 1930's. In the subsequent decade and a half, Europe has found itself choked by the motor car, both literally and figuratively. The plague of congestion and air pollution created by cars, trucks, and busses has engulfed one urban area after another. Massive programs entailing the construction of new superhighways and the reconstruction of older streets and roads have been carried out in country after country. Many a stately row of ancient oaks or Lombardy poplars has fallen victim to a bulldozer making way for a broader strip of asphalt or concrete. Just finding space to put the burgeoning masses of automobiles when they are not in use has posed such headaches that many an imposing piazza or medieval marketplace now doubles as a parking lot. In the wake of the motor car have come the inevitable automobile-oriented business enterprises—the gas station, the supermarket, the motel, and the drive-in (theater, restaurant, or bank)—fortunately, in most instances accompanied by an esthetic sense that is largely lacking in Anglo-America. (On the other hand, the multiplying trailer courts and automobile junkyards are no more attractive in the European countryside than they are in America.)

Profound as the purely physical aspects of its impact have been, the automobile has had an even greater economic, psychological, and cultural impact on Europe. This has come about because the motor car has opened a whole new dimension of spatial interaction in Europe. Today the Dutch office worker spends his vacations on the Costa del Sol in Spain or on the beaches of Mamaia in Romania, and the coal miner of the German Ruhr consumes fruit and vegetables from Bulgaria rushed to his local market by refrigerator trucks. A rapidly increasing volume of foodstuffs, industrial raw materials, and finished manufactured goods is moving between the countries of Europe by road, in most instances with as little complication as between the United States and Canada and in many, with as little difficulty as between the individual states of the United States. But by far the greatest volume of traffic consists of private automobiles—tourists motoring in foreign countries for pleasure. So great has this tide of motorized visitors become that in several of the economically less diversified countries of Europe, tourism now ranks as the largest single industry, and in almost all of them it makes a significant contribution to the national income. (In the countries of Eastern Europe, for example, tourism is the chief source of "hard" Western currencies, so travel restrictions have been minimized and every effort has been made to roll out the red carpet. Ideologically, the "peoples' democracies" seldom miss an opportunity to berate the "Western imperialists," but from a practical business viewpoint they literally outdo themselves to cater to the foreign tourists' whims as regards service and hospitality.) It is almost ironic, therefore, that the same diversity that once provided the rationale for the Europeans' fears, suspicions, and distrust of one another has now become a major factor stimulating tourism. Probably for the first time in Europe's history, it can be said that its multitude of physical and cultural differences are contributing in a positive manner to the spiritual and psychological unification of the subcontinent. Whether this will ultimately set the stage for the development of firmer bonds of an economic and political nature, only time will tell.

Economic, Social, and Political Patterns in Contemporary Europe

Earlier chapters attempted to delimit and describe the regions of individual European countries, their personalities, and their significance. In this final chapter it behooves us to attempt to discern the broader, supranational patterns of the subcontinent as they exist today—economic, social, and political patterns that enable us to see Europe not only in a more encompassing view but also in context with the other major regions of the world. In making such an attempt, however, it should be kept in mind that it is all but impossible to compartmentalize such a discussion neatly into "economic," "social," and "political" patterns per se, for all of the aspects of modern Europe—as of any region—are so interwoven as to be one continuous fabric. Here it can only be hoped to selectively emphasize those aspects with greatest relevance to our understanding of the whole.

In the post-World War II period, three distinct supranational economic unions, or trading blocs, have emerged within Europe (see Figure 17). Inevitably, each of these has developed in response to a given political impetus or orientation. Thus, the European Economic Community (EEC), or Common Market, was in large part the outgrowth of experience gained in such bodies as the European Coal and Steel Com-

principal trading blocs

EEC and associate (Greece).   EFTA and associates (Finland, Iceland).   COMECON.

Figure 17

munity, where the increasing interdependence of long-standing enemies (France and Germany) was seen as a means not only of reducing mutual tensions and distrust but also of sparing their smaller neighbors (the Netherlands, Belgium, and Luxembourg) from periodic involvement in their struggles. Indeed, as was pointed out earlier, it was the latter who, for reasons of self-preservation as much as for any abstract idealism, have been in the vanguard of the campaign for European unity. Together with Italy and their associate member, Greece, these five West European countries today constitute the core of an economic union as populous as the United States and second only to it in material wealth.

The European Free Trade Association, or Outer Seven, (EFTA) was formed as a reaction to the Common Market, for the nonmembers of EEC were quick to see the advantages of trading bloc partnership. Yet, it was not a "sour grapes" reaction, for when EEC was first formed, each of the Outer Seven states felt it had its own valid (most often political) reason for not joining. Britain had sincere reservations related to its ties with the Commonwealth, while Switzerland, Austria, and Sweden felt that membership would be incompatible with their neutrality. Norway, Denmark, and Portugal, all of whom were more strongly oriented toward the British economy rather than toward West Germany or France, preferred to adopt a wait-and-see attitude. Once EFTA had come into being, Finland, with the approval of the Soviet Union, applied for and was granted associate membership, for Finland too is strongly oriented toward the British economy. Similarly, Iceland found it was no longer possible to risk exclusion from EFTA, and was accepted into membership under very favorable terms in 1970. Thus, today the only West European states remaining outside both trading blocs are an Ireland adamantly intent on demonstrating independence from Britain, and a politically "untouchable" Spain.

In Eastern Europe, the countries of the Warsaw Pact military alliance likewise constitute the membership of the Council for Mutual Economic Development, or COMECON. Here too, political orientation is the all-important prerequisite, for both Communist states that are outside the Moscow orbit (independent Yugoslavia and China-tied Albania) are excluded.

Some of the interplay of economic and political factors in modern Europe can be discerned from the patterns of foreign trade on the subcontinent. Figures 18 and 19 show the leading customers of each of the individual countries in 1967 (buyers of exports and suppliers of imports, respectively). For example, Figure 18 shows that the United Kingdom ranks as the chief buyer of exports from seven European states, her six EFTA associates and Ireland. West Germany and the Soviet Union each act at the principal purchaser of exports from six European countries—West Germany from four of its Common Market associates and its two neutralist neighbors Switzerland and Austria, and the Soviet Union from its six COMECON partners. France, in turn, is the largest individual buyer of West German exports; the Netherlands is the best customer of Belgium and Luxembourg; and Italy is the leading purchaser of Yugoslav goods. Only in the United Kingdom, Spain, and Albania is a pattern of overseas trade orientation found—the first two having the United States as their principal buyer and the latter, Red China. However, with these three exceptions, the main point to be made is that the largest purchaser of exports from any individual European state lies within Europe itself or immediately adjacent to it (i.e., the Soviet Union).

From Figure 19, much the same conclusion can be drawn, only here we see the heightened economic and political impact of the United

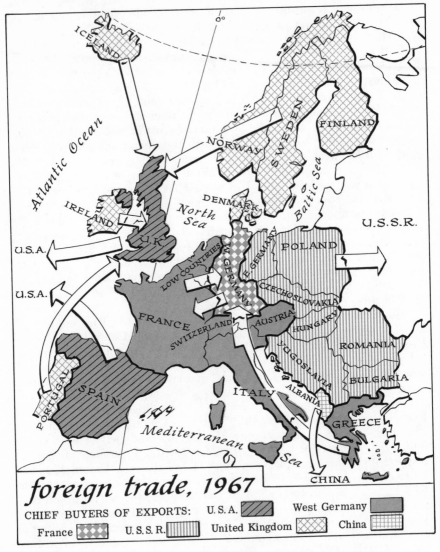

Figure 18

States. The United States acts as the chief supplier of imports for the two major industrial nations of the subcontinent and its two foremost military allies in Europe (West Germany and the United Kingdom), and also for its military ward Iceland, and its bilateral military ally Spain. In each instance, strategic geopolitical considerations probably weigh as heavily in this pattern of orientation as do purely economic ones. Nonetheless, West Germany remains the largest supplier of imports for no fewer than twelve European states (five of these are its associates in the Common Market,

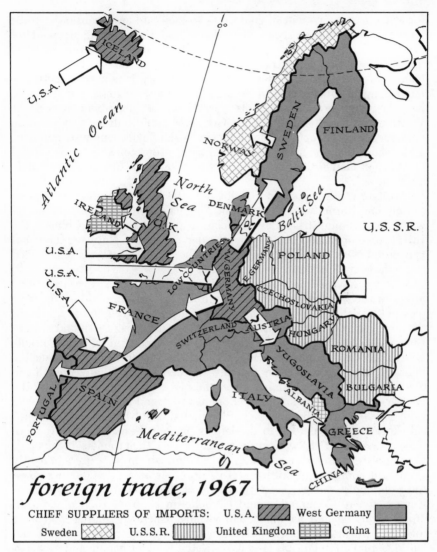

foreign trade, 1967

CHIEF SUPPLIERS OF IMPORTS: U.S.A. | West Germany
Sweden | U.S.S.R. | United Kingdom | China

Figure 19

six are members of EFTA, and the twelfth is Yugoslavia) once again confirming its importance as the economic keystone of the subcontinent.

The Soviet Union is the chief supplier for all COMECON countries, although it is questionable that it would be if all the political restraints were removed. (For example, the use of the ruble as the basic currency keeps the East European countries economically oriented toward the Soviet Union, because the ruble is not freely convertible with Western hard currencies. The Poles, in particular, have been pressing the Soviets for at least part payment in gold, so as to facilitate an expansion of trade with the West. There seems little doubt that the growing demand for variety and quality in consumer goods in Eastern Europe could be filled more easily by the industrial nations of the West, especially West Germany, than they could by the Soviet Union, which is now conscientiously attempting to satisfy its own pent-up consumer demands. Nevertheless, an economic reorientation of its East European neighbors toward the West, and especially toward West Germany, could only be viewed as an ominous and unacceptable development in the Soviet Union. It might be added here that the same kind of thinking prompted the Soviet refusal of Marshall Plan aid in the reconstruction of Eastern Europe immediately after the war.)

Britain ranks a poor fourth, for it is the largest supplier of imports to only one European state—Ireland. Albania's ideological orientation toward the communist hard line is seen in the fact that Red China is the chief source of its imports. Finally, the dependence of Norway's merchant marine on Swedish shipyards explains the former country's specialized trade tie to its Scandinavian sister-state.

As we have seen, language and religion continue to remain vital forces in the social and political geography of Europe, dividing the peoples of several countries. On a supranational scale, religion is no doubt the stronger force, particularly the ties that most of southern and eastern Europe have with Rome. In Iberia the conservatism of the Catholic church, bolstered and effectuated by the large landowning class and the military, has helped to stifle virtually all change. There, any liberalizing tendency needed only to labeled "communistic" to justify excesses by the Salazar or Franco regimes, and seldom has any condemnation been evoked from the clergy. In those Catholic-dominated countries where free political expression is accorded to the leftists, namely France and Italy, more than a quarter of the electorate regularly cast their ballots in favor of Communist-sponsored candidates. (In contrast, in the predominantly Protestant countries of northwestern Europe, it is front-page news when the Communists muster even 5 per cent of the popular vote.) In eastern Europe, where Communism and Catholicism confront each other head on, a *modus vivendi* has been achieved by which the church is at least tolerated by the authorities. However, there, as in many parts of the world, actual attendance is largely restricted to older people and especially women, although a lively academic interest in religion and philosophy characterizes many of the younger people in Eastern Europe. (Perhaps one sees a parallel here to the mystic appeal that certain Eastern religions, particularly Zen Buddhism, holds for the youth of the West. In both instances this interest probably symbolizes but one further manifestation of the rebellion of youth against the *status quo*.)

In the East European countries, the confrontation between religious groups (a forceful argument can be made that Communism is essentially a "religion," replete with its own hierarchy of "saints" and body of dogma) has involved the direct and open challenge of one group's teachings and beliefs by the other. On the other hand, in Western Europe "politeness" has prompted all but the most radical partisans to minimize the struggle between religious groups, at least in public, though this has not prevented insidious economic and political maneuvering from going on behind the scenes. The unfortunate "procreation race" between Catholics and Protestants in the Netherlands is a case in point. Pope Paul VI's reiteration of the church's condemnation of *all* birth control measures in July, 1968 could only provoke increased dissension and hostility between Catholics and Protestants, just as it must inevitably provoke increasing debate among many Catholics themselves.

As a comparison between Figures 6 (Religion) and 16 (Purchasing Power) reveals, there is a striking correlation between Catholic Europe and "poor Europe." (In Figure 16, the data from the original Chase Manhattan map of Purchasing Power in Western Europe has been re-mapped to show the highest and lowest quartiles of income distribution.) It will be noted that all of the counties and provinces of the Republic of Ireland, Portugal, and Spain rank in the lowest quartile of per capita purchasing power, and that this is also true in most of Catholic Italy and Austria, as well as in Orthodox Greece. Catholic France, on the other hand, has some of the sharpest disparities in income in Western Europe, with several *departements* lying at each extreme. In the predominantly Protestant countries, on the other hand, there are fewer extremes in wealth, and most of their inhabitants enjoy a standard of living well above the West Eurpean average. Unfortunately, comparable data are not available for the countries of Eastern Europe, but if they were, they would no doubt demonstrate a relatively uniform level of purchasing power in the intermediate range (i.e., below northwestern Europe but above Southern Europe).

To be sure, it is not suggested here that the correlation between religion and poverty is the only one which exists in Europe, or that it is even the most important one. There is, for example, a strong inverse correlation between purchasing power and degree of industrialization. In Eastern Europe, where a "forced draft" expansion of industry has been carried out by the communist regimes since the war, the standard of living has risen markedly and the birth rate has also fallen sharply. In Southern Europe, where limited economic opportunity coincides with a rapidly growing population, the long-term prospects for social and political stability will remain in doubt unless genuine reforms are carried out. As long as the church adopts an essentially negative attitude toward such programs, it can but expect ultimately to alienate yet larger numbers of its people.

The supranational political configurations that have developed in postwar Europe essentially represent the demarcation of the spheres of influence of the two superpowers, the United States and Soviet Union. The latter, in its desire to guarantee the security of its exposed western frontier, installed Communist regimes in the countries of Eastern Europe following their liberation from the Nazis. This Soviet preoccupation with defense also found expression in the 1944 peace treaty with Finland and in the twenty-year treaty of friendship and mutual security subsequently signed and since renewed by the two countries. For its part, the United States was quick to interpret these moves as the Soviet Union's first steps toward world conquest, and it reacted by drawing its allies into the North Atlantic Treaty Organization, and by creating the state of West Germany and initiating its rearmament. These moves, in turn, could only result in heightening East European fears, thereby giving Moscow the rationale for welding its partners into the Warsaw Pact alliance, and thus further solidfying the division of Europe. However, the underlying defensiveness of the Soviet position was well illustrated when Tito broke out of the Moscow orbit and went unpunished, simply because Yugoslavia does not occupy as strategic a position on the western approaches to the U.S.S.R. as do Hungary, Poland, or Czechoslovakia. In the latter three countries, any real or imagined threat to Soviet security immediately strikes a sensitive nerve in the U.S.S.R. and is dealt with promptly. Conversely, the intransigence of its Romanian ally is viewed with far greater deference, for Romania does not occupy a vulnerable position between the Soviet Union and its feared West German rival. Thus, their very location determines in large measure what degree of freedom Moscow's East European allies may be permitted to enjoy. (The reader is reminded that this in fact is the essence of geography—where a place is and why it is important.)

In Western Europe, the specter of Soviet military aggression gradually lost its threat to America's allies, although events in Czechoslovakia in 1968–69 did have a sobering effect on all of them. As the prospects of invasion faded, so did the *raison d'être* of NATO. While statesmen from other NATO countries sought to find some new cement with which to perpetuate the alliance, Charles de Gaulle of France withdrew his nation from the pact. His move, of course, was not only an admission that NATO had outlived its usefulness, but also a means of divorcing himself from a distasteful "junior partnership" with the Anglo-American powers and a new leverage for independent dealings with other nationalists, both in the West and in the East. While de Gaulle's grand design for a "Europe of the Fatherlands" stretching from the Atlantic to the Urals may appear to have been a vainglorious attempt to re-elevate France to Great Power status, it does typify a growing awareness among many Europeans that the time is fast approaching when a united Europe must arise to act as an intermediary between the capitalist West and the Communist East. What form a united Europe may take will, of course, depend in large part on how it is conceived and by whom it is sponsored. If it is to be a nuclear-armed power whose most immediate goal is the reunification of Germany, as visualized by the former West German defense minister, Franz-Josef Strauss, it can only anticipate continuous and forceful opposition from the Soviet Union. If, on the other hand, it develops as a middle ground of democratic socialism, typified by such countries as Sweden and Switzerland, Europe could, indeed, usher in a new era of ideological bridge-building between the two superpowers, which find it so difficult to relax in each other's presence. Instead of again becoming the focus of world calamity, Europe may at last point the way to brotherhood and peace through tolerance, trust, and reason.

index

References to maps and tables
are printed in *italics*.

Provence, 56–58
Purchasing Power, 153

Regions, 1, 22–23
Religions, Dominant European, 21
Reykjavik, 148
Rhine graben, 102–3
Rhone valley, 58–59
Romania, 122–23
Rome, 36

Sardinia, 32
Scottish Highlands, 81
Serbia, 125
Sevilla, 44
Sicily, 32–34
Significance of place, 1–3
Skåne, 139
Slovakia, 121
Slovenia, 125
Sofia, 124
Soils, 9–10
South (Greece), 28–29
South (Iberia), 44–45
South (Italy), 32–35
South Swedish Highland, 139
South Tyrol, 39
Southeast (France), 56–59
Southwestern Peninsula (England), 82
Spain, 40–50, 52–53
Stockholm, 140
Styria, 106
Sweden, 139–42
Switzerland, 107–11

Temperature, 4–5
Thessaly, 29
Thrace, 29–30
Topography, 10–13
Trading Blocs, Principal, 156
Transylvania, 122
Tröndelag, 145
Turin, 39
Tuscany, 35–36

Ulster, 80
Umbria, 36

Vegetation, 9
Vienna, 106
Vienna basin, 106

Walachia, 123
Wales, 81
Warmth Index, 7
Warsaw, 117
Weald, 88
Wessex, 86
West (France), 61–62
West (Greece), 30
West (Iberia), 50–52
West Country (Norway), 145
Western Fringe, Selected Statistics, 72
Winds, 4–5

Yorkshire, 84
Yugoslavia, 124–26